SOUTHEAST ASIA
Crossroad of Religions

SOUTHEAST ASIA

Crossroad of Religions

BY KENNETH PERRY LANDON

THE UNIVERSITY OF CHICAGO PRESS
CHICAGO, ILLINOIS

THE HASKELL LECTURES IN COMPARATIVE RELIGION
DELIVERED AT THE UNIVERSITY OF CHICAGO IN 1947

THE UNIVERSITY OF CHICAGO PRESS, CHICAGO 37
Cambridge University Press, London, N.W. 1, England
W. J. Gage & Co., Limited, Toronto 2B, Canada

Published 1949. Composed and printed by THE UNIVERSITY OF CHICAGO PRESS, *Chicago, Illinois, U.S.A.*

PREFACE

MY PURPOSE in this volume is to describe a few of the developments among the peoples of Southeast Asia when their villages were invaded by alien religions and cultures. I selected for major attention the three areas of Sinicized Annam, Hinduized Siam, and Islamized Indonesia. Because of the purpose of the study, I deliberately slighted all primitive tribes. Out of Indonesia I selected the Javanese for special attention, feeling that what might be said of the Javanese could be said with modification of the religious progress of other developed parts of Indonesia.

There is only passing mention of the non-Annamese parts of Indochina and Burma because what may be said about religious development in Siam might also be said, with qualification, of them. They have most of the same elements that are found in Siam, but in different proportions. Of course, as any housewife knows, a different mix will result in a different cake. Ancient Cambodia was more highly Hinduized than Siam ever was; and modern Cambodia is a faint shadow of modern Hinayana Buddhist Siam. Burma has kept somewhat apace with Siam, and Laos has a history of retarded development.

The Malay element of Malaya has changed, in general, along with the peoples of Java and Sumatra. The preponderant alien elements of Indians and Chinese in Malaya did not seem to warrant much attention in a study of this sort.

My chief regret is that the limitations of time and space prevented me from devoting a section to the Philippines, the only area in Southeast Asia as completely won to Catholicism under Spanish influence as Indonesia was won to Islam. The Philippines, unlike most of the rest of Southeast Asia, was never Hinduized. Its experience might be compared to that of the non-Hinduized Annamese areas, where the folkways of the people were pressed into new forms by an alien people who conquered and then governed them. Although the Catholicism of the Philippines came from the West, the Westernization of the islands, as I have defined the term in this study, did not precede the Westernization of other parts of Southeast Asia to any great extent.

In order to carry out my purpose in this study, I have attempted to set the scene historically by describing the lands and the peoples involved in all Southeast Asia. The folkways of the peoples have been recounted in some detail in order to indicate the foundation on which invading sophisticated religions had to build.

I have tried to show that until modern times invading religions failed to convert the peoples to new points of view but were rather converted by them to serve old ends. It seems to me that the modern West is affecting Southeast Asia more profoundly than any previous invader because it has promoted the dynamic idea of the integrity of the individual as opposed to the authority of the village or clan and because there were such accompanying developments as the breakdown of village autonomy, the loss of land tenure, and the new function of money in an economy which previously was able to subsist without it.

Westernized persons in Southeast Asia in some instances have simply discarded their old religious attitudes and have accepted the humanism of the West. Many of them, however, carry their eggs in two baskets, between which there are no exchanges: one basket is filled with the usual local religious produce and the other with odds and ends picked up from the West. They make no attempt at reconciliation.

There are also persons who accept the new terms, the new gods, the new cult practices, and use them to clothe their old ideas. Rather than being converted to the new, they convert the new to old purposes.

A fourth sort of Westernized persons turn back upon their traditional religion and regard it with a new understanding.

They examine it as a Westerner might. They then attempt to re-think it, rationalize it, discard those things about it which are unusable anachronisms, and, finally, present it triumphantly to their neighbors as the equal of any other modern religion.

KENNETH PERRY LANDON

WASHINGTON, D.C.
October 1, 1948

TABLE OF CONTENTS

I. The Lands, the Peoples, and Their Folkways 1

II. Annamese Folkways under Chinese Influence 32

III. The Hinduization of Southeast Asia 61

IV. Siam, a Hinduized Nation 100

V. The Islamization of Southeast Asia 134

VI. Westernization and Modern Trends in Southeast Asia 165

Bibliography 204

Index 213

I

THE LANDS, THE PEOPLES, AND THEIR FOLKWAYS

SOUTHEAST Asia includes the Indochina Peninsula, the islands of the East Indies, and the Philippines. The northern part of the area is semicontinental, but the major part is maritime in character. The peninsula and islands form a circular sweep from Burma through Sumatra, Java, Bali, the Moluccas, and the Philippines to Indochina. This physical formation has tended to create a "Mediterranean" in the Far East in which intercommunication was encouraged rather than hindered by the waters of the Bay of Bengal, the Java Sea, the Gulf of Siam, and the China Sea. These waters have not tended to prevent the populations of the widely scattered areas from getting together but have been veritable highways for bringing them together.

The earliest records indicate that civilization has always been riverine and maritime in character throughout Southeast Asia. The great rivers leading deeply into Burma, Siam, and Indochina fostered a way of life which led naturally to the sea and to the coasts and rivers of the islands to the south and southeast. The peoples passed freely in their small craft along the sea routes connecting India with Burma, Malaya, Sumatra, Java, Bali, Borneo, Siam, and Indochina. Less frequently they seemed to reach the Philippines. The interchanges among the diverse peoples of the area tended to develop similarities of culture. There are certain beliefs and ritual which are found in all parts of monsoon Asia. It might even be said that a community of culture was developed between India and Farther India.

Travelers' records from China show that the Chinese were also familiar with the sea routes and with the principal kingdoms of the peninsula and archipelago. Their reports are invaluable sources of information on the early centuries of the Christian Era.

It is customary to stress the differences rather than the likenesses among the peoples of Southeast Asia. This is natural in this scientific age in which scholars strive for more exact definition of their subjects. The sharper the definition of each subject, the more different it appears from every other subject. By stressing the differences, it would not be difficult to convince one that Southeast Asia is a hopeless hodgepodge of human complexities. In fact, many people are certain that it is a congeries of disassociated peoples. To prove it, we might list the peoples resident in Southeast Asia.

Burma, before World War II, was supposed to have a population of about sixteen million, including ten million Burmese, one and a third million Karens, a million Shans, a million Indians, two hundred thousand Chinese, and scores of minor racial groups.

The East Indies had a population of seventy million, made up of countless tribes of Indonesians speaking about two hundred and fifty different languages and dialects. There were a million or more Chinese, less than a hundred thousand Arabs, and about two hundred thousand Europeans.

Siam had a population of sixteen million, which number included two million who considered themselves Chinese and who behaved like Chinese; three hundred thousand Malays, whom the Siamese dubbed Thai-Malays to indicate that they were a Malay branch of the Siamese; fifty thousand Indian British subjects; and thirty thousand Laos, Cambodians, and Annamese, who were French subjects.

Indochina had a population of twenty-four million, of which twenty million were Annamese living in Tonkin, Annam, and Cochin China, less than three million were Cambodians, three hundred thousand were Chinese, less than a million were Laos, and forty thousand were French. The remainder were hill tribe peoples.

Malaya had a population of five and a half million, including two and a quarter million Malays, two and a half million Chinese or Sino-Malays, and less than a million Indians.

And, lastly, the Philippine Islands had sixteen million Mongoloids who spoke no less than eighty-seven different languages and dialects.

Here we have, then, one hundred and fifty million people, speaking between three hundred and four hundred languages and dialects and having so many tribal differences that no one has ever been able to compute accurately the actual number of tribes. How can they possibly be studied regionally? And, of all things, how can they be studied in terms of their religion, which involves their basic attitudes toward life?

It all depends on what one is looking for and how one looks. The man with his eye to the microscope is correct when he states that every snowflake is different from every other. But the average experimenter with snowflakes who tries shaking them out of his collar probably thinks that every snowflake behaves like every other snowflake. They all melt. In a mass they provide excellent sledding. I feel certain that the Byrd expedition in Antarctica planned its safety in terms of the general behavior of snowflakes rather than in terms of their remarkable differences.

It is the intention of this book, in the description of the religions of the peoples of Southeast Asia, to emphasize those common features which make this region a sort of cultural "Mediterranean" of the Far East. Raymond Kennedy in *The Ageless Indies* wrote that the Malayo-Polynesian was one of the most widespread linguistic families in the world. "Its hundreds of branches extend all the way from Madagascar, off the coast of southeastern Africa, through the East Indies and the Philippines to Formosa on the north, up through the Malay Peninsula to the borders of Burma and Siam, and clear across the Pacific from Indonesia through Melanesia and Micronesia to the distant outposts of Hawaii and Easter Island. In the whole Oceanic area, only Australia,

New Guinea, and a few interior districts of the Melanesian islands have languages not belonging to the Malayo-Polynesian stock."[1]

The Thai language stock reaches from the Ahom of Assam through the Thai of Yunnan, the Shan of the Shan States in Burma, the Laos of Indochina, the Laos of northern Siam, and the Siamese, who extend halfway down the Malay Peninsula. The Tibeto-Burman stock in Burma, the Mon-Khmer stock in Burma and Indochina, and the Annamese in Indochina make up the other major groups on the mainland of Southeast Asia.

These people live in tropical lands which lie across or near the equator, either north or south of it. All of them are subject to monsoon or trade winds which bring about the changes of the seasons and which tend to create similar climatic conditions. Winds blow from the southwest from May to October (or from the southeast in the Southern Hemisphere) and from the northeast from November through April.

The amount of rainfall any area receives is a matter partly of topography and partly of exposure. The windward slopes have the heaviest precipitations of two hundred or more inches a year. On the plains nearly a hundred inches falls, but they may get less if there are mountains near by which cause premature precipitation.

Burma and the western side of the Malay Peninsula are affected by the southwest monsoon, which brings rain from May to October. The eastern side of the peninsula all the way to Tonkin is affected by the northeast monsoon and the trade winds and has a rainy season from October to January. In Java and adjacent islands there is rain from October to April. Some of the areas are affected all the year round by the moist winds and experience no dry season. In the Philippines it rains throughout the year on the eastern coasts, while on the western coasts, which receive their moisture from the

1. Raymond Kennedy, *The Ageless Indies* (New York: John Day Co., 1942), p. 7.

southwest winds, the rainy season lasts from May through September. All the peoples of Southeast Asia have had to adapt themselves to moist tropical living.

Hot weather is a year-round experience. Maximum temperatures seldom reach 100° F., and minimum temperatures are rarely lower than 65°. Clothing is necessary for aesthetic rather than practical purposes. There is something about this climate that tends to wilt all kinds of people down into the same damp pattern.

Life in the continental portion of Southeast Asia is profoundly affected by the great and small rivers which flow from north to south through deep valleys leading chiefly from the southeastern corner of Tibet. The extreme northern regions are very rugged and mountainous but rapidly give way to wide low plains and deltas ideal for rice culture. Some of the more important and better-known rivers are the Irrawaddy in central Burma, the Sittang in eastern Burma, the Salween on the Burma-Siam border, the Chao Phya in central Siam, the Mekong on the Siam-Indochina border, and the Red River in central Tonkin, Indochina. Each of these rivers has fostered a way of life which is characterized by riverside villages, village or commune administration, and rice culture.

The people, in general, derive most of the protein in their diet from fish. Their houses usually stand on stilts to make allowance for high water and seasonal inundation and are constructed generally of bamboo and leaves. Some of the rivers have been so fruitful that great cities such as Rangoon, Moulmein, Bangkok, Saigon, and Haiphong have developed on their banks. In each case the delta-plain civilization has dominated the hinterland.

The islands to the south have a somewhat different geography, although there, too, the rivers, short though they be in most cases, have furnished the communication system and have been the scene for the developing life of the people. Geographically, the chief variation in the islands is the volcanic element. Java alone has more than a hundred volcanoes, some of them active. The typical landscape is composed of rice fields backed by coconut palms, with volcanoes bunched up against the sky.

Most maps, because of their scale, lead us to think that Southeast Asia is a small portion of our world, an appendage dangling without significance from a corner of Asia. It is much more than that. Extensively it spraddles out over three thousand miles from east to west and about half that distance from north to south. What the one hundred and fifty million people in this vast area think is important. It will become increasingly important as they take a larger place in the commerce and politics of the world.

Siam has been an independent nation since the thirteenth century. The Philippines achieved political independence in 1946. That same year the French made an agreement with the Vietnamese of Indochina in March and supplemented it with a *modus vivendi* negotiated in September and made effective in October, taking cognizance of the Viet Nam Republic. Negotiations were then undertaken to determine the nature of French-Vietnamese relations in the future. Unfortunately, those negotiations have broken down, and both sides have resorted to force. Similar cognizance was taken of the Cambodian kingdom in January, 1946. The Dutch and Indonesian negotiators arrived at an agreement in March, 1947, which laid the basis for the clarification of Dutch and Indonesian relations. The agreement provided for the establishment of the United States of Indonesia, which would be made up of three states: the Indonesian Republic, Borneo, and East Indonesia. This agreement was never implemented and was followed by police action taken by the Netherlands authorities to restore order. Appeal was made for intervention to the United Nations Security Council by India and Australia. The Security Council called on the antagonists to cease fire and suggested that a Good Offices Committee representing three nations be established to bring them together. The Netherlands named Belgium, the Indonesian Republic named Australia, and the two selected chose the United

States as the third member. As a result of the work of the Good Offices Committee, the Netherlands and the Indonesian Republic agreed on January 17, 1948, to the Renville Agreements, which included eighteen principles as the basis for a political settlement. Negotiations then began on the details of a political agreement which would provide for a sovereign United States of Indonesia and a Netherlands-Indonesian Union of which the United States of Indonesia would be one part.

As for Burma, Prime Minister Attlee announced in 1946 that Burma would be given the right to be independent either within or outside the Empire. He invited Burmese political leaders to go to London to engage in negotiations. The negotiations were successful, and Burma became a sovereign nation in January, 1948.

British authorities laid plans for a union or a federation of the states of Malaya and eventually settled on the Federation of Malaya, which was formed on February 1, 1948. The Federation included all Malaya except Singapore, and its government was made responsible for all administration with the exception of such matters as military and international relations.

New nations are being born. Old ways of life are being altered or exchanged for new ways. Old religious ways are no longer capable of meeting life's needs in many instances.

Always in the past it has been said that the peoples of Southeast Asia were peaceful agriculturists who had no interest in world affairs and who had little contribution to make to such affairs. But it seems that now these peoples are full of ideas about their place in the world and their relations with great and small nations. Their ideas about themselves are going to become increasingly important to other peoples. It is not the intention of this book to deal with their political thinking and aspirations. Its responsibility is to examine their past and present religious attitudes and perhaps to attempt to plot the direction of their religious thinking into the future a few inches of time.

India, China, and the Western world in turn have affected and still are profoundly affecting the lives of the people of Southeast Asia. Burma, Siam, and part of Indochina are regarded as Hinayana Buddhist countries as a result of Indian influence. The majority of the Indochinese population is said to be Confucianist, Taoist, and Mahayana Buddhist at one and the same time as a result of Chinese influence. All the areas to the south, with the exception of the Philippines and Bali, are Moslem because of Indian Moslem and Arabian influence. The Philippines are Roman Catholic due to European influence. And the tiny island of Bali tenaciously maintains a Hindu character which is a result of Indian influence. It would seem as though older cultures have been submerged under these newer religions.

Let us begin to examine the religious traffic which has crowded the crossroads of Southeast Asia. If a large amount of time is spent describing the folkways of the people, it is because the folkways contain an element essential to an understanding of the people.

Religion in this book is not limited to religions which claim to have a supernatural revelation or enlightenment such as Christianity or Islam. For the purpose of this study religion is any cult used by man to explain and to solve his relations with the seen and unseen world about him. There is the same sort of religious enthusiasm, sense of awe, and satisfaction with the approved techniques for dealing with the surrounding universe in such widely different cults as the spirit cult of the Annamese addressing the ancestors, the cult of Jehovah's Witnesses addressing deity, and the cult of physical scientists in solemn conclave addressing themselves to the sacred principles of evolution. One is just as much a religion as the other. In each instance the true believer must have a measure of faith. Certain things have to be believed.

Probably the best place to begin is at the beginning. If we turn back to earlier times, we must return to a simpler way of life and to fewer people leading that life. Java, which now has fifty million persons, had a population at the beginning of the nineteenth century of only five million. Thus one of the most densely populated areas in the world today was severely underpopulated only a century ago.

The same is true of all the other areas in Southeast Asia. The Mekong and Red River deltas in Indochina, which are today densely populated, were previously underpopulated. In fact, the deltas themselves were probably only partly there. The rich rice-growing area of Burma, which made her the greatest rice-exporting nation in the world, was not even above the sea in the early centuries of the Christian Era. At the beginning of the nineteenth century Indochina had a population of about seven million, Siam about six million, Burma about five million, Malaya about a million and a half, and the Philippines about five million. A century ago, instead of the one hundred and fifty million people of modern times, there were certainly less than fifty million and probably not much more than thirty million in all Southeast Asia. The best we can do is to make a guess at the population figures of the preceding centuries. It must be an estimate in the direction of severe underpopulation because such underpopulation was one of the chief reasons for making war. War was an annual event. The dry seasons were the occasions for raids on neighboring lands to acquire manpower. The victor literally "swept" the country of the vanquished of its population. This is one reason that so many diverse peoples have come to live together and to share some cultural practices.

The capital city of Siam in the seventeenth century, for instance, was surrounded by communities of aliens who had been gathered there by war or by the lure of trade. There were Mons, Burmese, Laos, Cambodians, Annamese, Chinese, Japanese, and Indians as well as Europeans. These alien peoples took an active part in the new way of life. They were frequently used as servants about the house and consequently imparted their own concepts of life to those around them. Wars and trade helped to develop cultural similarities.

If we turn back to the earliest times near the beginning of

the Christian Era, before Hinduization began, we may ask: "Who were the people in Southeast Asia?"

Some persons believe that many of the ethnic groups in Southeast Asia came from India before the Aryan invasion of India. Others think that, as the Aryans entered India by the northwest, they pushed before them the aboriginal populations, who pressed on into Farther India to effect a pre-Aryan Indianization. Another point of view holds that maritime contacts between India and Farther India from the earliest times produced similarities of culture even before the development of Hinduization. Such constant close relations are of the utmost importance in understanding the people and the problems of Southeast Asia. It can be shown that Hindu influences not only came from India but also that Islam was introduced from India. It is therefore not difficult to believe that there was a pre-Aryan Indianization of Southeast Asia perhaps as a result of constant maritime and overland communications.

The peoples in those early times who were affected by influences from India were the Malays of Sumatra, the Sundanese, Javanese, and Madurese of Java, the Balinese, the Jakun Malays of the peninsula, the Chams in what is now the province of Annam in Indochina, the Cambodians in Cochin China and Cambodia, the Thai in Yunnan Province, the Mons (also known as Peguins or Talaings) in Lower Burma and the Chao Phya River Valley, and the Pyus (the advance guard of the Tibeto-Burmans) in the Sittang and Irrawaddy river basins.[2] The Annamese or Vietnamese then resident in southern China and Tonkin were not culturally influenced by India during the period of Hinduization, but they are mentioned at this point because their native folkways have much in common with the folkways of the other peoples in Southeast Asia. These peoples all had pressed south in successive waves and were in this approximate geographic relationship at the beginning of the Christian Era.

2. George Coedes, *Histoire ancienne des états hindouises d'Extrême-Orient* (Hanoi: Imprimerie d'Extrême-Orient, 1944), pp. 15 ff.

In material things these peoples held in common the culture of rice by irrigation, the domestication of the buffalo and bullock, the elementary use of metals, and the employment of boats.

In social things there was the important role of the female in the family, and relationship and inheritance were frequently in the maternal line. The community itself was organized for the raising of rice.

In religious matters there were spiritism, the ancestor cult, the cult of the sun-god, the establishment of "high places" for cult practices, and the burying of the dead in jars or in cairns.

In mythological matters there was a cosmological dualism in which the mountains and the sea were opposed. The winged people were against the people of the water. The people of the heights were opponents of the people of the seashore.

Not all the peoples named had all the foregoing cultural elements. But each of them possessed some of these practices.

It was without doubt this general similarity of culture which led the Chinese to refer to all the peoples of Farther India by the term *K'ouen louen*. The exact meaning of the term is not known. The Chinese referred not only to the writings of the *K'ouen louen* but also to their commerce and to their pirates as though the term had an ethnic reference. It is true that the term was applied by travelers after Hinduization had spread over the area, so that the cultural implications of its use might have to be limited to that period and, if so, would have less significance.

The Hindus, and later the Moslems who came over from India, did not find uncivilized savages but people with an organized society who had some practices which were familiar to them. These cultural elements which were common to the peoples of Southeast Asia and many of which were also common to India made it less difficult to introduce religions from India. The acceptance of the new religions, however, need not imply the relinquishment of the old.

Raymond Kennedy wrote in 1942: "The native peoples of the islands have withstood, over the past two thousand years, successive and strong intrusions of Hindu, Chinese, Mohammedan, and European Christian civilizations without losing their own cultural and social identity. . . . Waves of imperialistic expansion have swept over the Indies for hundreds of years; Hindu, Arab, Portuguese, British, and Dutch captains of empire have 'taken' the islands in succession; but underneath the surface shifts and struggles the native communities have gone their traditional ways relatively undisturbed. The masses of the people in their countless little tribes and settlements have been left essentially untouched by foreign governmental systems—the pulse of native life has varied hardly a beat despite the surface disturbances and the changing complexion of the higher government. These people are rooted to their native soil; their horizon of social and political concern stretches scarcely beyond the village or small district where their ancestors lived and died for long ages before them. To them, beyond the next hill lies the end of the world."[3]

That was probably true until World War II. It was written on the assumption that Westernization had had no more profound effect on the lives of the people in their villages than the Hinduizing, Moslemizing, and Sinicizing of the previous centuries. There was a tightness about the village or commune which made it self-sufficient. "Scratch a Mohemmedan Javanese, and you find a Hinduist; scratch the Hinduist, and you find a pagan" is an old saying in the Indies. "This pagan substratum," wrote Kennedy, "is the most important element in the whole superimposed system of religious beliefs and practices, and it gives the tone to the later layers; for the dogmas and rituals of Mohammedanism, Christianity, and Hinduism are all recast by the essentially pagan Indonesian into an ancient cult pattern that would hardly be recognized by a 'true believer.' "[4]

Dr. Fay Cooper-Cole wrote somewhat the same thing:

3. *Op. cit.*, p. ix. 4. *Ibid.*, p. 106.

"The Malayan has found it possible to accept foreign ideas —such as that of state and overlord—and foreign religions without sacrificing the fundamental village organization and many ancient beliefs. Most outside ideas and institutions that have become integral parts of the culture are those that harmonize with native custom and belief or have been built on native foundations."[5] Dr. Cole termed this a fundamental Malayan culture, basically of the village type. In this village type of culture the people practiced the spirit and ancestor cults.

These observations as to the tenacity and endurance of the pristine culture may be extended to refer to the peoples on the peninsula as well as to those in the islands. Although the religious beliefs of the people were little influenced by the Hinduizing, Moslemizing, or Sinicizing of their nations, their ceremonial and vocabulary were transformed. For instance, during the Hindu period the gods and spirits were given Hindu names, and the ceremonial became Hindu in character. In the Moslem period the gods and spirits received Moslem names, and the ceremonial assumed Moslem characteristics. It is impossible at this late date to sieve out only those pristine elements from the later additions, but enough can be identified, even with elements of other religions clinging to their ritual and vocabulary, to give us an idea of what the people in general have always thought about their world. We will proceed regionally so that comparisons can be made and similarities and differences in basic religious attitudes can be noted.

INDONESIA

The Indonesians believe that spirits dwell in the objects of the physical world as well as in persons, both living and dead. Some spirits are benevolent and some are malevolent. It is very important to understand something about the spirits in order to know how to treat them. The first thing to learn is how to communicate with them. Anyone who knows

5. Fay Cooper-Cole, *The Peoples of Malaysia* (New York: D. Van Nostrand Co., 1945), p. 293.

how can do it, and so there is no special spirit priesthood, although there are experts.

If one does not know how to communicate with spirits, he goes to someone who he believes does and learns from him. This person is a medicine man or sorcerer. By his help one can win a wife, call back an erring spouse from a distant place, make one's self seem handsome and attractive, appear to be powerful and fearsome, find money or jewels which have been lost, take revenge on an enemy, cure an illness, or cause sickness in some hated person. To begin with, the sorcerer may point out that feeble-minded or insane persons are not diseased but are possessed by spirits. One needs to learn how to secure the help, or to ward off the attacks, of spirits.

The medicine man may be male or female. Usually the females predominate because they officiate at birth as well as at sickness and death. They claim to be able to remove all obstacles to a successful life. They are for hire by anyone who has the price, and they miss no opportunity to make a profit.

Suppose that one wants to get rid of a competitor for a girl's love. One hires the sorcerer to do it for him by his control of the spirits. Or suppose that one wants to hurt an enemy. To cause an enemy a wound on the leg, the witch sticks a toadstool with a needle and then secretely mixes a portion of it into the victim's food. Potions may also be concocted to engender passion for a lover, hatred against a spouse, madness, or even death. It depends on how far one wants to go. The natives have studied their poisons and have actually discovered formulas which have physical effects on their victims. To offset witchcraft, the best thing for one to do is to hire a better witch than the other fellow. Expert witches use for their purpose only such toadstools as grow near each other in pairs. Of such a pair, one is the prince and one the princess. The prince is the worker of evil, and this the poisoner gives to his customers to work destruction on their enemies. The princess, which provides the antidote, is then hidden by the witch. If he has no scruple about defrauding his customer—which he usually does not—he sells the princess to the victim for a handsome fee.

The Javanese refer to spirits as *yang*. There are many classes of them: the *danhyang*, which protect the village; the *ratu demit*, which are protective spirits; the *jakalbakal*, which are the spirits of the founders of villages; and the *buta*, which are the giants which devour the heavenly bodies during an eclipse. And there are countless others.

In swamps and creeks spirits reside in dead wood floating around. A person first realizes that he is attacked by these spirits two days after the event by feeling pains in his legs. Other spirits lurk in great trees of hard wood and attack passers-by. One gets dysentery by having a passing spirit blow on him. The cure is to blow away the spirit by magic. Great creepers in the jungle are dangerous places for spirits, especially if they have thrown themselves across a creek. If one drinks from such a stream, he will get goiter. If one becomes feverish, then he is probably being attacked by the spirit of someone who died a violent death, perhaps a woman in childbirth. As the attacking spirit would know better than anyone else the cure for his own attack, it once was the custom for executioners to ask their victims what remedy should be applied if they attacked anyone.

Cholera is believed to originate from the battles between warring spirits. To get rid of their violence, offerings are made to all the spirits without distinction.

The spirits of the dead are important because of their effect on the living. The Javanese refer to the soul of the living by the word *soemangat* and to the soul of the dead by the word *njawa*. When the *soemangat* leaves the body, the person dies. A dead person is very dangerous to the living. Those who are on watch by a corpse dare not sleep because their own souls or spirits would be carried away at the moment they fell asleep. It is also customary to prevent a person who is gravely ill from sleeping in the belief that, if he falls asleep, his spirit will depart.

A spirit is a thing of lightness and fineness. It can therefore fly off into space like a butterfly. Javanese often describe the spirit of a person as a bird or a butterfly, and, in attempting to call the spirit back into a dead body, they call to it as they would to the hens. The spirit has an independent existence and may travel about while the person sleeps. All that it sees en route represents the thoughts of the owner of the spirit. A sneeze is regarded as a sign that the spirit has returned. If one has been napping and on awakening sneezes, it means that the spirit is present and wants something.

Because of fear of the dead there are many practices to protect the living, such as the purifying bath of the corpse and the distribution of the ashes at the end of a cremation ceremony to dissipate fearsome forces. The Balinese still cremate. Cremation used to be practiced in Java during the period of Hindu dominance, but generally now the Javanese bury the dead near their own village communities so that their spirits will find old friends and be satisfied and happy and leave the living alone.

The spirits of the defunct are able to maintain communication with the living. Certain domestic animals, such as the dog, the pig, and the hen, are able to see spirits and to let the family know when they are lurking around. Whenever the people have a feast, they always offer some of the food to the spirits, particularly their own ancestors. In every house there is a place set aside for offerings to the spirits of the ancestors. In the village temple, which is usually a Moslem mosque, they make offerings to the spirits of those who have been of importance to the village.

Some of their spirit-houses, if not most of them, are crude things made of bamboo and leaves with a little porch where the offerings are put on a bamboo table or on a piece of stone. Offerings in behalf of a village are generally made by the head of the leading family or by the chief of the village. If a wedding is held in the Javanese village and the married couple wish to show honor to the spirit of the founder of the village, the *jakalbakal*, they offer steamed rice, red and white, with the appropriate accompanying dishes. This is a very important offering for the future welfare not only of the village but of the newly married couple.

One of the most important of all the spirits dwells in a large tree near the village or in the village and is known in Java as the *danhyang desa.* The idea is that this spirit dwelt there before the village existed. The fact that the village was successfully established in his presence is proof enough that he is its protector. All blessings in the village come from the spirit of this great tree. If there is a flood or a drought, it is because the villagers failed to show him honor. The average Javanese villager is unable to distinguish between the *danhyang desa* and other spirits, such as the *jakalbakal* or *Gusti Allah* of Islam. It is probable that the villager has listened to talk about the gods—Hindu, Moslem, and Christian—and understands them in terms of the *danhyang desa.* And what more does he need if his village continues to prosper with plenty of rice and with people in good health?

The cult of the tree spirit is carried out at the foot of the tree itself. Perhaps two stones are set on edge, a third one is placed across the top, and flowers or food are offered. The villager murmurs his needs or tells his troubles or asks where his true love has gone. Since he has direct access to his unseen helper, no priest is necessary.

The numerous spirit ceremonies when planting and harvesting rice show that the people consider that the plants themselves have spirits. When they cut the paddy, they first unite some heads to represent a pair of rice spirits newly married. A processional carries this united "couple" to a little place prepared for them in the barn, where the "couple" must pass symbolically a conjugal life during the following year in order to make the next crop a rich one. The Javanese hold the spirits responsible for all rice-crop failures. A rice disease called *mentek* is believed to be an evil spirit which behaves like an irresponsible child and ruins the crop. Even mice in the field are blamed on spirits.

Among other spirit-beings in Java there is Njai Lora

Kidoul, goddess of the Indian Ocean. She commands legions of spirits and lives on the rocky south coast of Java, where high waves pound. The noise is thunderous, and the water which is forced into caves in the cliffs comes shooting out with considerable strength. The people carry on an extensive cult which centers around the business of collecting birds' nests. After a long preparation of offerings, prayers, and fastings they render their homage. The people at Surakarta believe that the Susuhunan, the prince, unites carnally with her. That prince and the Sultan of Djokjokarta are said to send their cloaks to her annually. More than one prince of the House of Mataram has gone to consult the goddess in the famous grotto of Karang.

The Indonesians believe that the spirits of the dead seek to reincarnate themselves in living bodies and that there are persons actually possessed by spirits. This belief has led many to claim that they are the reincarnation of some famous person in history. Some individual may set himself up as a mystic. His predictions begin to take on a messianic tone after he has had some success at finding things people have lost or in predicting future happiness or sorrow. Perhaps he prophesies that the signs of the times indicate that a great change is coming into the world. And then some phenomenon of nature, such as a volcanic eruption, occurs to excite the imagination of the people. In order to take advantage of this happy event, he may then announce that he himself is actually the reincarnation of some personage such as, in Java, Ratou Adil, who was a sort of pre-Islamic Messiah. If he is successful, the people go wild over him and throng about him, asking for healing, for help in finding lost objects, or for aid in retrieving an erring spouse. High officials have been known to resort to the same sort of magic to claim that they have a more powerful spirit in order to subdue the people.

This belief in the reincarnation of spirits explains why the Indonesians believe that spirits are in innumerable objects such as tigers, crocodiles, snakes, certain areas of ground, mountains, grottos, rivers, stones, lakes, fish, boats, statues, woods, road crossings, marsh, caverns, craters, pits, jewels, the creese, and cannon. In Batavia there is a sacred cannon which I have seen whose fecund power has been proved by countless women who have burned incense there and rubbed its butt smooth with their hands.

Some people who know that death is approaching claim that a werewolf or tiger inhabited by a spirit has eaten their liver. And sometimes persons accused of being werewolves are made to undergo tests to prove that they are or are not. In Sumatra some villages are supposed to be inhabited by people who know how to take on the form of beasts. They acquire these powers by means of incantations. Most of these persons are said to have no dimples on their upper lips.

The idea that the creese has an indwelling spirit has been mentioned. The creese is frequently featured in stories and is often described as sacred or magical. The creese now is less a weapon than a ceremonial object. But the making of a creese has always been done with great care. The person goes through a mystic, almost yoga, program of fasting and meditation in order to purify himself so that he can make a sacred weapon. He begins making the weapon on a lucky or propitious day according to good omens. A creese so made possesses a special power or spirit which is transferred to the person wearing it. A propitious creese brings good fortune and is feared by thieves and dishonest persons.

Tied in with the idea of spirits is that of auspicious times and lucky days. Indonesians place enormous importance on good and bad, lucky and unlucky, days. There are many complicated Javanese calendars, and, by manipulating these, they figure out that certain days of the year are unlucky. Then they calculate what hours of the unlucky days are the unlucky hours, because the spirits may not know what hours are unlucky, and so one can take advantage of them even on an inauspicious day.

Suppose that a thief wants to steal something and wishes

to select a good time to do it. If he wishes to steal on Tuesday, he must first know if it is a lucky day for him and then at what instant on that day will be his luckiest moment.

According to the day of one's birth, one can determine all sorts of things, such as illnesses which will befall, offerings which should be made, and amulets which should be carried for protection. In Java, among objects to be avoided, there is a class of objects called *ringkel* which vary for different persons. It is the thing which contains disaster for a certain individual. For instance, if one is born on a Saturday and if his calendar cycles work out so that his *ringkel* is the tree *siwalan*, he must carefully abstain from touching the tree, eating its fruit, or even coming near it on Saturday.

Among the Sundanese there is a variation in that their calculations for good luck depend not on the calendar but on the alphabet. Each one of the consonants of the Sundanese alphabet is given a numerical value, and, by adding up the values of the consonants, one discovers the numerical value of one's name. If two persons are to marry, magicians work over the values of their names to discover whether they can be happy together.

All these determinations of lucky and unlucky days and acts and associations have an enormous practical importance because these are the things by which the people actually live, work, marry, and bury. And they are by no means only for the lowly and ignorant. In 1938, when the daughter of Mangkou Negoro VII of Surakarta married on June 1, the wedding ceremony took place at 6:00 A.M., although there were formal ceremonies all day. The explanation for this was that the magician had figured out that that hour, before sunrise, was the auspicious moment for the marriage.

An important element in the spirit cult are amulets. Certain objects are supposed to have a spirit and possess supernatural power and so be able to ward off evil. These charms are generally preventive in function. Amulets may be made of small pieces of wood, small stones, or of odd-shaped roots. Or they may be written in Arabic on bits of paper and carried in a tube hung from the neck. The purpose may be more than protective if the charm is written; it may be used to cause harm to fall on someone who is hated. A charm of this sort, if it is very effective, may gain fame and become known over a large area.

Most of the seventy million people in Indonesia support the spirit cult to some degree. Not all the things that have been described are practiced by all the people. But all of them are practiced by some of the Indonesians. Modern sophisticates may carry out some of these practices "just for good luck" or because it is a "family custom." The people have been Hinduized. And after that they were Islamized, so that most of them regard themselves as orthodox Sunnites of the school of Shafei. Many of them have been Westernized and are familiar with modern progress in technological matters. They have accepted new ritual and new vocabulary. But most of them have not been remade as human beings. They hold tenaciously to their traditional outlook on the seen and unseen world about them and solve their practical problems in life as they have always solved them—in terms of the spirits.

Spiritism of the twentieth century is not the same as the spiritism of the first or the tenth century. New names, new gods, new rituals, new courts of justice, new holy places, and new ancestors have come into existence. But in the process of time conversion has not been of the people from the point of view of spirit cultists to the point of view of Hindus or of Moslems or of Westerners. The invading practices have been converted to the uses of the Indonesians. They have had to learn to placate new spirits, to use new charms, to engage in new rituals, but all to the same old end—the happiness of the people dwelling in the midst of myriads of spirits.

BURMA

Even though Hinayana Buddhism has been the established religion in Burma for centuries, spiritism has retained a firm hold on the minds of the people. Spirits in Burma are known as *nats*. The propitiation of *nats* is a daily process and is involved with the problems of day-to-day living. Buddhism is something that is more ceremonial and pertains to the life to come. As the people are concerned with the life that they are leading, they propitiate the *nats*.

There are *nats* of the house, the water, the forest, the trees, and of other things as there are in other Southeast Asian countries. Spirits are generally malevolent, and so the people do not worship them but fear them and try to keep out of their way. All nature is filled with *nats*—every stone, every pool, every tree, every stir of air. To keep them quiet, the people offer them liquids to drink, meat to eat, incense and flowers to smell, and knives to fight with among themselves.

Not only the hill-tribe peoples but the more sophisticated Burmans themselves are aware of the presence of *nats* and take appropriate steps to mitigate their evils. At the edge of every village there is a *nat* shrine and sometimes at the edge of the property of every home in the village. The shrine may be a small house set on a post or hung in a tree. In this the people make their small offerings of morsels of food. Sometimes puppets are made to represent *nats* which have gained a considerable reputation such as Shwe Pyin-ghi and Shwe Pyin-nge, the younger and elder royal brothers who are feared in Upper Burma. Usually, however, the *nat* houses are empty because, after all, a spirit has no body.

Shway Yoe mentions a number of the more prominent spirits.[6] There are the *kosaung nats*, or the spirits of a person, six of them good and six of them bad. There is Min Magayi, or the *eing saung nat*, who is the guardian *nat* of the house. As he usually dwells in the tops of the house posts, these posts are kept covered with white cotton cloth. Most houses have a water pot full of sacred water over which various religious formulas have been muttered by the astrologer. This water is occasionally sprinkled around the house to fend off disease or to bless a person who is going on a journey.

6. Shway Yoe, *The Burman: His Life and Notions* (London: Macmillan & Co., 1910), pp. 253 ff.

The people in the house keep their household *nat* appeased with offerings, believing that, if he is not propitiated, he might do them harm. If a stranger or a chief suddenly appears in the house and disturbs the *nat*, the *nat* is expected to attack him in some way—perhaps with plague, cholera, or dysentery.

There is a *nat* of the village known as the *ywa saung nat*. All Mons before eating offer some of their food to the *nat*, just as many Christian families say grace. In both cases the food is eaten by the humans present. The spirits get only the essence to sniff.

If there should be an epidemic of sickness in a village, a special ceremony is carried out which is marked chiefly by yelling to scare the wits out of the spirit. Certain Buddhist elements have been added to the ceremony which are to be understood not in terms of their Buddhist reference but in terms of their magic effect on an evil spirit. If the epidemic continues, the village is deserted, and the people build another elsewhere. Or, if they feel they must return to the old village, they hire a Buddhist monk to read the law in the streets. This is supposed to drive all *nats* away. After a safe period the people return and set up a new spirit shrine and make a new start.

The spirit is regarded as a sort of bird or butterfly which may be caught and controlled. In some villages, when there is an epidemic, a great feast is held, with the food first offered to the *nats* outside the village. The villagers all take new names for the occasion, and no one is called by his own name for fear the spirits will know who he is and do him harm. At a certain point in the ceremony there is shouting and confused running around, terminating with one or more persons catching a "butterfly" of a spirit in his bathing cloth. This is carefully shaken out over the head of the ill person or persons in the belief that, by so doing, their spirits will return to dwell within them.

Burmans take care when they carry on their trades or as they travel about to propitiate the *nats* which they believe are about them and upon whom they are intruding. Just before rice-harvesting time the people have a feast for the *nats* so that the crop will not be damaged. Often a puppet figure is made before which the feast is laid out.

Persons who suffer a violent death are supposed to have had especially dangerous spirits. In former days when a town was founded, people were buried alive at each of the four corners of the city walls and under the gateposts. There the spirits were supposed to hover around and to bring disaster on anyone with evil intention. As people are forever dying in miserable and unhappy condition, these vicious *nats* are always in great number in all parts of the country.

Omens are sought for in order to know the future. Perhaps the best way for a Burman to find out about the future is to ask the local witch who claims to be able to explain signs and to control the spirits. Every district has a witch who dances at *nat* feasts and is ready to give advice on where lost objects are, where a missing spouse is, in what world a deceased person is, and what time is the auspicious moment to begin a trip. There are also men who dignify their sorcery with an astrologer's book. Sorcerers lay down the rules for almost every human activity in the village.

Instead of Buddhism displacing the ancient ideas about spirits, Buddhism has been gratefully used as a prophylactic against too violent spirits. When all else proves of no avail, there is nothing like some water blessed by a monk or a chanting of the law to drive off the spirits.

"*Nat* worship," according to Cecil Hobbs, "is found to be not only incorporated into Buddhism but also determines some of the most significant religious expressions of the people. One observes the fact that celebrated festivals in Buddhism in which all share alike are not Buddhist in origin at all but are really *nat* festivals. The Water Festival held in April is in honor of Thagyamin, king of the *nats;* while the Festival of the Lights is in honor of another *nat*, Sulamani. Both festivals are accepted by the Buddhist religion."[7]

7. "Christian Education and the Burmese Family" (unpublished thesis; Colgate-Rochester Divinity School, 1942).

Buddhism was used to dress up traditional ceremonies aimed to propitiate the *nats*.

Perhaps the place of spiritism in Burma can best be stated by quoting an old Burmese saying: "At the front door a pagoda, at the back door King Magari [a *nat*]."

SIAM

Before the Siamese ever heard of Buddhism or Brahmanism they had a religion by which they adapted themselves to this inexplicable and sometimes hostile world. Reginald le May wrote of northern Siam: "In spite of the vast numbers of temples built, the innumerable images of the Lord Buddha fashioned and venerated, the endless pilgrimages to the more famous shrines, the countless store of money spent on gold leaf and incense, and the armies of priests that have been ordained, the Laos people remain at heart what they have been from time immemorial—animists."[8] To a lesser degree the same may be said of southern Siam.

The Siamese seem to feel that, while it is good and right to live a life of virtue and to lay up merit for the future, the dangers and evils of the present must be met. The world to them is full of evil spirits that help or hinder. Spirits are ghosts of the dead or the astral bodies of the living. The birth of a spirit was described by Le May as follows:

"When a Laos villager dies, his family washes the body with water and dresses it in a panung and a new coat, which latter is put on inside out with the buttons facing inward. This is because the dead man has become a 'phi' and spirits always wear their clothes inside out. The wrists were tied together, and flowers and candles were placed in the hands. The body is laid in the center of the room and a string is fastened to either wall running across the center of the body at a height of six inches, supporting the cloth that covers the body. A small basket of wicker frame is made and hung across the doorway to keep the evil 'phi' out. Sometimes this basket is never taken down. The body remains alone for one night.

8. Reginald le May, *An Asian Arcady* (Cambridge: W. Heffer & Sons, Ltd., 1926), p. 135.

The next day the coffin is made and four priests are called to chant over the dead. The body is nailed up in the coffin. Cremation takes place after six months or longer."[9]

There are a number of spirits included in the category of ghosts of the dead. The term *phi lawk* is applied to those spirits that haunt old houses or ruins; they love to frighten people by sitting on the end of the bed and pulling their toes. The *phi am* is a spirit that sits on the chest and liver of a person on a journey, and the afflicted one can do nothing but groan and utter inarticulate sounds.

The *phi pret* is a giant about twenty-five feet high, the ghost of an evildoer. Its mouth is as small as the eye of a needle, and thus it is always hungry. It makes a noise like a whistle. Little red spots on the arms and legs are the result not of some mosquito's activity during the night but are tiny holes through which the *phi pret* has been getting as much of a meal as his small mouth would allow.

The *phi tai hong* are the ghosts of those who have died sudden or violent deaths. They are very malevolent.

Sorcerers are interested in *phi prai* or *phi put*. The sorcerer goes by night to the spot haunted and by incantations calls the spirit to appear. He then places a torch under the chin of the spirit, which, to the untutored eye, is a corpse, whose fat is melted and allowed to drip into a waiting vessel. This fat is mixed with sweet-smelling oils. This is a powerful charm which may be used to drive men mad or to attract the love of women. In one instance of which I know a grave was guarded by relatives with shotguns for three nights after a funeral to prevent a sorcerer from practicing his art upon the corpse buried in it.

Then there are spirits that exist of themselves and are not the ghosts of the dead. There is the *phi ruen* that is the guardian spirit of the house. Every home has one, and it may often be heard grumbling to itself. There is a guardian of the land named *prapum chao ti*.

Siamese medical ideas came from India according to which

9. *Ibid.*, p. 120.

the body consists of the four elements of wind, water, fire, and earth. As spirits have control over the elements of the world, they may control the elements of the body too. A spirit may cause a disproportion of some bodily element and bring on sickness. When this happens, the thing to do is to exorcise the spirits and expel them by incantation and the sprinkling of holy water which has been blessed by the monk. This is an example of spiritism taking the new teaching and the new ritual and adapting it to spiritism.

Dr. Henry R. O'Brien tells of one of his cases in which the birth of a child was incomplete. The doctor removed the placenta just before the woman died. To his surprise the family was grateful beyond measure for his help in delivering them from a danger which he had not apprehended at all. The spirit of a woman dying in childbirth is fearsome. If she dies with the placenta within her, she is twice dreadful. The most terrible spirit of all is that of a women dying with child unborn. The family hardly regarded the death because they were grateful to have been saved from a malevolent spirit that would almost certainly have returned to trouble relatives and friends. In what would probably have been a futile effort to escape the spirit, they would have had to lower her body through a hole torn in the floor, take it out of the compound through a hole ripped in the fence, presumably to confuse the spirit so that it could not find its way back, and then dispose of the body by burial instead of cremation.[10]

Persons dying violently or in great misery were supposed to have violent spirits. This belief led in former times to the curious practice of deliberately creating such spirits with a view to having them guard the fortified gates, the city wall, the royal treasury, and other important military objectives. Every old city had a Lak Muang, which was a post in the heart of the city, sheltered by a small structure of permanent materials, such as brick. The idea was to drive the post through the body of a living victim after first having fed him

10. "The Evil Pees," *Siam Outlook*, April, 1929.

well and treated him royally to gain his favor. His spirit was then expected to guard the city.

The story is told that in 1865 the king and the French consul had a grave misunderstanding, so that the French threatened war. The king called in his ministers, who advised a new fort and gate. Six men were seized at night. In the center of the new gateway a deep ditch was dug, and over it an enormous beam was suspended with two cords. The victims were fed an elaborate banquet and then led to their fatal post of honor, The king and all the court made obeisance, and the king begged them to guard the gate with devotion. The cords were cut, the beam fell, and the six men became guardian spirits. Such practices have long since ceased.

In the same older period it was common practice in the courts of justice to exorcise a person believed to be inhabited by an evil spirit. Such an exorcism was described in great detail by Anna Leonowens in reporting on the trial of a slave girl who had cut out her tongue so that she could not be forced to confess her crime or to name her accomplices.[11]

R. Lingat in his "History of Wat Mahathat"[12] recorded of that earlier period that if any person stabbed another in the precints of the royal palace or if a female slave had a miscarriage there, offerings were to be made to the gods. Pavilions were to be erected at each of the four gates and flowered offerings placed under the gates. A sacred thread was to be passed around the palace and a chapter of Buddhist monks invited to chant for three days. The Brahmans also were to come and offer sacrifices to the guardian spirit. And there was to be dancing and music and the beating of gongs. At the end of the ceremony, if it were over a miscarriage, the fetus would be carried out of the city and cast away and thus the evil averted and the city saved from calamity.

One source of information which indicated the strong belief of the people in spirit-gods was the oath of allegiance to the king which was taken twice yearly until 1932, when it

11. *The Romance of the Harem* (Boston: Jas. R. Osgood & Co., 1873), pp. 197 ff.

12. *Journal of the Siam Society*, Vol. XXIV, Part I (1930).

was discontinued. The civil officials taking the oath said: "We beg the land, the forest, and the atmospheric deities, and the four great guardians of the world, whose power extends to all the worlds of the gods, to the sacred foundations, forces and rulers of powerful nations, and the deities stationed in the great white parasols of royalty, and the guardian deities that protect His Majesty by night and by day, and the deities that protect the palace, and the deities stationed to protect the twelve royal treasures, and all the deities, the armories, the ministers, and great royal property; we entreat you all. . . ."

Here were listed the chief guardian spirits of the kingdom which were regarded as efficacious and powerful and fearful enough to require the loyalty of the government officials of all ranks. Anyone taking this oath and drinking a cup of the magic water of allegiance, which had been made potent by Buddhist monks chanting over it and Brahman priests plunging royal weapons into it, had to be sure in his own mind that he had no rebellious thoughts. If he had such thoughts, his perfidy would be revealed by the spirits causing him to choke as he drank the water or to die suddenly shortly after drinking.

Even in these modern times the speech of the common people is revealing of their belief in spirits. One hears such sayings as: "Three days, demon's child; four days, human child. Child of whom let them receive it." This is said when a babe is born and after it is washed and laid on a tray. The father and the relatives then come forward to receive the child, and it is supposed to resemble the person who takes it. If no one takes it, it is a demon's child.

There is also this saying: "If we wish to comb our hair at night, we must first scratch the comb on something three times, or we shall do an injury to our parents." Failure to scratch the comb is supposed to stimulate a spirit into malevolent action.

When Siamese are building homes, one of them will probably say: "We must have an odd number of steps for the house, else they'll be demon stairs." Siamese houses that I have visited always had an odd number of steps.

If one is ill, or if disaster comes in some form, it is common practice to promise valuable gifts to the spirits. Herds of elephants, a hundred buffalo, or fine houses may be promised. When recovery is complete, paper elephants, buffaloes, or houses are made and given. Sometimes the gifts are burned; sometimes they are placed on a river and allowed to float away to the spirits.

For most of the people in Siam, Buddhism has provided, among other things, new ways of controlling evil spirits. A Buddhist amulet or a necklace of metal cylinders containing Pali sutras may be hung about the neck for protection. If one becomes ill, some lustral water made potent by the chanting of monks may be sprinkled on him to drive out the spirit. In cases of severe illness a chapter of monks may be invited to chant for the recovery of the person. It is the rare child in Siam, even in modern times, who does not wear a charm or amulet at some time or have lustral water poured over him.

Many practices and beliefs in connection with the spirits have passed or are passing. Their passing is expedited by the fact that the ancient folkways had no literature. However, certain aspects of the old folkways continue to find favor. With most people there is a continuing sense of the reality of a spirit world and a desire to make some recognition of it. Some of the contemporary ceremonies in connection with the spirit cult are also an expression of social friendliness.

For instance, in 1946 an American was honored with a dinner party in a Siamese home in a small town. After dinner he was informed that, if he were willing, the Siamese would hold a good-luck ceremony for him. He was willing. In a large room cushions were set out for him to kneel on, and silver vases of flowers were grouped behind the cushions. There were also candles lit and some incense sticks stuck into buckets of sand. A Buddhist monk sat crosslegged near by, while the American knelt on the cushions. Siamese men gathered around, and a man on either side gripped an elbow of the American and in turn was gripped by another standing beside him. Everyone in the room then touched the person next to him until a closed circuit of about one hundred persons was formed from the American around the room and back to the American. The Buddhist monk began to chant and then mumbled something as he tied a string on each of the American's wrists. All during the ceremony both the American's elbows were firmly gripped by the men on either side of him. After the monk was finished, an old woman came up and tied strings on each wrist, and she too mumbled something. Then two young girls approached and also tied strings on the American. These strings were to be left on until they rotted off and were supposed to ward off evil spirits and keep him safe while traveling. The American was warned not to remove the strings but to let them rot. He was told that, if he took them off, a calamity might befall him. Another person received the same ceremony later in the evening. After going home, the other person removed the strings from his wrists. The next day he became violently ill. The American who did not remove the strings was so impressed that he was still wearing them a month or more later.

A Siamese graduate of an American university who was appointed in 1946 to an important foreign post had the foregoing ceremony carried out in his home for his wife and children in preparation for their trip abroad. He and his wife are modern sophisticates, and both have an excellent education. Both consider themselves devout Buddhists. At the ceremony in their home a Buddhist monk or two conducted the ritual. But Buddhism was being used to garnish a ceremony as ancient as the race.

II

ANNAMESE FOLKWAYS UNDER CHINESE INFLUENCE

WRITERS on the religion of the Annamese of Indochina distinguish three religions: Buddhism, Confucianism, and Taoism.[1] Generally the three religions are described along stereotyped lines, but the descriptions do not necessarily have a vital relation to the living religion actually practiced by the people.

All three of the standard Annamese religions were imported from China. The Chinese Empire controlled Annamese affairs from the second century B.C. until the tenth century A.D. Chinese occupation left an indelible impression on the Annamese people. The Annamese, however, were not entirely converted to the Chinese point of view. They accepted the Chinese format and put into it the content of their own racial inheritance.

It is generally conceded that there is a strong element of spiritism in the Annamese religions. The abundance of that element makes it difficult to classify and evaluate. One of the best statements in brief of the Annamese religions was made by M. Madrolle in his guidebook *Tonkin du Sud*, in which he stated that there was a rich mixture of the ancient traditions of the race with the systems imported by the Chinese

1. There are no studies of Annamese religion in English. French scholars have been making excellent studies of every aspect of life among the Annamese. Among those which I found especially valuable were *La Cochinchine religieuse* by Louis Eugène Louvet; *Variétés tonkinoises* by E. Souvignet, who provides a remarkably concise summary of Annamese life; *Tonkin du Sud* by M. Madrolle, who in his various guidebooks shows a most unusual understanding of the peoples of Indochina; and, best of all from the point of view of the folkway of the people, *Croyances et pratiques religieuses des Annamites* by Leopold Cadière. M. Cadière arrived in Annam in 1892 and remained there for fifty-three perceptive years, during which he won his way inside the Annamese mentality. Other works consulted were *Rituel domestique des funérailles en Annam* by E. C. Lesserteur and *Essai sur l'esprit du droit sino-annamite* by an Annamese, Tran van-Chuong.

when they were sovereign. He said that, aside from Buddhism, Confucianism, and Taoism, there was a belief in beneficent and malevolent spirits and in the immortality of the soul which dominated all their religious practices and which was evident in their cult of spirits and cult of ancestors.

The religion of the Annamese is essentially the cult of spirits and one which dates back to the origin of the race. The Annamese believe that all organized matter is inhabited by spirits. Spirits are everywhere and are supremely important to man's welfare. Spirits fly in the air and ride with the winds. They move along the middle of roads and float down flowing streams. They hide in the cool depths of the waters. They wait at the edges of whirling water to suck in persons. They ride on the tide rips along the coast and dash small craft upon treacherous reefs.

Spirits lurk in tranquil seas and toss up high waves at the unwary. They love the mountain tops, and they can be heard singing in the climber's ears as he scales the heights. They wait in the deep shade of the forests, and their presence can be felt as they stand quietly by one who is resting. They keep step with the huntsman going along the forest path.

The Annamese venerate a legion of spirits: spirits of men, spirits of the forces of nature, spirits of stones, of trees, of animals, of heaven, of air, of earth, of high rank and of low rank. A complete list would be impossible because there are new ones coming into being daily.

The spirit cult is carried on in many places. When one venerates a natural object, one places the offerings to the spirit on that same object, on the branches or at the foot of the tree, before the rock, or on the hillock.

Heaven is usually represented by a hillock, while earth is represented by the composition of the hillock. The method of showing veneration differs from time to time and from place to place. In the seventeenth and eighteenth centuries heaven was venerated at Hanoi in a temple, but in modern times the sacrifice known as *Nam-Giao* is offered on a hillock.

Most villages consecrate a hillock to Confucius, but the official cult of the philosopher is celebrated at the capital and in the provincial centers in temples. The hillocks used for ceremonial are often bare, and the offerings are placed on the ground or upon a wooden altar table carried there for the occasion. Some altars are built of concrete and are permanent fixtures.

The most usual place for carrying on the spirit cult is a temple, but it may not be a temple in the usual sense of the word. It may be a part of the house which has been dedicated to the practice of the cult of ancestors and to the patron of the trade in which the owner of the house works. There are also little structures erected especially for the spirit cult. The most simple of these is a small house of wood, somewhat like a bird house, which is hung from one of the walls of the house or is set up on a post outside the house.

Cult houses are named according to their function. The *Nha-tho* are the repositories for the ancestral tablets of the clan of the family. The *Dinh* are for spirits which protect the village officials. The *Mieu* may be consecrated to a number of different spirits. The *Den* or *Phu* are dedicated to the spirits of the Taoist cult. Buddhist shrines carry the name of *Chua* or *Am*. Some of these terms are used indifferently in various parts of the country.

Taoist shrines are filled with grimacing images. The others contain nothing but altar tables, some in cheap wood and others in rare woods which are deeply carved, lacquered, or gilded. On these are deposited the tablets bearing the names of the spirits. The official spirit cult does not permit representation of the figure of the spirit. The popular spirit cult does not use images either except in such rare cases as in the cult of the patroness of childbirth, of the god of fire and sun, or of the tiger, or of the patron of a trade or craft.

Why are certain ordinary objects selected for veneration? It is not difficult to see why rocks which menace navigation and which have caused frequent wrecks are venerated. And there are other rocks which because of their peculiar shape or odd coloring might well attract veneration. But usually the stones which are venerated seem ordinary in character and look like any other stone or rock. It is not the rock which determines its quality but the sorcerer who ascribes supernatural virtue to it and says that in it dwells a spirit capable of saving a child from death. Often a legend grows up around a rock near a village ascribing to it all sorts of miraculous cures. Cults like this are born spontaneously and die out without anyone knowing exactly why.

The tree cult is more specific than that of the rocks. Particular attention is paid to certain species of trees which have great vitality, such as the *Ficus*, which is an immense tropical tree. The somber green *Garcinia* or the *Artocarpus* have such an unusual appearance that they draw attention to themselves. Their obvious vegetative energy is the cause of their veneration.

The cult of spirits pays a great deal of attention to feminine spirits of a dangerous sort such as the spirits of young girls who died before marriage and who seize upon young men to satisfy their desire for children. The Ladies of the Five Elements—fire, water, earth, metal, and wood—also receive a great deal of veneration. In this group of old ladies it is particularly the Fire Dame who is venerated. There is hardly a town or village which has not dedicated to her a temple, an open-air altar, or a hillock. This is because of the terrible destruction caused by fire in bamboo villages.

Certain awe-inspiring animals are also venerated. The whale, being an unusual creature, is venerated by fishers as their protector. The tiger cult is practiced on the edge of the forest where the beast itself is encountered and where it is easy to believe that it is a god with supernatural powers who carries off helpless villagers. The picture of the tiger is painted on many protecting screens as a magical defense against spirits.

We see, then, that spirits are venerated because they are believed to affect man's destiny. They attach themselves to man from the time of his birth. If we are happy, it is because of them; if we eat bitterness, it is because of them. They make all the difference between life and death. They cause sickness, destroy the harvest, cause the ax of the woodsman to slip and cut his artery, plague women with sterility, come in a chattering host to simulate cholera and plague, and make articles vanish into queer places. They are always restlessly active.

The Annamese accordingly live in two worlds at all times. They live in the world in which the rest of mankind lives, the world of nature, the world we see. They live also in the world of the supernatural, the world we do not see but sense. They believe that a man may work and plan and study and save but that the results do not depend on man alone; man works in vain unless the spirits about him are agreeable. There are invisible forces which work for or against him. These mysterious forces are at work in his tools, in his domestic animals, in his fields, in the very fishes he catches. As the invisible is more powerful than the visible, the invisible is the important force. Man's part in a job is not so important as the invisible powers which work for or against him. Every ritual act in the religious life of the Annamese must be understood in terms of their belief in spirits.

Religion to the Annamese is not a formal thing which is performed once a week on Sunday morning at eleven o'clock. It is expressed in every act of the daily life. On all occasions the Annamese harmonize their ritual, deportment, and inner attitude. This is true of all classes of people. The nobles, the artisans, the administrators, the teachers, the woodcutters, the carpenters, the ubiquitous market women selling cakes and vegetables—all conduct their affairs with a sense of the presence of the unseen. The most sophisticated and highly educated are equal with the peasant in this respect. One who drives a modern locomotive is no different in his inner attitudes toward the spirit of his locomotive than the driver of a bullock cart toward the spirit of his cart.

As in other parts of Southeast Asia, no intermediary is necessary for one to carry on the cult of spirits. In this respect the cult is different from Buddhism, in which the person who wishes to perform a religious act does so through a monk who gets him in touch with the deity. In the spirit cult the communicant speaks directly to the spirit. Since he himself directs his plea to them, there is no priest.

The Annamese brings before the spirit his modest offerings in order to secure his aid. His comments to the spirit are spontaneous and in terms of his own needs. Perhaps he has offended the spirit and desires to be friends again, or perhaps his child is ill, and he wants some help. He states the case simply.

When a number of persons address themselves to a spirit, they usually do not do it in concert like Methodists saying the Lord's Prayer. They select someone who they feel is representative of their group to speak for them all. He is no priest. He is their spokesman who says what they tell him to say. Such a person may be the head of the family, the village chief, a mandarin, or even the emperor. None of these spokesmen possess any special qualifications themselves which make them a priestly class, different from other men. They are indistinguishable from their fellows. By one mouth the group addresses itself to the spirit. Even the guardians of the Taoist temples who lay out on the altars the objects offered to spirits, who make the ritual gestures and utter various well-known formulas, are not intermediaries but are there to be of service as the communicants address themselves to the spirits. This is the closest that the Annamese come to using an intermediary. These persons are almost indispensable for a successful service, however, because they make the right gestures at the right moment. Furthermore, they possess specialized knowledge which is available for a price.

The Taoist cult is complicated with magical rites which require trained personnel. Perhaps one wishes to know the future, is bent on selecting a good burial place, or is anxious to know whether a certain young man and woman will be happy together. If he goes to a Taoist temple, he usually hires an expert to help him.

Perhaps one knows that he has offended a spirit, because he can hear the spirit grumbling around him at odd moments and because he himself is terribly unhappy and can find no relief. But he is ignorant of what he has done to offend the spirit and is uncertain of what to do to please the spirit and win his favor. And, above all, he does not know what spirit he has offended. The inexperienced cannot find answers to these questions. Special knowledge is required.

There is also special ceremonial for occasions of great importance with which the ordinary man can scarcely cope. In the spring the villagers chase away malicious spirits which bring epidemics. This requires special knowledge by someone who has unusual control over the spirits. Since only a few people have acquired such control by long experience, the ordinary man has recourse to sorcerers, diviners, witches, and geomancers.

Magical practices are handed down from generation to generation in special books or are transmitted orally and are accordingly distorted by each transmitter. Elements are lost because of faulty memory, accretions are picked up out of the experience of each new generation, and borrowings are made from neighboring peoples. The purpose of magical ceremonies is not to express the noble sighings of the soul but to get a quick answer to pressing needs, to regain a lost article, or to satisfy a hate, a jealousy, or a passion. These practices sometimes border on the criminal and may cause death or injury and bring legal action against the practicer.

This is the way one uses a witch or sorcerer. Suppose that a spirit has caused a person to be ill. The object is to appease the right spirit, with the right offerings, with the right promises, and at the right time, under circumstances which will make the acceptance of the offering certain. Is the evil spirit that of a dead ancestor who rests uneasily? Is it perhaps the paternal aunt, the old lady who died without having any children and who is now seeking a child? Is it a spirit in one of the local temples? Is it the spirit of a tree, and, if so, which tree? The sorcerer performs various rites and makes certain puzzling calculations and then names the spirit which has been offended. He also indicates the nature of the offering which the spirit requires. Maybe a simple offering of food will do, or perhaps it is necessary to offer a substitute if the spirit is busy destroying the ill person in order to get his services in the next world. They have servant problems in the next world too! One makes a paper image and burns it in order to provide a substitute servant. Maybe the spirit has merely been trying to attract attention to the need to move his dead bones to a drier spot. Then all one has to do is to move them.

After the sorcerer has given his diagnosis, the application is left with the inquirer. In the case of an ill person the parents perform the offering. They prepare the usual things: a chicken, some rice, some wine, some gold and silver papers, and some incense sticks. They make their offering at the place indicated by the sorcerer. When they make their offering, they also make promises to do certain things if the spirit will not trouble the ill person any more. The work of the sorcerer ends when he points out which spirit to appease and what to do to appease him. In most cases, however, a sorcerer is not used at all.

How can one know when a spirit will accept an offering? For official offerings to spirits court astrologers determine the day and the hour. The imperial calendar also provides the general public with indications as to the times for making offerings. But in most cases this is not enough. Sometimes it helps to consult the fates or charms. One common charm is in the form of two Chinese coins made white with lime on the face side, that is, the side which bears the characters. The inquirer places the two coins, face side turned up, on the middle finger of the right hand, which is rested on the extended left hand in front of the chest. The inquirer then addresses the spirit in a bass voice while sucking in air with his mouth and informs him that on a certain day a certain person proposes to offer him a sacrifice. He asks whether the spirit will accept the sacrifice. Then he jerks his two hands apart, causing the coins to fall to the earth. If one is tails and the other heads, it means that the spirit will accept the offering. If the omens are negative, the person tries several times in order to see whether the spirit will weaken in his rejection of the offering. If after repeated trials the spirit always rejects, then the inquirer may wait to attempt it another day. Or he may, if he is impatient, wait only a few minutes and try again and again until the spirit is forced to accept the offering.

The religious act itself almost always takes on the form of an offering of food, but there are certain exceptions. The religious act may rest within the heart and never rise to the surface for others to see. A market woman carrying her baskets of vegetables on a pole across her shoulder as she trots along the road may mentally address the spirit in a temple, a tree, or a stone as she passes and ask it to help her make a good profit. If she has good luck doing this once, she may do it every day until she feels as though she and the spirit are old friends—or old enemies.

Another example of inner worship which is simple in its elements and which is rendered to heaven is carried out when a person is on the point of death from some serious illness. The parents or relatives of the ill person go out of the house and stand before heaven. Holding a bunch of grass in their mouths, they cry with real tears, "Biting on a bunch of grass, we prostrate ourselves before you; we plead with you to come to our help and save us."

This simple religious act is usually accompanied with a vow. When one makes a request of a spirit, one also makes a commitment. If one is granted certain things, one will perform certain acts of service. Perhaps the spirit of a stone is believed able to help children who are ill. The father and mother of an ill child may carry on a tray a chicken or a duck roasted, some glutinous rice, some bananas or other fruits, some rice wine in a small bottle, some sticks of incense, some silver and gold paper leaves. These are deposited on the ground in front of the stone. The offerer makes four complete prostrations. He then kneels beside his offerings, pours some wine in one or two little cups on the tray as an offering of libation, and makes his prayer in a deep voice, the way one speaks in addressing a superior, sucking in air noisily two or three times in order to show how much emotion and faith the offerer has.

Then he says: "I salute you, in prostrating myself here, Spirit of the Rock. I am So-and-so, of So-and-so family, of such-and-such a village. I have a son of such-and-such a name whom I find difficult to raise. I pray that I may intrust him to you, Sir, Spirit of the Rock, with the prayer that the Spirit of the Rock will be pleased to make him strong and vigorous. Each year on such-and-such a day, I vow that I will come to make an offering to the Spirit of the Rock. When the child is twelve years old, I will come to thank the Spirit of the Rock to pray him to release me from the agreement which I make this day."

After this prayer is completed, the offerer makes four complete prostrations on the earth, arises, burns the paper of gold and silver, and stands before the rock, bending his body forward. He thanks the spirit and asks permission to withdraw. He then drinks the wine which he previously poured into the cup. The other offerings are carried home and eaten by the family.

Perhaps the vow or promise was not uttered in words but was implicit in the act of offering. The worshiper is expected to repeat his offerings and to continue the cult if the spirit grants him the favor he asks. This sort of unspoken vow is included in the ceremony practiced by the guards at the mouth of the Imperial Canal at Hue when they make offerings to the spirit guards who watch with them. The offerings are placed before the rock on which is inscribed the name of the mouth of the canal and where it is believed the influence of the canal's spirits is concentrated. The guards offer some bananas, some wine, some sticks of incense, some gold and silver paper leaves. The person officiating burns some incense, makes four prostrations, and then, standing, with the body bent forward, hands joined on chest, eyes lowered in an attitude of the most profound respect, he addresses the spirit while sucking in air a number of times. Perhaps he says:

"Lord of Rivers at the Mouth of Waters, we who are entirely unknown come before you and prostrate ourselves. Our offerings are of little value, but our hearts are right. We have prepared some bananas, some areca nut, some wine and tea, some gold and silver paper. We offer them all to you. We ask of you that which is good; keep away from us that which is evil and let it be far from us." The officiator then prostrates himself, after which he pours wine into a small cup which he places before the rock. He offers some tea in the same fashion. Finally, he burns the silver and gold papers. The officiator then stands and bows his head and body a number of times while shaking his own hands which he holds against his chest as he thanks the spirit. He concludes by asking the spirit's permission to withdraw.

Offerings to the dead differ somewhat from offerings made to spirits in a direct fashion. In making an offering to the spirits of the dead, one begins by preparing a feast for the ancestors. This is made up of all the usual things that are offered to spirits but may also include glutinous rice which is colored in a number of harmonizing colors so that it will look attractive.

The family altar on which rest the tablets of the ancestors is fixed up, care being taken that each tablet is in its right place. Incense sticks are lighted which send their fragrance all through the house. After the various dishes are placed on the altar in the order prescribed, the ceremonial is ready. The offering is usually made in the morning at sunrise. The head of the family, hemmed in by all the rest of the family, stands before the altar and pours wine into three small cups and then recites the following:

"Today is the anniversary of my ancestor So-and-so. I invite all my ancestors to come with that ancestor to take part in the reception which I respectfully offer to him." Then the officiator and all the family make three prostrations. The head of the family lights the incense sticks and says:

"Today is the anniversary of my ancestor. I, So-and-so, light these fragrant sticks so as to pray his spirit to return to the chief male, to come and accept my offerings, and to protect his descendants." Then he pours a little wine on the earth and continues:

"Today is the anniversary of my ancestor. I pray his shade to return to the principal female, to come and accept my offering and to be favorable to his descendants."

Then the ancestors have their feast which has been prepared for them. Naturally they are content simply to smell the odors from the plates of food. Everything is done with the greatest gravity just as if the ancestors were seen actually eating the food placed on the altar. The head of the family, assisted on the right and left by the two nearest relatives, then makes a number of prostrations and offers the food, a plate at a time, to the ancestors. When the ancestors are supposed to have had their fill, the plates are carried to the dining-room to be served to the family. Each person prostrates himself three times before the altar to say goodbye before going to the family table to engage in the feast.

What lies behind the ancestor cult? The Annamese believe that if a man lives it is because of superior vital principles called *hon*, which are three in number, and of lesser vital principles called *via*, which are seven in number for men and nine for women. These concepts are not clearly defined.

The lesser vital principles are related to the functions of the body and its members and express the vital energy which is used in the functions of the body and its members. These principles control the healthy life of a person. They are not totally dissipated at death but persist indefinitely. Some of them, on passing out of the soul, may be made to attach themselves to the funerary tablets. Others remain attached to the corpse and make witchcraft a very ghoulish profession. Others of the principles are able to travel around. The Annamese do not know which of the principles do which things, but they are sure that they do them. These vital principles after their disincarnation continue to have the same needs that they had when they were united with the body. Their energy is in no wise lessened and indeed might even be augmented by their passage into the world of the supernatural. They continue to take an interest in the affairs of the living and particularly in the affairs of their own family and their friends. Naturally they are animated by good wishes and desire to make their relatives prosper. However, if the living do not carry out their duties toward the ancestors, the ancestors exact justice from them and punish the guilty with sickness, with evils of every sort, with financial ruin, and in extreme cases even with death. As a consequence the living are interested in seeing to it that the dead rest in peace and that their every need is satisfied. The cult of ancestors has for its objective the satisfaction of the requirements of the dead. The motives are not only love of those who have died but fear of beings who have acquired supernatural powers and who can exert a beneficent or malevolent influence on the living.

Every family venerates the souls of the dead. But there are groups other than the family which venerate the spirits of the dead. Villages or towns which have produced superior citizens who are distinguished for their abilities and who might be considered the fathers of the community are venerated by the village fathers. Some village or town spirits are so influential that they are referred to as the "father and mother of the community." These are the spirits of persons who have gained the position of mandarin and have served their community with outstanding ability. The state and the commune may even render homage to them because, if neglected, the state itself might suffer. Each year, on the ritual day, the commune or in unusual cases the whole nation, on instruction from the Emperor, offers homage to the spirit of the departed.

All the individuals mentioned so far are fortunate persons

who have the high regard of the family or the commune or the state. But what of the spirits of those unfortunates who have disgraced themselves? What of the spirits of beggars who have fallen down dead at the side of the road? What of the spirits of young girls who have died without being married? Particularly what of the spirit of the old-maid paternal aunt who died without children and who all her life wanted some? What of the spirits of children born dead? What of persons who died suddenly in an accident? What of the spirits of persons who died while committing a crime? What of the spirits of persons who fell on the field of battle or who were tortured to death? Here is a vast multitude of abandoned spirits. What can be done to protect the living from them?

These spirits all suffer. No one offers them food, clothes, gold, silver, perfumes, garlands of flowers, or sticks of incense. Accordingly, pious persons organize ceremonies on the hillocks for these abandoned spirits. On the first day of the year, each family places at the entrance gate of the garden some offerings for such wayward spirits. In the ceremony they throw them grains of rice, some salt, some gold and silver paper. But will that be enough to satisfy the spirits of these frightful dead? These are terrible beings capable of damaging the living. They make their curses fall on their descendants and on their neighbors. It is up to each person who is plagued by them to discover by divination what spirit is causing the trouble from which he is suffering at the moment and then to attempt to appease that spirit. If unappeased, spirits may cause cholera, plague, or dysentery and may desolate a whole region. These demons and devils are human souls who have been forgotten by their families and have become bitter about it. It is against them chiefly that the sorcerers employ their magic talents.

As the worship of the spirits of the ancestors is one of the most important forms, culturally speaking, of spirit worship, the following pages will describe in some detail how ancestor worship functions.

The Annamese recognize two types of families, as do the Chinese: the large family and the small family. The large family is the clan. Everyone descended from a common ancestor bears a common name. There are not a hundred families as claimed for China but only about a dozen. Among these dozen, however, there are only a few which are really common, such as Nguyen, Tran, and Hoang. The fact that many Annamese bear the same name, however, does not mean that they belong to the same clan and are related. They are like the Smiths and Joneses in this respect. There are many family clans bearing the name of Tran. The clans which bear the name of Nguyen are so common that the Siamese refer to all Annamese as the "Yuen" or "Nguyen" people.

The family clan includes all persons, male and female, descended from a common ancestor. The females by marriage tend to pass over into the families of their husbands. The clan includes not only the living but the dead and is a religious organization because it includes supernatural members. The poorest Annamese coolie is related to the gods. His ancestors are persons above the ordinary world, and he knows that after he dies his descendants will consider him as a supernatural being to be honored and placated. The family thus understood has great dignity and strength.

According to funeral ritual, when the chief of the clan is on his deathbed, the eldest son becomes the Master of Mourning. He murmurs in his father's ear his posthumous honorific name. He takes a remnant of white silk cloth and places it over his father's stomach at the time his father is dying. After the chief has died, he knots the cloth to make a doll-like figure with a head, two hands, and two feet. This is known as the "silken spirit" and is supposed to catch the spirit of the departed and retain it. The eldest son then bathes the body of his father with the five fragrant waters and clothes the body and covers it with a cloth. He then lifts the cloth covering the figure of the deceased, opens the jaws and slips in a small wooden block, and places a small lump of rice first in the right side, then in the left side, and then in the middle of the mouth. He closes the jaws, covers the body with the cloth, and then leads in the wailing.

After the body has been put in the coffin, the silken spirit is put on a spirit couch. Each morning the Master of Mourning invites the spirit to come out and eat; each evening he invites the spirit to return to rest. This is continued for ten days. When the time for the funeral has come, the silken spirit is carried to the ancestral temple, and the Master of Mourning addresses the spirit and says: "As you approach the shadowy shore, come and present yourself in the temple of ancestors." After the visit has been made, it is reported before the coffin. In the funeral cortege the silken spirit is carried in its own chair.

When the burial is half completed, that is, when the grave is half filled up, the silken spirit is replaced by the ancestor tablet. At that moment the engraver gives a few light blows with his chisel and traces on the tablet the last strokes needed to complete the inscription which otherwise has already been traced. The Master of Mourning then has the tablet transported on the spirit litter or chair after having removed the silken spirit, which he tucks in the chair behind the tablet. He then advances and burns some incense and kneels and offers wine and rice before the tablet. Everyone else then gets down on his knees, and the Master of Mourning recites the sacred hymn whose sense is that the children cry with great sadness for their father and request that, as the body has been buried, the spirit should dwell in the tablet and return to the house with them.

The tablet is then carried to the house, where another ceremony takes place. All kneel before the spirit chair and pray: "Let us be permitted to place the tablet and the silken spirit in the place of the spirits." They then carry the tablet in and put it on the altar. The deceased has left the house, physically speaking, but his spirit has returned to dwell in the midst of the clan in a mysterious fashion.

A hundred days after burial the Annamese celebrate the

ceremony of "peace of heart." The tablet of the ancestor is uncovered, and the Master of Mourning and the rest of the family stand each in his place according to rank and weep and wail. Then the Master of Mourning takes incense, lifts it to the height of his forehead, and prays: "May the soul of my father descend from the upper regions and reside in the tablet." He then makes two prostrations and gets up. Then they all get down on their knees, and the Master of Mourning pours some wine into a cup, takes it in his hands and lifts it to his forehead, and prays: "Let the soul of my father ascend from the lower regions and dwell in the tablet." After this ceremony has been completed, the silken spirit is interred, since the spirit is now secure in the tablet.

Not only are the ancestors honored on their anniversaries as previously shown, but they are included in all important family events. This sort of recognition is carried to a high level in the royal family. The emperor makes known to the ancestors all marriages, births, and deaths in the royal family and informs them of all other happenings which might have an effect on the national life. He reports all wars, treaties, and accessions to the throne.

The family clan is a strong and vital element in the national life of the Annamese. The clan includes the living and all the venerated ancestors, whether they are in the funerary temple of the clan, where the tablets of the ancestors more than five generations back are stored, or on the ancestral altars of the heads of the various branches of the family, where the tablets of the ancestors of less than five generations back are kept.

Everyone in the clan has a responsibility toward the ancestors. The Master of Mourning is always the eldest son by primogeniture in Tonkin and Annam, or he may be the eldest male, as in Cochin China. The younger brothers who have small families and who do not have ancestral tablets in their homes must assume their responsibilities also and appear at appropriate seasons in the house of the elder and stand behind him in the course of the ceremony and offer incense sticks.

The women, too, have their place. They prepare the offerings and the feasts and arrange them on the altars. During the ceremony they stand in their proper place and make the prostrations required. It is a common sight to see a lone woman in a graveyard offering incense, areca nut, silver and gold leaves. She stands there head bowed, with hands joined on her chest. The deceased may be her husband, her son, her father, or her mother. Why does she do this? She is probably living alone, without male children. The anniversary day has arrived, and, if she takes no notice of it, dire results may occur. She does what she can to assure the peace of the dead and the happiness of the living.

The lines which draw the Annamese clan together are many. Family terminology is very detailed. Each degree of relationship has a special term to designate it, and these terms are employed in daily usage. To make an error in designation in addressing anyone is considered rude or even a personal injury. Each member of the family knows perfectly his place in the family and knows what is due him and what is due the others. The clan provides each member with assured status.

The members of the clan are drawn together by lines of authority also. The eldest has almost civil or penal powers over the members of the family. He has great moral authority which he may use in directing the affairs of the family. He is their executive director.

The strongest cords holding the members of the clan together are religious in nature. The cult of ancestors not only unites the members of each branch but pulls all the branches together and makes them an effective instrument for action. Clan gatherings on anniversary days are impressive affairs. In times of happiness and in times of sorrow the clan acts as a unit either to rejoice together or to help each other. A member of the clan in trouble discovers how effective the solidarity of the family is.

The family makes a tremendous impact on the children, who are trained along traditional lines. The child is surrounded with affection and is taught respect for his elders and his ancestors. On ceremonial occasions he has his place in the affair, and in feasts he has his seating also. The living and the dead unite to affect him and to convince him of the moral principles necessary for the perpetuation of a strong family.

Another type of spirit offering is a formal one made to the spirits of heaven, earth, the mountains, Confucius, and the protecting spirits of the village. Besides the ritual already described in connection with offerings to spirits, there are certain additions which are peculiar to this sort of formal offering. It is always a collective act, an offering made by the nation or by a group of citizens. There is a parade of flags, a band of musicians, and a host of officials dressed in uniforms with all their decorations on their chests.

The most complete and colorful of these formal offerings is the sacrifice to heaven, *Nam-Giao*, offered on a hillock. Formerly it was held every year, but recently it was held every three years. It was done by the emperor or by his delegate, assisted by a number of lesser ministers. This ritual was imitated more or less faithfully in the provinces and even in remote villages. The ceremony was discontinued upon the abdication in 1945 of the emperor. In general, the main ceremony was as follows.

The emperor and his aides purify themselves first by a fast of three days. During this period they abstain from sexual relations, from intoxicating liquors, from condiments, and from highly spiced food or food with a strong odor. In traveling about, they take care not to go along the middle of the road, which is the route reserved for spirits. They live in a special place selected for the occasion, a place of temporary imperial abode. They remove the veils which cover the tablets of the spirits, sound the bells, and beat the drums. They roast the whole carcass of a young buffalo on fragrant woods piled high. They then inter at a designated place a part of the blood and the hair. The emperor burns incense in a pan, and the spirits are invited to come by the following song which is sung in the name of the emperor:

"Respectfully obedient to the mandate of heaven, and prospering in thriving times, on this occasion of fragrant sacrifice which is first in excellence, we piously present these offerings to their majesties of the bells and drums. Let the spirits who come regard with favor our hearts which are full of veneration." Then the emperor and his assistants make four prostrations because the spirits have arrived.

The emperor then mounts the rounded hillock where are located the altars of Heaven, of Earth, and of the Ancestors of the dynasty. He offers them jade and silk while chanting goes on in his name as follows: "O Boundless Immensity of Heaven! O Calm Profundity of Earth! We offer you these precious objects with a sincere veneration to the end that, always worthy of your exalted world, we shall receive from you happiness, prosperity, and peace." The offering is then placed on the altar or before the altar, after which the officiator, on his knees, lifts the offering to his forehead and bows profoundly. Following this there is a first offering of wine, and then dancers dressed in ancient insignia perform rhythmic dances while the following is chanted:

"Spirits of blue Heaven and yellow Earth! Deign to cast on us your penetrating look and send happiness without and upon us. O Spirits! Deign to remain tranquilly here and observe our sincere hearts. Taste of our offerings! Send us a calm and wholesome atmosphere, with happiness and lasting favor to the end that we shall be forever prosperous."

The emperor then gets down on his knees, and in his name a reader who speaks in a falsetto voice says the following: "On such-and-such a day and month I dare to permit myself to present to the Supreme Emperor of the celestial world and to the august Lord of the terrestrial world my profound and respectful salutations. I have the great honor of presenting to the Supreme Spirits offerings of jade, of silk, of slain victims, of glutinous rice, of flowers, and of fruits. I take the occasion to ask also that the shades of my ancestors will also be willing to accept the offerings which I have placed on the altars."

The reader then withdraws, and the emperor prostrates himself. At that moment the emperor's aides perform the ceremony of presenting the offerings to the altars dedicated to the spirits of the celestial and terrestrial universe. Then they perform for a second and third time the offering of wine, during which the dancers execute ritual dances. They give the emperor a part of the offerings, a bit of food and a little wine known as "the food and drink of happiness." The emperor eats these after he returns to his palace.

The text of the offering formula which the reader has read and a portion of all the things offered on the altars are then carried in processional to the burning fire and hurled into the flames. By this time the emperor has left the Hillock of Heaven, but he stops a moment in his march and turns and gazes on this the final act of the sacrifice. During this period a chorus sings the Song of Approbation and the Song of Celestial Aid, which are as follows:

"We are ashamed of our poor offerings . . . but the Spirits have approached us. . . . The grand ceremonies are successfully completed. . . . Great is Heaven, principle of activation! Immense is Earth, principle of generation. May they send us happiness and prosperity with supreme peace!"

Such is the official spirit cult of the Annamese which renders to supernatural beings the honors which are their due in the hope of winning their favor. The elements of the ceremonial are simple and the ritual understandable at every step. The words which are uttered express sentiments that reveal the human spirit in the presence of the mysterious and unknown. In this ceremony there are elements of praise, humble abasement, spontaneous offering, prayer, and ardent faith which give the communicants the joy of feeling secure. The foregoing ceremony is spiritism on a high religious level.

One of the most practical aspects of the spirit cult is in connection with everyday work. The Annamese believe that each trade should have a cult in honor of the founder of that trade. The cult might be in honor of the person who introduced the trade into a new region or into a certain commune. In many cases they have in mind a particular person in history whom they refer to by name. Frequently, however, they create a mythical character whose spirit they honor.

Such spirits are honored because the Annamese believe that the success of their work depends upon them. This is especially true in specialized trades which require sureness of hand and long training. All tradesmen and artisans venerate a patron saint or spirit. Each year on certain fixed days they perform ceremonies and make offerings to the patron of their particular trade. Some trades have patrons that are very particular and have to be appeased not only annually but on each job and on each stage of the work on each job. The artisan thus may have to address the spirit at each level of his work to get his continuing favor. The builders of junks at Quang-binh after the first stroke of the ax on the wood perform the ceremony of quartering the wood in honor of the "Venerable Lady the Mysterious Virgin of Ancient Heaven" and of "Messers Lo-Ban and Lo-Boc."

As the work advances, they mark the beginning of each new operation by special offerings. For instance, there is the ceremony of joining the mortises which is done when the three pieces of the keel are joined. There is the ceremony of placing the beam when placing the central beam which holds up the great mast. There is the ceremony of opening the heart and of light when the two great eyes are painted on the prow which permit the junk to direct itself and avoid reefs. There is the ceremony of removing the cradle when the junk has been put into the water. And there is the ceremony of peace for the junk when they dismiss the spirits of the wood so as to drive far away all malevolent spirits which might have been lodged in the wood and which might interfere with the good sailing qualities of the junk.

Another example is found among the makers of norias or Persian wheels of the bucket type, which are made at Quangngai. At the beginning of the year all those who work in the forest for a living perform the ceremony of the opening of the mountain. The ceremony is so named because these people search in the Annamese Chain for the woods which they need. They believe that by this ceremony they attract to themselves the favor of their patron, who will give them supernatural guidance in their trade.

They perform the ceremony of the ascension of the mountain when they set out for the forest and the ceremony of planting the posts after they have gathered their woods and are ready to begin building norias. These posts are used to support the wheels of the norias. Then there is the ceremony of the establishment of the mill race, which refers to the channels which lead the waters onto the paddle boards of the wheels. There is the ceremony of joyous reception to the water when all the rice fields are irrigated by the water. A ceremony of prayer for blooms is held when the rice begins to head up, and one for the beginning of the harvest occurs when the harvest is actually begun. And, finally, there is a ceremony of removal of the cult house when they end the year and venerate the patron of the norias. These are not all the ceremonies in connection with the norias and the growing of rice, but they are typical.

There are countless examples of this sort of detailed veneration of the spirits at all stages of the work in a trade. The cult of the spirit of agriculture with its diverse ceremonies might be put in this category also. Another which might be added is the cult which the mother of a family renders to the "Twelve Female Sages," who are the patronesses of childbirth. In all these ceremonies not only the actions of the workers are put under the protection of the spirits but even the instruments of their work are dedicated, particularly at the beginning of the year. The blacksmith pastes gold and silver leaves of paper on his anvil, on his bellows, and on his hammer. The master of a small ship pastes such leaves on the planks of his ship. The keeper of transport ships hangs garlands of flowers on the stakes where he ties up the boats. The mother of the family pastes silver and gold paper leaves on her pans and on her jars, on the doors of the granary—in fact, on everything which has an influence or a part in the well-being of the family.

The act of pasting silver and gold paper leaves on things is a religious act. It is an offering which one makes to a supernatural being in order to attract his favor. The cult which the soldiers render to the flagstaff, to the gates of the citadel, to the cannons, to the mortars which announce the opening and closing of the gates, and to the spirits of prison gates all imply belief in mysterious forces whose assistance is necessary for success. How can a prisoner be kept in prison if the spirits jar the doors open all the time to show their dissatisfaction with the jailer?

The engineer on the modern railroad lines of the country hold the traditional belief, and they burn incense sticks as offerings to their engines. The builders of steel bridges also placed their work under the care of the spirits—spirits which until recent times were unknown among the Annamese because they came into being with the creation of the bridges.

One of the more noble aspects of the spirit cult is the veneration of great nature spirits. Villagers worship three principal nature spirits depending on where the village is located, whether in the mountains, on the plain, or along a river. These three are the Master of the High Palace, the Lady of the Great Drought, and the Lord of Rivers. Their names indicate their function. The state officially venerates the spirits of rivers and mountains, the spirits of stars and constellations, the spirits of clouds, rain, wind, and thunder, and the spirits of hillocks, hills, and fertile plains. The most popular of all the nature spirits are those which the people in the villages call vaguely "spirits of river and mountain" and regard as protectors of their commune. They may not render a distinct cult to them, but they are always being mentioned in daily conversation as well as on formal occasions. Whenever an Annamese wants to show his love for his corner of the world which is his birthplace, he refers to the spirits of river and mountain in connection with that place.

The god of the sun is another nature spirit which is known under different names and venerated in different ways. This is a spirit whose attributes are vast. The general idea is that it is the sun on which the Annamese look and that it is the earth which they cultivate. The sun is the true master of the earth, and the Annamese are but occupants for a day. They must then on every occasion show their dependence on the sun. Whenever they cultivate a piece of land, catch an animal in the chase, cut a tree in the forest, build a house or a tomb, or raise a temple to a spirit, they also make mention of the sun.

Heaven is even higher than the sun. The concept the Annamese have of heaven approaches the notion of a supreme being. Heaven is not a spirit but is a sort of personage known as Lord Heaven. He seems to belong to a transcendent order. The emperor pays homage to him in a formal cult, but the common people do not honor him with a formal ceremonial except in the most exceptional cases. They do, however, refer to him constantly in their ordinary daily language. He is known as the provider for mankind and as the immanent cause of all that happens to man, including life and death, happiness and unhappiness. The witness of heaven is appealed to because heaven is not far removed from man. Lord Heaven sees all and is witness of every act, even of secret thoughts. He is good and compassionate and can be appealed to. He can assist because he is all-powerful. His judgment is requested because he is not vengeful. He examines; he reflects; he decides; he is just. He punishes faults and rewards good intentions. Thousands of times each day the unhappy in the Annamese community cry to heaven for justice and mercy. Without doubt this idea has been strongly influenced by the Chinese, but it is too old and too deeply laid a concept to be other than indigenous. It manifests itself in the language with a spontaneity which shows that, to the common Annamese people, heaven is one of the principal elements in their lives, and certainly one of the most noble.

One who is familiar with Chinese ways of thought will

doubtless feel that Annamese practices are remarkably similar to those of the Chinese in many respects. Certainly the Annamese have accepted much from the Chinese religions.

Confucianism has not appealed to the Annamese in its philosophical aspects so much as in its advocacy of ancestor cult, spirit cult, and the cult of heaven and earth. That is not to say that educated Annamese are unaware of the profound teaching of Confucius, because they are. Many Annamese are veritable Chinese philosophers. Such a person, for instance, is Ho Chi Minh, who seems to personify the classical concept of a Chinese philosopher devoting his life to the reform of government.

Confucius reinterpreted the beliefs and practices of the ancients. The followers of Confucius read and criticized him, discussed him, added to and detracted from his teachings, each explaining in his own fashion the teachings of the Master. Finally, Chu Hsi made a definitive statement which was effective in China and in Annam for many centuries.

The Annamese accordingly came to venerate Confucius and to include him in their cult of ancestors. Annamese liked what they read about Confucius and especially references to the cult of heaven and earth, to the spirit of agriculture, to the seasons, to the shades of great men, to the spirits of nature, and to ancestors.

For instance, in the *Analects* there occurred the statement: "Let there be a careful attention to perform the funeral rites to parents, and let them be followed when long gone with the ceremonies of sacrifice; then the virtue of the people will resume its proper excellence." And this statement: "He sacrificed to the dead, as though they were present. He sacrificed to the spirits, as though the spirits were present."

On one occasion Tsze-kung wished to do away with the offering of a sheep connected with the inauguration of the first day of each month. Confucius said: "Tsze, you love the sheep; I love the ceremony."

On another occasion the Duke of Ai asked Tsai Wo about the altars of the spirits of the land. Tsai Wo replied that the

Hsia sovereign planted the pine tree about them; the men of Yin planted the cypress; and the men of Chau planted the chestnut tree, meaning thereby to cause the people to be in awe. When Confucius heard of it, he said: "Things that are done, it is needless to speak about; things that have had their course, it is needless to remonstrate about; things that are past, it is needless to blame."

As a final instance, Confucius, speaking of Chung-kung, said: "If the calf of a brindled cow be red and horned, although man may not wish to use it, would the spirits of the mountains and rivers turn it aside?" It is this aspect of Confucianism which appeals to the Annamese more than any other because it gives them authority for what they already think.

Closely related to Confucianism is Taoism. Confucius explained the world and man after one fashion, while Lao-tse, the founder of Taoism, did it in another way. A number of persons with a strong interest in magic collected about Lao-tse. These people believed in a complicated pantheon of immaterial beings which personified the forces of nature or were the spirits of great men of ancient times. To such beings priests and priestesses rendered a religious cult. The cult involved exorcisms, incantations, divinations, charms, philters, amulets, and magical formulas. These rites were supposed to secure for poor human beings, no matter how humble, safety and happiness in birth, sickness, and death. By these means they could find lost objects, cure diseases, and drought, ease floods, prevent accidents, and wisely select a site for a house or a grave.

In Taoism all the religious manifestations and all the supernatural beings encountered in Confucianism are also met. These include the forces of nature personified, the souls of the dead, and the spirits of ancestors.

The Annamese are Confucianists in the sense that they hold to the Confucianist philosophy and adhere to the interpretation which is popular in China. They render an official cult to Confucius and to his principal disciples on certain days of the year. They also render, whether officially or in ordinary daily practice, sacrifices to the forces of nature personified, to the shades of great men, and to ancestors.

The Annamese are not Taoists in their philosophy, since in this they are Confucianists. But they take advantage of the various Taoist techniques and have recourse to the practices of sorcery and magic. They refer to Lao-tse as the founder of this aspect of their religious life.

The third major religion imported from China was Mahayana Buddhism. Buddhism has doctrine, ethic, and ritual which should distinguish it from the spirit cult and make it a distinct religion. But the average Annamese is entirely ignorant of the significance of Buddhism. In the Buddhist temple the Annamese see statues of Buddha and of abstract entities. He sees lines of bodhisattvas or arhats, painted or sculptured. There are statues of Quan-Am, the enigmatic goddess of mercy and maternity. Often enough in an upper gallery he is able to kneel before one or more Taoist or Confucianist gods which are on good terms with Buddhism. He feels at home. The Buddhism of the Annamese furnishes new window dressing for old stock.

Buddhism as such makes little impression on the Annamese. In almost every Annamese village there is a Buddhist temple. At least once or twice a year a representative of the village goes to the Buddhist temple to perform a ceremony. In some of the large cities there are Buddhist temples which are served by a community of monks, but this is not the usual practice. The people living near such temples voluntarily make offerings to them or invite the monks to their homes to celebrate religious ceremonies. In such a community a wealthy person would not wish to go to his grave without Buddhist monks in the funeral procession. But all these manifestations are superficial.

The Buddhist religion does not affect the essential life and the inner being of the Annamese. In the provinces almost all Annamese live and die without ever having performed a religious act in connection with the Buddhist religion. The Annamese ignore the Buddhist temples in general, and the temples are not kept in good repair. The tourist who forms his judgment according to the richly endowed temples about Hue would form an opinion very different from the person who knew the nullity of Buddhist life in the small towns and villages.

The Annamese are Buddhist in the sense that the Buddhist religion is patronized by the state. In all parts of the country Buddhist temples may be found where persons go, usually officially but occasionally privately, to carry out a religious rite. However, the Annamese should not be included among the Buddhist peoples of the world, because Buddhist religious life is comparatively unknown to the common people. Even those who frequent the Buddhist temples interpret the ritual in terms of their own spirit cult and never penetrate to the doctrine and the ethic of the religion. Buddhism for the Annamese is an accessory to the spirit cult to which they are at all times faithful.

The Annamese probably regard Mahayana Buddhism, which is supported by the state, much as they regard Roman Catholicism, which is supported by the French. Both religions belong to the official class. The Annamese view them disinterestedly as alien products. At best they look on them as providers of new spirits and ancestors to be appeased. The images of the saints and of the Christ in the Catholic churches, like the images in the Buddhist churches, promote that impression.

An American visiting in Saigon in 1946 had tea at the home of Dr. Tron Van Ty, vice-president and minister of the interior of the Annamese government in Cochin China. He had been minister of justice in the previous government. Mme Ty served tea and Annamese food and cakes. Before serving her guest, she offered some of the food and tea to her ancestors at the family ancestral shrine which was in the same room where she was entertaining. She was a Roman Catholic, but, if she had been a Buddhist, she would have done the same thing.

Confucianism, Buddhism, and Taoism are all importations from China. All three religions have been used by the Annamese to express their traditional spirit cult and cult of ancestors.

III

THE HINDUIZATION OF SOUTHEAST ASIA[1]

WHAT was Hinduization? In brief it was an extension of organized Hindu culture. This included an acceptance of the Hindu conception of royalty, the divine king. Tied in with this was the Hindu idea of administration according to which the administration was as completely swallowed up by the king as the footprints of all other creatures were swallowed up by the footprints of an elephant. Hinduization involved the acceptance of the Hindu or Buddhist religious cults. It also included an acceptance of the mythology of the puranas. The puranas were the third of the four classes of shastras which dealt with cosmogonic, theological, astonomical, and physical knowledge. The secondary puranas included two of the most popular works in Southeast Asia, the *Mahabharata* and the *Ramayana*. Hinduization also included the observances of the dharmashastras, which

1. The subject of Hinduized nations in Southeast Asia has received considerable attention in recent years. One of the outstanding scholars in the field whose views I have generally accepted is G. Coedes. Coedes has spent a large part of his mature life in Southeast Asia and has been resident chiefly in Siam, Cambodia, and Tonkin. In Siam he was employed by the Siamese government in the National Museum, where he translated difficult inscriptions of historical interest. More recently he has been associated with the École Française d'Extrême-Orient at Hanoi, where I met him again in 1946. There I secured copies of his latest work *Histoire ancienne des états hindouises d'Extrême-Orient* published in 1944 at Hanoi. Thanks to his courtesy, I was able to bring to the United States copies for the Library of Congress, Yale University, Harvard University, and the University of Chicago. His volume is one of the best on the subject of Hinduized kingdoms in Southeast Asia from the point of view of history. Other works of his which I consulted are listed in the general bibliography.

Two other writers on this general subject whose works were constantly consulted were G. H. Quaritch Wales and R. C. Majumdar. Two of Mr. Wales's volumes on Siam were consulted more frequently in connection with chapter iv, but his *Toward Angkor* was very thought-provoking in connection with the present chapter. R. C. Majumdar's *Champa*, *Suvarnadvipa*, *Hindu Colonies in the Far East*, and *Kambuja-Desa* all were useful in supplementing Coedes' history and were especially valuable in their description of the various Hindu colonies. Mr. Majumdar raised a number of questions of a historical nature, especially in connection with the location of Srivijaya, which are far from being settled.

contained the canonized common law. And, finally, Hinduization involved the use of the Sanskrit language.[2]

How did Hinduization occur? Did the Indians establish mission boards to convert the heathen? Did they send out colonizers to start a new and little India to the east? Were masses of Indians driven out of India to the east in the bloody conquests of Asoka or by other invasions?

Hindu expansion during the first centuries of the Christian Era was probably commercial in nature. In the course of expanding their trade, the Hindus carried their way of life with them. As a result of certain political and military developments in India and the Near East, a new trade in luxury goods developed. The campaign of Alexander established contact between the Mediterranean world and the Orient. The empires of Asoka and later of Kanishka organized India on a large scale and made an expanding commerce possible in India. The birth in the West of the empire of the Selucides gave organization to the Mediterranean end of the commercial line. The development of trade in gold, spice, sandalwood, and camphor benzoin prospered in the isles beyond the Ganges. This luxury trade was deplored by the Latin moralists of the first century. Place names in the isles indicated the nature of the trade which lured the merchants of India. Takkola (Takoa Pa on the Bay of Bengal), for instance, means "cardamom mart." Karpuradvipa means the "isle of camphor." Another place name, Narikeladvipa, means the "isle of coconut palms." The general designation of the whole area was significant of the trade in gold because the Hindus called it Suvarnabhumi, or "land of gold." They also used the term Suvarnadvipa, or "island of gold."

Farther India had a great reputation for its wealth in gold, and both Greek and Latin geographers have mentioned it. The search for gold played a large part in Hindu expansion into the Indochina Peninsula and the Indonesian Archipelago. The names of the streams and rivers registered by Ptolemy in many instances contain allusions to gold. It was gold above all that attracted the Indians to the East.

2. Coedes, *op. cit.*, pp. 17 ff.

In these modern times when we are familiar with the scanty production of gold in these regions, we may have doubts about the stories referring to this metal. But we are prejudiced by our familiarity with the rich deposits of California and South Africa. In those earlier days gold was very rare, and at the beginning of the Christian Era India had lost its principal source of gold. India had been buying its gold from Siberia, whence caravans carried it by a route across Bactria. The great movements of the peoples of Central Asia in the two centuries before the Christian Era had the effect of cutting off that caravan route and so of depriving India of its usual gold imports. Perhaps that was one reason why India in the first century sought to import money from the Roman Empire. K. M. Panikkar in his *India and the Indian Ocean*[3] mentions the discovery of great caches of Roman coin in South India, especially on the west coast.

The drift of money out of Rome into India was so alarming that Emperor Vespasian in A.D. 79 attempted to stop the export of money on the grounds that it was having a prejudicial effect on the imperial economy. In attempting to find other sources of gold, adventurers turned toward the Golden Chersonese and, in so doing, carried Indian ways of life with them.

Circumstances favored their going. At that time Chinese and Indian shipping had been developed in which there were junks capable of carrying from six to seven hundred passengers. The construction of these ships was based on the techniques in use in the Persian Gulf. A Chinese text of the third century gave a description of the rigging which was a sort capable of long expeditions in dangerous waters.

Furthermore, it is known that in the middle of the first century the Greek pilot Hippalus had discovered the periods of the monsoons, a knowledge which the Arabs had had for some time but had kept as a trade secret. With this knowledge and with good ships there was a prodigious increase of maritime commerce between India and the ports of the Red Sea, the gate of the Occident. This commerce drove the Indians to the peninsula and archipelago to the east of them for

3. (New York: Macmillan Co., 1945), p. 25.

raw products to satisfy the rich trade. A veritable economic revolution followed. It would be another fourteen centuries before such an impetus would be given again to world trade by the Portuguese.

A further circumstance of a moral nature which made commercial lines out of India possible for the caste-conscious Indians was the development of Buddhism. In abolishing the barriers of caste and the exaggerated ideas of racial purity, it destroyed at one stroke the shackles of fear of pollution by contact with barbarians. The Hindus were psychologically freed for overseas travel.

A great many of the Jataka tales dealt with adventures of the sea, showing what a large place the sea had in the life of India. One Jataka tale, for instance, told the story of a king of Videha being defeated and killed in battle, and how the widowed queen fled in disguise to Champa (Bhagalpur) with her treasures. When her son had grown up, he asked her to give him half her treasures so that he could go to Suvarnabhumi to become rich in order to regain the kingdom. The mother pointed out the dangers of the sea and the small chance he had to succeed but eventually gave in to his pleading. He put his stock-in-trade on board a ship bound for Suvarnabhumi and in the course of events was shipwrecked, became rich, and did at last regain the kingdom of Mithila.

Although sea routes were used in traveling to the archipelago, land routes were also employed in reaching points in the peninsula or in crossing the peninsula to take a short cut to China. The peninsula was a natural barrier closing off sea routes between India and China, and the only way to get by was through the narrow channel at what is now Singapore or up through the Sunda Straits in the archipelago. Although the peninsula was covered with mountain ranges, deep rivers, and wild jungle, travelers were not deterred. Persons in search of gold or trade or plunder have never been stopped by such things. Neither the deserts of Asia nor the snows of Pamir were able to discourage the silk merchants in pursuit of trade or the Buddhist pilgrims in search of sacred texts.

The difficulties encountered were graphically described in the *Brihatkatha*, a treasure-house of old Indian stories dating from a period before the Christian Era. In the adventurous story of Sanudasa our hero crosses the sea and lands at the foot of a mountain. He scales mountains, falls into ravines, fights enemies, and swims rivers, and ends up by the hut of a hermit who has the true gold of knowledge.

The geographic obstacles were less formidable than the pirates in the straits and the commercial tyrants located at Palembang who took heavy toll on all passing vessels. These were compelling reasons for cross-peninsula routes. The routes forced through at that time were in constant use through succeeding centuries. In the seventeenth century the famous Three Pagodas Pass was used by the adventurers at the court of Ayuthia in Siam, and the notorious "Siamese White" at Mergui used this route frequently. It was also along this route that the Japanese built Death Valley Railroad from Siam to Burma, where over a hundred thousand Allied prisoners of war died in World War II. When the Japanese began to cross the peninsula toward Burma, it was possible to predict exactly where they would go, because they had to follow back along the same ancient routes the Indians had made on their passage east.

Probably all the eastern ports of India contributed to the eastward expansion of Hindu influence, but the southern ports possibly furnished most of the travelers. Hindu expansion was not a simple historic fact which happened in one day or even in a decade. It went on for centuries. It was aided by centers of distribution created by the first waves of travelers which acted as relay stations. For instance, the Brahman Kaundinya, a Hinduizer of the kingdom of Fou-nan, came from the kingdom of Phan Phan situated on the peninsula. In southern Sumatra, Palembang in the seventh century was a great center for the diffusion of Buddhism where foreign scholars went to study.

How were merchants in quest of spice and adventurers in search of gold able to establish communities so strongly organized as to give birth to Hinduized kingdoms? Certainly the commercial ventures were not undertaken with missionary ends in view. Nor was there any great mass emigration which would have modified the physical types found in the regions.

The newcomers did business with the chiefs of the countries and made themselves acceptable by their rich presents, by their ability to heal disease, and by their gifts of amulets to ward off evil. The stranger in every century who has penetrated the East successfully has passed as wealthy, as a healer, and as a magician. To this day all Presbyterian missionaries in Siam are called "Doctor" because the mission was established by medical men whom the natives regarded as men of wealth and of magic. These Hindus, without a doubt, also posed as of royal descent to impress their hosts.

They needed interpreters in order to live successfully among the indigenous peoples. Marriage with the daughters of the chiefs was the natural step, and it was only then that the culture and religion of the strangers could have influence. The local girls became familiar with Hindu ways and unconsciously acted as missionaries. Being high born locally, when they asserted that Hindu ways were superior to their own, they were seldom contradicted. The indigenous people had no language for the new religious and ritual concepts, and so they naturally adopted the Sanskrit terms. After two thousand years the Hindu terms are still in use.

If a Hindu lived in a community for some time and had several wives and made himself and the community rich with his trade, it would not be unnatural for him to set himself up as chief of the region. Or perhaps a local chief who was enriched by the Hindus adopted Hindu ways for himself and his state. The usual practice was to elevate the local chief to the rank of Kshatriya by a Brahman rite for the admission of aliens into the orthodox community. The rite was known as *vratyastoma*. Many inscriptions made reference to such a ceremony and recorded Sanskritized indigenous names. King Mulavarman, who left some Sanskrit inscriptions in Borneo at the beginning of the fifth century, had a grandfather whose name was the un-Sanskrit one of Kundunga. He probably was a Hinduized local chief. And Sanjaya, who founded in the eighth century the Javanese dynasty of Mataram, was the nephew of Sannaha, whose name sounds like a Javanese one which has been Sanskritized.

In general, the social framework of India dominated by the caste system underwent profound modifications in contact with the indigenous societies. The genealogies of ancient Cambodia present a curious mixture of Sanskrit and Khmer names which show that the Brahmans of Cambodia were not overscrupulous in maintaining the purity of their blood lines. In fact, if the Brahmans wished to found families, they could not pay serious attention to the rules of endogamy. A Chinese text of the fifth century stated that in the kingdom of Touen-siun there were more than a thousand Brahmans from India. The people of Touen-siun practiced the doctrine of the Brahmans and gave their daughters to them in marriage. This kingdom was a dependency of Fou-nan in the Indochina Peninsula.

In the wake of the early merchants there must have followed cultured Hindus of the two upper castes. Otherwise it would be difficult to account for the introduction of the Hindu religion and Sanskrit literature among the indigenous peoples. The part played by Buddhism in leading Indians to ignore caste difficulties is evidenced by the presence of images of Buddha Dipankara of the school of Amaravati which were in great favor among navigators. But most of the kingdoms were not slow in adopting the Sivaistic conception of royalty based on the linking of Brahman with Kshatriya and expressed in the cult of the royal linga.

The tribes of the jungle admired the cultured Hindus and aspired to possess the Brahmans as their own. Led on by hope of gain, the Brahmans were not unwilling and began by recognizing in the fetishes of the clan an avatar of their own divinities. They developed for the aggrandizement of the chief of the tribe a genealogy which identified him with epic cycles.

In payment they expected him to observe their practices. Certainly the communal traits of these countries were not those of Hindu colonies but of indigenous peoples who accepted certain aspects of Hindu culture. And only a small percentage of the people were affected. In this connection W. F. Stutterheim said of Bali that only the members of the court had Hindu blood and that the mass of the people were indigenous. The upper castes, including those of mixed blood, formed less than 7 per cent of the population, with the rest being dubbed "Sudras."

Parallel with the travel of Hindus to the East, there was considerable travel of Indochinese and Indonesians to India. These travelers picked up Hindu attitudes and practices and returned home to Hinduize their own associates. In modern times there is a parallel seen in the students returning from Europe and America who have more effect on China and India in introducing Western manners and customs than the Europeans visiting or living in those countries. The most effective missionaries are indigenous persons who have gone abroad and have been thoroughly indoctrinated and who then return home to affect their home communities.

A further factor in the process of Hinduization was the propensity of the Hindus to put in treatises or shastras the various aspects of their civilization including law (*dharmashastra*), politics (*arthashastra*), and even pleasure (*kamashastra*). A volume by H. B. Sarkar on *Indian Influences on the Literature of Java and Bali*[4] gives an idea of the extensiveness of Hindu literary influence. During the Hindu period the *Ramayana*, the *Mahabharata*, the *Harivamsha*, and the puranas were the principal if not the only sources of local literary inspiration. In all Hinduized Indochina, in Malaya, and in Java this epic and legendary literature was the inspiration for the classic theater, the dance, the shadow play, and the marionettes. From one end to the other of Farther India the audiences wept over the misadventures of Rama and Sita. Stutterheim went so far as to believe that these books and

4. (Calcutta: Greater India Society, 1934).

manuals were more effective than the Hindus themselves in Hinduizing Southeast Asia. It seems more likely that not only the books of the Hindus but the Hindus and the indigenous persons who went to India worked together to produce Hinduized kingdoms.

How profoundly did Hindu civilization penetrate the general population in Farther India? It is believed that one reason for the sudden disappearance of the Hinduized kingdoms was the weakening of the position of the élite, leaving the mass of the people still strangers to Hindu culture. Certainly it is not doubted that under a Hindu varnish the native society retained its essential characteristics. This is the view of N. J. Krom for Java, of W. F. Stutterheim for Bali, and of G. Coedes for Cambodia. Hindu culture was for the upper classes and never became a possession of the masses, who were attached to the cult of spiritism and of ancestor worship.

The royal Hindu cult was essentially an aristocratic religion. This explains the ease and the rapidity with which Singhalese Buddhism and Islam supplanted it when the Hindu world was shaken by the Mongolian conquests and the Moslem invasions. Nevertheless, Hindu influence was not negligible, since it contributed to the peoples of Southeast Asia their script, a large part of their vocabulary, their calendar, their cosmological myths, the great epic themes of the *Ramayana* and of the puranas, certain artistic standards and techniques, the administrative and legal forms, and a social system with a hint of the caste system in it.

It seems astonishing that in nations so close to China which entered into commercial and diplomatic relations with her from the first century that her cultural influence was weak compared to that of India. There has been a great deal of speculation why this was the case. No one knows why. Coedes has commented that the Chinese proceeded by conquest and annexation, as in the country of the Annamese, while the Hindus went peacefully, and that that made the difference.[5]

5. *Op. cit.*, pp. 40–42.

That may be so. It is certainly true that many of the peoples of Southeast Asia had drifted south for centuries, fighting a rear-guard action with the tempestuous Chinese. The Hindus whom they met they met peacefully.

The Hinduized kingdoms which were created in Farther India in the first centuries of the Christian Era were bound to India by nothing more than lines of tradition and admiration. There was no political dependence. The exchanges of diplomats between the two shores of the Bay of Bengal were on an equal footing. Diplomats to China were regarded as barbarians and were required to offer tribute when they appeared at court.

The Chinese-controlled areas of Indochina were administered by Chinese governors, while the Hindu kingdoms of Farther India were governed by independent sovereigns of native origin or of mixed blood who were surrounded by Hindu advisers of their own choosing. The areas conquered militarily by China were required to adopt copies of its institutions, its manners, its religions, its language, and its writing. Those areas conquered peacefully by Hindu penetration adopted Hindu institutions, manners, religions, and writing voluntarily. Both areas, however, actually conserved their essential characteristics and developed according to their natural inclination within the framework of the foreign culture.

Another consideration is the possibility that Hindu civilization of that period, as compared to Chinese civilization, was more missionary in spirit and more dynamic in reaching out beyond its own borders. Hindu missionaries at that time were penetrating into China, and Chinese scholars were making pilgrimages to India to learn of the new culture and to secure sacred texts. One does not hear of Chinese missionaries bearing Chinese texts trying to win India to the Chinese way of life.

There is no easy explanation why Hindu culture and not Chinese culture affected the peoples of Southeast Asia. All one can do is to point out certain obvious differences in the method of promotion and in the reception of the two cultures.

The history of the first Hindu kingdoms in Southeast Asia began in the second century. The most ancient and the better known, thanks to Chinese historians, were Fou-nan and Lin-yi. Fou-nan was the predecessor of Cambodia in the basin of the Lower Mekong River. It extended its conquests as far as the Malay Peninsula and seemed to constitute a sort of empire or federation of petty states, all of which were Hinduized to some degree.

Lin-yi was the ancient kingdom of Champa and was roughly located in the modern province of Annam in Indochina. The Chams sought to extend their control northward at the expense of the Annamese and so started the drama of conflict between the Sinicized Annamese and the Hinduized kingdoms of the south and west.

In the Indochina Peninsula during the first fourteen centuries of our era, Fou-nan and its successor Cambodia, Champa, and Burma were the principal Hinduized nations. In the archipelago perhaps the greatest of the kingdoms was that of the Sailendra Empire. It is not the intention of this chapter to describe the historical developments of these nations in any detail, but some mention should be made of their relations.

Fou-nan was the dominant power in the peninsula for about five centuries. Following generations held its memory in high esteem. Various Hindu cults thrived there simultaneously. The two Kaundinya who at different times supposedly Hinduized the country were Brahmans who introduced Sivaistic rites which were flourishing there in the fifth century. The *History of Ts'i* records that, during the reign of a king named Jayavarman, the custom of the country was to worship the god Mahesvara or Siva. The god was supposed to descend ceaselessly on Mount Mo-tan, which was located near the palace and marked the center of the kingdom. This was the palace where heaven communicated with earth. The god was materialized in the form of the linga of Siva. Images of the god referred to in the *History of Leang* were those of Harihara or of Vishnu and Siva united in a single body. The existence of the cult of Vishnu was also attested by inscriptions left by a prince named Gunavarman. The Buddhism of the Little Vehicle, using the Sanskrit language, was also flourishing there in the fifth and sixth centuries.

Fou-nan was replaced, probably by an internal revolution, by the kingdom of Cambodia, in which Hinduized culture eventually reached its highest level in Farther India.

The other important Hinduized nation on the mainland to the east of Fou-nan was Champa. Its wars, its struggles for survival, and its loss of great numbers of citizenry to its neighbors, who on occasion of victory would "sweep" away tens of thousands of persons, cannot be related here. All we can do is to attempt to show the kind of kingdom it was.

Champa was an absolute monarchy administered by two chief ministers, one for military and one for civilian and religious affairs. Justice was meted out according to the Law of Manu, and their king was supposed to be expert in the dharmashastras.

The caste system was practiced in theory but not in fact, since only the two upper castes, the Brahman and Kshatriya, actually existed. There was constant intermarriage between the two upper castes which formed the aristocracy and patronized Hindu culture. The real social distinction lay between the aristocratic Hinduized society and the mass of people who continued as usual in their folkways. The aristocracy was easy to identify because sumptuary laws reserved for them certain rights and privileges of clothing, of jewelry, of materials for their houses, and of access to the king. The rules for building were strictly enforced. Durable materials were reserved for religious edifices, for royalty, and for high mandarins.

The upper class was familiar with Sanskrit literature and wrote in an alphabet derived from India. The kings considered themselves literary and religious patrons and were themselves said to be familiar with the Vedas, Buddhist texts, and the traditional philosophies of India. The scholars were conversant with the *Ramayana*, the *Mahabharata*, the religious literature pertaining to Siva, Vishnu, and Buddha, as well as with the puranas and the text of Manu.

Siva was the supreme god in Champa and was referred to

in inscriptions as the chief of the Trinity. He was represented both as a figure and in linga form. One famous linga was established by King Bhadravarman in the fifth century. This linga was named Bhadresvara, which was a combination of the name of the king and of the god, showing that the king regarded himself as a divine king or *devaraja*. This particular linga became a national deity, and eventually a mythical origin was claimed for it. In the course of events the linga went through wars and fires. One inscription explained that Siva himself gave it to Bhrigu and that Uroja received it from Bhrigu and established it in Champa. King after king declared himself to be an incarnation of Uroja and restored or further endowed the temple of Bhadresvara and glorified this national deity. Here were magic and ancestor cult on a noble order, indeed, and they were successful in holding the awe and devotion of the population.

Although not so popular as Siva, Vishnu was not unknown in Champa and was incarnate as Rama and Krishna, both of which were frequently referred to. Many kings of Champa compared themselves favorably with Vishnu. Brahma was also referred to, and, although he was the third god of the Hindu Trinity, not much attention was paid to him.

To show how eclectic the religion of Champa was, we need to take note also that a victorious Chinese general carried away with him 1,350 Buddhist works in A.D. 605. There was a community of Buddhist monks, and statues and temples were erected to Buddha.

A point worth noticing is that the characteristic feature of a Cham temple was its storied roof of several stages, in gradually diminishing proportions. This was characteristic of indigenous architecture throughout Southeast Asia. And it was also characteristic of the Indian structures of Mamallapuram Raths and the temples at Conjeeveram and Badami. The style of Champa and the early Dravidian style of India arose about the same time in history, and, in view of what we know about communications back and forth, there might be some connection.

In the archipelago the Sailendra Empire became a great

naval power and extended its control all the way from Java and Sumatra to Cambodia and Champa in the eighth century. Its capital for a time may have been at Srivijaya or Palembang, Sumatra. The struggles between the kingdoms of Java and Sumatra and between the Javanese kingdoms for supremacy over the island empire need not be related here. But the extension of Javanese influence should be indicated.

An Arab merchant, Sulaiman, who traveled through the islands and visited the center of the empire which he called Zabag, perhaps his pronunciation of Javaka, returned home in about A.D. 850 and related what he had seen. He and other Arabs told of the wealth of the "king of the mountain," the Sailendra monarch, whose kingdom was the center of the spice trade. According to the Arabs, the king sat every morning in his palace facing a lake which was tidal in character. An attendant brought him a gold brick which he ordered to be tossed into the lake. When the tide was high, the bricks were all covered, but, when the tide was out, the bricks shone and glinted in the sunlight, and the king admired his treasury. On the death of the king the gold bricks were supposedly collected and divided among the members of the royal family and among high officials. According to H. G. Quaritch Wales, the same custom prevailed in Champa. And in Siam a golden image was cast to commemorate each anniversary of the reigning king's accession. This latter custom was still going on in Siam in the twentieth century.[6]

According to Sulaiman, in the last quarter of the eighth century the king of Cambodia, who was young and rash, was discussing with his minister the wealth of the Sailendra kings who were resident about twenty days' travel away by sea. The Cambodian king was supposed to have said that he would like to see the head of the king of the Sailendras on a plate. The story got around and eventually reached the ears of the Sailendra monarch. The latter fitted out his navy and released a story to the press of the day that he was going to inspect the other islands in his empire. The Cambodian mon-

6. *Towards Angkor* (London: Harrap & Co., 1937), p. 180.

arch heard the news and had no suspicion of his own fate until his capital city was suddenly invested and the Sailendra monarch was sitting on the Cambodian throne.

The Cambodian monarch was beheaded, and the head was washed and embalmed and placed in a receptacle and presented to a new Cambodian king selected by the Sailendra monarch to rule in his behalf. As the story goes, when the kings of India and China heard of these events, they held the Sailendra kings in great veneration. And the Cambodian kings were said to turn their faces toward the Sailendra monarch and to bow to earth to do homage every morning on rising.

Hindu civilization in the island world reached a high level under the Sailendra Empire and during the succeeding Javanese dynasties of Kadiri, Singhasari, and Majapahit, which continued, with Hindu influence dominant, until the fifteenth century. The caste system was introduced, but, as in Bali, where the three upper castes amounted to 7 per cent of the population, the common people continued their usual way of life. There was no purdah system, and the position of women was superior to that of women in India. A woman was even a ruler on one occasion. Women could choose their own husbands. The usual indigenous practices were continued in social affairs.

The administration was that of a highly organized bureaucracy with a divine and absolute monarch overriding the whole system. Under the king there were three ministers, or *mantri*, who were represented by three executive officers who actually carried the burdens of government in military, civilian, and financial affairs. Two other classes of officers were responsible for the courts of justice and the religious institutions, both Sivaistic and Buddhist. The Code of Manu was highly regarded, and an Old Javanese text known as *Kamandaka* was the basis for the exaltation of the king. In the *Kamandaka* political principles were illustrated by the characters from the *Ramayana* and the *Mahabharata*.

The residences of the king and the nobility were built of

durable materials, but the dwellings of the common people were of bamboo and leaves, as was usual in all the Hinduized kingdoms of Southeast Asia. The people amused themselves with gambling, chess, and cockfighting, and music and dancing were popular. One type of group singing which is still in vogue was that wherein one person would sing a first line and the rest would join in on the chorus.

Buddhism preceded and accompanied Hinduism. Buddhism of the Little Vehicle using Sanskrit was prevalent in the islands by the seventh century. When in 671 the Chinese pilgrim Yi-tsing made his initial voyage from China to India, his first stop, less than twenty days after his departure from Canton, was Fo-che, where he stayed for six months to study Sanskrit grammar. He said that in the fortified city of Fo-che there were more than a thousand Buddhist monks who devoted themselves to study and good works. They studied all possible subjects exactly as in India. The rules and ceremonies were identical. If a Chinese priest wished to go to the West to study the original Buddhist texts, he could not do better than to stay at Fo-che for one or two years to practice the rules and then proceed to India.

On his return from India, where he spent ten years at the University of Nalanda, Yi-tsing stopped again at Fo-che between the years 685 and 689, during which time he copied and translated into Chinese some Sanskrit Buddhist texts. In 689, after a brief trip to Canton, he returned to Fo-che to write up his memoirs on the eminent religious persons who went in search of the law in the countries of the West. The only known kingdom of that period which fitted the description of Fo-che was Srivijaya at Palembang.

A group of inscriptions in old Malay, of which three were found in Sumatra, attest that in that period there existed at Palembang a Buddhist kingdom which conquered Jambi and Bangka and launched an expedition against Java. The kingdom bore the name of Srivijaya.

An inscription of the year 684 was the first evidence of the existence of Buddhism of the Mahayana in Farther India. It confirmed the statements of Yi-tsing on the importance of Srivijaya as a Buddhist center and showed that there existed diverse Buddhist schools of thought. It affirmed that the Mulasarvastivada, one of the sects of the Hinayana, used the Sanskrit language which was generally adopted. It also mentioned some sects of the Mahayana in Malayu and stated that at Srivijaya there existed the *Yogacharyabhumisastra*, one of the principal works of Asanga, the founder of the mystical school of Yogacharya or Vijn'anavadin.

This was the period of the rise of the Sailendra monarchs who carried to fame with them the Mahayana type of Buddhism. In 778 the Maharaja Panangkaran, at the request of his spiritual guides, founded a sanctuary for the Buddhist goddess Tara and consecrated to her service the village of Kalasa. This was the monument of Chandi Kalasan situated east of Jogyakarta.

In the second half of the eighth century, when the Sailendras were consolidating their position in Java, they erected some great Buddhist edifices in the Plain of Kedu. Borobudur was built, a Buddhist microcosm, a mountain of stone which was ornamented with bas-reliefs illustrating some of the great Buddhist texts of the Mahayana such as the *Jatakamala* and the *Lalitavistara*.

Borobudur was located on a hillock in the Plain of Kedu and was without a doubt the greatest monument of Indo-Javanese art. On the hillock there was a high rock, which was used to form the core of the immense structure which would otherwise have been architecturally impossible. The temple was actually a facing or outer covering of the virgin rock. The structure had a series of nine terraces, each set in from the one beneath it. At the peak was a bell-shaped stupa. The six lower terraces were square and the upper three circular. The three upper terraces were circled with stupas, and in each stupa was an image of Buddha. The balustrade on each terrace consisted of niches, and each niche contained an image of Buddha—over four hundred in all. Sculptured panels in the galleries were a striking feature, and they depicted the life of Buddha and his deeds, and also the life of Sudhanakumara, who obtained enlightenment from Manjusri. The images of the Buddha in this temple are some of the finest products of Indo-Javanese sculpture.

Near Borobudur was built Chandi Mendut, where a magnificent triad of pure Gupta style showed the Buddha preaching between two bodhisattvas. From the religious point of view these structures exalted the esoteric Buddhism of Vajrayana which was codified later in a treatise known as *Sang Hyang Kamahayanikan*, one of the most famous pieces of Javanese religious literature.

The entire hierarchy of the Mahayana gods was developed in the islands. As time went on, Buddhism adopted the Hindu gods in the Buddhist pantheon and with it also developed a tantric form of worship.

The close association of Buddha with Siva was a characteristic of Javanese religion, and some of the literature, such as *Kunjarakarna* and *Sutasoma*, identified them as one. The Brahmanical religion that developed was similar to that evolved in India at almost the same time. It was sectarian in character and recognized a chief deity, which in the islands was generally Siva. Elaborate ritual based on the puranas was developed which gave great pomp to the cult. This sectarian Brahmanical religion slowly triumphed over Mahayana Buddhism and gradually assimilated it.

As an expression of the growing Brahmanical influence there was erected in the tenth century the Lara-Jongrang group of temples in the Prambanan Valley, which are probably the finest example of Brahmanical temples left in Java. There are eight main temples, two rows of three in a row, and two temples between the two rows. Of the three main temples in one row, the central one contains an image of Siva, while the other two have images of Vishnu and Brahma, so that the whole Trinity is represented. The central place is given to Siva. The temples contain a wealth of sculpture in relief depicting parts of the *Ramayana* story. The workmanship is not finished and rounded, but the story in stone is told with great feeling.

The rise of Brahmanical influence coincided with the shift of political power to eastern Java under the kings of Kadiri, Singhasari, and Majapahit between the years A.D. 1000 and 1500. During that period a high level in Hindu influence was reached in the field of Indo-Javanese literature. In no other part of Southeast Asia did Hindu culture produce such a wealth of literature, most of it religious. The writers were chiefly Sivaists or Buddhists. The literature of this period is known as Old Javanese. Moslem conquests brought the period to a close in Java and forced the Hindu scholars to flee to Bali for refuge, where they continued their literary activities on a reduced scale.

The Old Javanese literature (called *kawi* if in prose or *kakawin* if poetic) derived its subject matter chiefly from Indian literature. It used many Sanskrit words and quoted Sanskrit verses. One of the most famous books of the period was a version of the *Ramayana*. It was not a translation but a new rendering of the old story in Javanese setting. It was so well done that the Javanese people thought that the events were all local. Another production was a prose translation of the *Mahabharata*. Certain parts of the epic were played up and produced as separate volumes. An example of this was the *Arjuna-Vivaha*, written by Mpu Kanwa under the patronage of King Airlangga about A.D. 1020. It dealt with an episode from the *Mahabharata* in which Arjuna helped the gods fight Nivata Kavacha.

Another great work was the *Bharata-yuddha*, which was based on certain sections of the *Mahabharata* which dealt with the great war. It was written by Mpu Sedah in 1157 by order of the king and was so well done that its fame lasted through the centuries.

In the fourteenth century the famed poem *Nagara-Kritagama* was written by Prapancha. It took as its theme the life and times of a famous king of Majapahit named Hayam

Wuruk and gave detailed information about the court life and life in the empire.

A famous *kakawin* work was the *Nitisastra-kawin* now known in Bali as *Nitisara*. It was full of wise moral precepts and religious doctrines.

One of the most important productions which reached full flower under Hindu influence was the wayang stories. *Wayang* means "shadow." It is derived from the root *yang*, meaning "spirit," to which the prefix *wa-* was added. The shadow was associated with the spirit in the minds of the Javanese. The wayang play was a natural expression of Indonesian concepts of the spirit world and its relation to the living.

The Javanese represented the stories by the *Wayang Purva*, in which leather puppets projected their shadows on a white canvas. Other forms of the wayang used puppet figures, masked persons, or even persons without masks. No medium more appropriately blended the cult of spirits of the Javanese with the Hindu stories than did the *Wayang Purva*, the "shadow show." Shadows of fantastic and monstrous figures were projected on a canvas. The player or players recited the story, cast the shadows, and made all the sound effects required. It is thought that the players were originally priests who offered worship to the spirits represented by the shadows. Certainly the show was opened by presenting offerings called *sajen* to the spirits, and incense was burned.

The shows were staged at night, preferably on a dark night when spirits were known to move about the earth in carefree fashion. These plays were a means of contact between the living and the dead. The figures were made as fantastic as the people thought the spirits were. Such shows were frequently arranged for curing diseases. It seems evident that the shadow shows originated in the worship of the ancestors. The modern form developed while Sivaism was the dominant religion of Java. In the beginning the figures of the actor Semar and his two sons, Petruk and Nalagareng, were the heroes. With the advent of Sivaism they became followers of the Indian epic heroes. The old spirit-gods persisted but in a less honored position.

This sort of play which has endured among the Javanese through the vicissitudes of time has spread to Bali, Siam, and Cambodia. The word *lakon*, which is used in Siam to refer to the play, is a Javanese and not a Siamese word, as has frequently been thought. The word has been assimilated into the Siamese language so thoroughly that few realize that it is not a Siamese word. Panji, known as Inao in Siam, was one of the important wayang figures in Java.

The Javanese shadow-show stories relate to early Javanese history. These stories have been worked over with the Hindu stories, so that it is difficult to distinguish the one from the other. A large number of the stories were borrowed from the *Ramayana* and the *Mahabharata*.

Hindu literature in a sense conquered the Javanese people and in a sense was also conquered by them. Hindu literature inspired the noblest of Javanese productions. And, whenever possible, those productions retained or at least reflected the essential point of view on life of the Javanese toward their ancestors and dressed it up in the new and elegant Hindu garment.

Architecturally the high art of Borobudur of the eighth century and of Lara-Jongrang of the tenth century represented the classical production of the best combination of Hindu inspiration with Javanese talent. As time went on and the inspiration became fainter, the native elements came to the fore, and the indigenous concepts of the weird aspects of the spirits began to affect their artistic productions. This became evident when they were building in eastern Java. The subdued and well-proportioned work shown in Borobudur was replaced by structures which had lack of proportion, careless arrangement, and profuse decoration which tended to obscure parts of the structure. This was evidenced in the Panataran collection located northeast of Blitar and in other temples of the thirteenth and fourteenth centuries in eastern

Java. The sculptured narrative reliefs showed vulgar, almost pornographic, human figures which were deliberately distorted like the wayang figures of the shadow show. It seems evident what the artists had in mind. They were expressing again through their artistic skill what they felt deep within about their spirit-infested world. They were paying tribute to the cult of ancestors. The figures were as distorted as they believed the spirits to be.

There was no symmetry or harmony among the figures. They were made to appear lifeless and to look like silhouettes. The busts were shown always in their bulging frontal aspect, even though the head and legs were turned sideways.

A most casual comparison of the artistry of the Panataran reliefs of *Ramayana* with those of Lara-Jongrang reveals the wide difference. The usual comment made by observers is that a fine art has been degraded from one of the highest to one of the lowest. That may be one way to put it. Perhaps, however, the Panataran reliefs indicate that it took a long time for the native spirit of art to absorb thoroughly the Hindu inspiration and make the fullest use of it to portray the world of ancestors and spirits.

Another point to keep in mind is that a remarkable number of the sculptured images did not take on the weird shapes of the sculptured reliefs. The rounded images of the gods and goddesses continued to be well formed. Many of these images were actually portraits of kings, showing that they regarded the cult they patronized as a personal cult. The Vishnu image of Belahan is one of the finest of them all, but it is not an abstract idealization of divinity. It is the figure of the famous King Airlangga of the eleventh century, a great Javanese ancestor to be venerated. The splendid feminine figure of Prajnaparamita of Singhasari with its serene beauty has also received great praise. It, too, was not an image of an abstract concept but was probably the representation of Queen Dedes of Singhasari of the thirteenth century. Another fine Siva image is supposed to represent King Anushapati of the latter part of the thirteenth century, also of Singhasari. And the

Harihara image of Simpin represents the features of King Kritarajasa of Majapahit, who reigned at the turn of the fourteenth century.

In eastern Java the Javanese took over the Hindu concepts and made them fully their own by transmutation. Under the Hindu format was the religious concept of the Javanese spirit world and cult of ancestors.

The freeing of Cambodia from Java was the work of Jayavarman II, the founder of the kingdom at Angkor at the beginning of the ninth century. The events of his reign were related in an inscription of the eleventh century. His Majesty came from Java to rule in the Cambodian city of Indrapura. Jayavarman II was of a family which had gone for refuge to Java during difficulties between the Sailendra and Cambodian monarchs. He doubtless was permitted to return to Cambodia on the understanding that he would rule the country for the Sailendras. At any rate, Cambodia was in a state of anarchy when he arrived, and he had to wage war before he could begin his reign.

After having achieved a strong military control over the kingdom, the king invited a Brahman named Hiranyadama, a scholar in the magical sciences, to carry out a ceremony to mark the end of the dependence of Cambodia on Java. Hiranyadama may have come from a Hinduized kingdom in Southeast Asia or even from India. The idea of the ceremony was to make the king a Chakravartin or universal monarch in his own right. Hiranyadama taught a clever local Brahman named Sivakaivalya the ceremonial procedure. The king then made Sivakaivalya his chaplain and agreed with him that he and his family and no others should celebrate the cult of the divine king. The result was that a powerful Brahman family was developed in Cambodia which gave authority for the divine position of the monarch, which intermarried with the royal family, and which, at times, was powerful enough to restrain the arbitrary actions of the king.

In the ceremony establishing the divine king it was necessary that the king, while on a mountain, receive from the hand of the Brahman a miraculous linga in which resided royal power. Ever after he would be known as "king of the mountain." The mountain in the ceremony was artificially built in the center of the royal city and was supposed to be the axis of the world. The miraculous linga was believed to have been obtained from Siva by the Brahman. Communion between king and god through the priest took place on the holy mount.

The ritual of the divine king was based on four texts: the *Vinasikha*, the *Nayottara*, the *Sammoha*, and the *Siraccheda*.[7] The four texts were inscribed on a stele known as the Four Faces of Tumburu, were of tantric origin, and were supposed to have been uttered by the four mouths of Siva; but they do not give sufficient detail to permit one to figure out the nature of the ritual instituting the divine king.

The *Siraccheda* mentioned decapitation as a part of the ritual. This might have reference to a ceremonial equivalent of the method whereby the Javanese kings were said to have wrested control of Cambodia by decapitation of the king. If Java did obtain control of Cambodia by that method, it is understandable why the ritual signifying the end of Java's control would have an element of decapitation in it. In the ceremony the effigy of the Javanese monarch might be decapitated, or someone might be decapitated in his stead.

Regardless of the details of the ritual, Jayavarman II instituted the cult of the *devaraja* in Cambodia. The sanctuary of the divine king, which marked the center of the royal city, was changed as the kings changed their capital city. Such sanctuaries for the cult are to be found in the Bakong at Hariharalaya, the Bakheng in the first city of Angkor, the pyramid at Koh Ker, the Phimeanakas, the Baphuon, and the Bayon at Angkor Thom. All these were pyramid mountains, and each had a place for the royal linga.

The Hindu religion was so fully developed in Cambodia that to describe it in detail would require a review of the religious history of India. The puranic form of Hindu religion

7. Coedes, *op. cit.*, pp. 126–30.

was stronger and Buddhism was weaker, in general, in Cambodia. However, there were times when Buddhism took the lead. This occurred, for instance, in 1181, when Jayavarman VII gained possession of the kingdom. This great monarch, whose authority extended beyond the actual limits of Cambodia to include part of Champa, of Laos, and of Dvaravati, was an ardent Buddhist. He erected the houses of mercy for pilgrims which marked the two main roads of ancient Cambodia. He also founded more than a hundred hospitals which were open to all four castes and were placed under the patronage of Baishajyaguru, the healing Buddha. The edifices erected during his reign carried the image of Lokesvara, the benevolent bodhisattva, with which he identified himself. He had the face of Lokesvara sculptured on the gigantic four-faced towers of Bayon and on the gates of Angkor Thom and of many other monasteries. The king considered himself to be an incarnation of the merciful bodhisattva. The maladies which afflicted the bodies of men became to him maladies of his own soul. Public sorrow became his personal sorrow. The king expressed the wish that he might be able by his works of merit to rescue from the ocean of existence all beings who were plunged into it.

The major act of the Buddhist monarch was to transform the cult of *devaraja*, instituted at the beginning of the ninth century as a Siva cult, into a cult of *buddharaja* or divine Buddhist monarch. The cult was celebrated in the Bayon, a Buddhist temple-mountain, in the capital city. The image of the central sanctuary was a Buddha which was substituted for the traditional linga representing the divine king. Each of the towers of the temple was sculptured into the four-faced image of Bodhisattva Lokesvara, who dominated and protected such Brahman divinities as Vishnu, Siva, and Parvati. The central Buddha was certainly a representation of the deified king, and in all probability all the bodhisattvas of the towers also carried the likeness of Jayavarman VII. These faces, looking in every direction, affirmed the omnipresence and omniscience of the king reaching out from the axis of the empire into all its parts. This adaptation to Buddhism of the old Sivaistic cult of the divine king did not survive the death of the king who instituted it.

At that time Buddhism went into a decline and was succeeded by an intolerant expression of Sivaism which had not previously been witnessed in the history of Cambodia. The majority of the Buddhist images sculptured on the monuments were systematically knocked to pieces or refashioned into the form of a linga. Perhaps because of their Sivaistic affinities the images of Lokesvara escaped these acts of vandalism. This violent reaction was the last powerful expression of Hinduism in Cambodia.

What caused this intolerance toward Buddhism? It seems out of character, for one usually associates tolerance with Hinduism. But is Hinduism really tolerant in the way in which we think of tolerance? Does it have a sense of respect for the conscience of another? Does it accord liberty to the beliefs and practices which it does not approve? This point has been seriously disputed. Certainly no Indian sovereign neglected to establish the dharma, or the good, and to exterminate the adharma, or the evil, because in India the march of the seasons of the year depended on man's virtue. The impression of tolerance is given by the fact that the Brahmans did not believe in any one god but venerated all the gods, making use of many liturgies. The kings permitted Buddhists and Brahmans to select their own gods just as sovereigns of the European Middle Ages permitted their subjects to select any of the religious orders within the true church. There was tolerance for those beliefs and practices which were approved.

The situation in Cambodia was complicated by political factors. The powerful Brahman House of Sivakaivalya, which had been second only to majesty in power, had been displaced by the Buddhists during the reign of Jayavarman VII. The opportunity of the Brahmans came with the death of the Buddhist king. They ruthlessly reinstated the old cult. It was a futile effort, however, because the nation was crumbling.

We have seen that for many centuries, in Cambodia, a cult was rendered to images which bore the attributes of the great figures of the Brahmanic and Buddhist pantheon. The names of these images recalled the titles of persons recently dead or even still living. Many of them were portraits of such persons in the framework of the characteristics of the cult god.

Innumerable statues of Vishnu, Siva, Harihara, Lakshmi, Parvati, and the bodhisattvas have been recovered in Cambodia. Only a small number of them represent impersonally the great figures of the Brahmanic and Buddhist pantheon. In most cases these images are images of kings, of princes, or of high dignitaries which bear the characteristics of the gods. The names of the statues are usually a combination of the name of a person linked with that of a god, showing how personal the cult was.

The great Cambodian monuments did not originate from the popular devotion of the masses. They were built by royalty, by princes, or by mandarins as mausoleums. In them they perpetuated the cult of ancestors and glorified themselves. Hindu religion had not displaced the ancestor cult or cult of spirits. Even persons in high position were converted only on the surface. They accepted the magnificent forms of the Hindu religions and used them to glorify their old points of view.

The Cambodian aristocrats experimented with every aspect of Hindu culture and absorbed every value they could find for their own use. Inscriptions referred to the proficiency of the Brahmans in Veda, Vedanga, Samaveda, and Buddhist scriptures. Kings and ministers were said to possess knowledge of the dharmashastras. There was daily recitation of the *Ramayana*, the *Mahabharata*, and the puranas, and copies of these texts were presented to temples as acts of merit. The inscriptions were in Sanskrit and have been described by some experts in the language as excellent examples of even the most difficult meters. The religious and mythological conceptions of India were faithfully presented in the inscriptions. This was a remarkable thing in a community separated from

India by thousands of miles. One embassy sent from Cambodia to India required four years for the round trip. But apparently hardships and long periods of travel did not deter travelers. As a result of cultural interchanges Sanskrit literature reached a high state of development in Cambodia, but it did not achieve the literary development found in Indo-Javanese productions.

Cambodia probably raised Indian culture and civilization to a higher level than any other colony. This is evident in the architectural marvels which are probably the greatest of all the ancient monuments constructed by man. The pyramids of Egypt, the ruins of Baalbeck, the famed remnants of Greek architecture, and the breath-taking Buddhist mountain of art at Borobudur are as nothing compared to the Angkor collection. The massive balance of Angkor Wat and the delicacy of carving at Banteay Sri were unsurpassed in the ancient world. The proportions of Angkor Wat are awe-inspiring. The moat surrounding the temple is more than 650 feet wide and is spanned on the western side by a stone causeway 36 feet broad. The length of the moat around the temple is about two miles and a half. A paved avenue runs from the western gateway over 1,500 feet to the first gallery. The first gallery measures about 800 feet from east to west and about 700 from north to south. The central tower rises over 200 feet above level ground, and near its peak is the place for the linga of Vishnu. It is an immense pyramid mountain, with concentric galleries uniting the towers. Despite the difference of level between the first and second galleries, cruciform galleries unite them by an ingenius overlapping of roofs. The galleries are endlessly decorated by bas-reliefs of a high level of excellence. One of the chief sculptured contributions is the peculiar smiling countenace of the gods with half-closed eyes. This unchanging and elusive smile is startling if one has been accustomed to images originating in India.

H. G. Quaritch Wales has ably evaluated the development of Hinduization in Farther India: "In the finest art of Java and Champa India certainly realized her soul; but it would seem to be a law of nature that the consummation of perfection requires the aid of a fitting mate. In Greater India it is in Cambodia that we find that ideal union of Indian inspiration with native genius, symbolized so poetically by the meeting of Prince Kaundinya with Queen Willow-leaf, which gave birth to Indo-Khmer culture, and produced as its outward manifestation one of the great arts of all times, culminating in the wonder that is Angkor."[8]

The only extensive eyewitness description in existence of Angkor when it was alive is that of Tcheou Ta-kouan, who visited the city in 1296. His description was translated into French by P. Pelliot in 1902. The principal section of this translation is appended to this chapter in English translation. When Tcheou Ta-kouan arrived at Angkor, Singhalese Buddhism had already invaded Cambodia. One of the sons of the great Mahayana Buddhist sovereign, Jayavarman VII, is reported to have studied at Ceylon and there to have become acquainted with young men from Burma and Siam who were there for the same purpose. En route home the son of Jayavarman VII visited Burma and probably also visited Siam. He and others like him returned to Cambodia and made easy the conquest of Singhalese Buddhism, which continues to be the dominant religion in modern times.

APPENDIX

OBSERVATIONS ON THE CUSTOMS OF CAMBODIA*

By Tcheou Ta-kouan of the Yuan Dynasty

The walled city.—The wall of the city is about 20 li in circumference. There are five gates, each one flanked by two postern gates. Two gates open on the eastern side of the city, while the other sides have but one gate each. Outside the wall is a great moat. Beyond the moat are causeways with large bridges. On both sides of the bridges there are fifty-four stone devils resembling stone generals, gigantic and terrible. The five gates are identical. The parapets of the bridges are of stone, carved in the form of nine-headed serpents. The fifty-four devils hold back the serpent with their hands and appear to be preventing it from escaping. On the gates of the wall there are five heads of Buddha in stone with their faces turned west;

8. *Op. cit.*, p. 237.

* Translated by K. P. Landon.

there is one in the middle decorated with gold leaf. On both sides of the gates stone elephants are sculptured. The wall is made entirely of blocks of stone, set one on the other, to the height of about 2 chang. The stones are very carefully and substantially joined, and there are no weeds growing between them. There are no battlements. On the rampart fishtail palms have been planted at certain places. At intervals there are small, empty, single-room structures. The inside of the rampart is a sort of ramp more than 10 chang high at the top of which there are great gates which are closed at night and open during the day. There are guards at the gates, through which only dogs may not pass. The wall is a regular square at the four corners of which rise four stone towers. Criminals who have had their toes cut off may not pass through the gates either. Marking the center of the capital there is a golden tower [the Bayon] which is flanked by more than twenty stone towers and hundreds of stone cells. On the eastern side is a golden bridge, on each side of which are two golden lions, while eight golden Buddhas are placed at the base of the stone chambers. About a li north of the golden tower there is a copper tower even higher than the golden tower and with a truly impressive view [probably the Bapuon]. At the foot of this tower there are more than ten small stone houses. Another li north is the king's palace. In the king's pleasure apartments there is another golden tower [the Phimeanakas]. We think that it is these monuments which have caused the merchants, since their arrival, to lavish praise on Cambodia's wealth and distinction.

About a half li from the southern gate there is the tower of stone which it is claimed was erected in one night by Lou Pan. The tomb of Lou Pan is about a li beyond the southern gate and measures almost 10 li in circumference. There are several hundred small stone houses. [The tower of stone corresponds quite well to the Phnom Bakheng almost halfway between Angkor Thom and Angkor Wat. Angkor Wat would then almost have to be the tomb of Lou Pan. Lou Pan is supposed to have been a contemporary of Confucius of the state of Lou and came to be regarded as the carpenter guild's god or sponsor. Tcheou Ta-kouan was probably informed by members of the flourishing Chinese trading community that Angkor Wat was Lou Pan's tomb. As the Chinese were probably forbidden to enter the temple, he fails to describe its wonders or to correct his misapprehension.]

The eastern lake is 10 li east of the wall and is perhaps 100 li in circumference. In it is a stone tower and also stone houses. In the tower is a bronze reclining Buddha from whose navel constantly flows a stream of water.

The northern lake is about 5 li north of the city. In it is a square golden tower, as well as dozens of small stone houses, a golden lion, a golden Buddha, a bronze elephant, a bronze ox, a bronze horse: nothing is lacking.

Residences.—The palace, the official residences, and the houses of the nobles all face east. The palace is north of the golden tower and the golden bridge. From the outer gate it is about 5 or 6 li in circumference. The tiles of the private apartments are of lead, while those of the other buildings are of yellow earth. The piers of the bridge are enormous. Buddhas are sculptured and painted on them. The main building is magnificent. The long verandas and covered corridors are bold and irregular, without great symmetry. The council chamber has golden window frames. At the right and left are square columns hung with forty to fifty mirrors placed at the sides of the windows. Below are depicted elephants. I have heard it said that inside the palace are many marvelous places, but there are very severe restrictions, and it is impossible to enter. In the palace there is a golden tower [the Phimeanakas] at the summit of which the king sleeps. The natives claim that in the tower dwells the spirit of a nine-headed serpent who is master of the soil of the whole kingdom. He appears every night in the form of a woman. It is with him that the king sleeps first and has intercourse. Even the king's first wives would not dare enter. The king comes out at the second watch and may then sleep with his wives and concubines. If one night the spirit of this serpent does not appear, then the king's time has come to die. If the king fails to come for a single night, some misfortune will happen to him.

The dwellings of the princes and of the chief officers are differently arranged and have different dimensions from the houses of the common people. All the outhouses and outside living quarters are thatched. Only the family shrine and the private apartments may be tiled. The official rank of each person determines the dimensions of his habitation.

The majority of the common people use only thatch and would not dare to use tiles. The size of a house depends on the owner's personal wealth, but a commoner would never dare to copy the plan of a nobleman's house.

Clothing.—Everyone, male and female, from the king down, wears the chignon [knot of hair at nape of neck] and keeps his shoulders bare. They wear only a loincloth. When they go out, they add a large strip of cloth which they drape low over the loincloth. There are many qualities of fabrics. Those which the king wears are worth two or three ounces of gold and are the most beautiful of all in color and texture. Although cloth is woven in the country itself, there is much imported from Siam and Champa, and the most valued because of its fine quality is that which comes from the West.

Only the king may wear a heavily flowered material. He wears a golden diadem similar to that on the head of the *rajradhara.* When he does not wear the diadem, he rolls garlands of fragrant jasmine flowers about his chignon. About his neck he wears strands of great beads weighing almost 3 pounds. On his wrists, ankles, and fingers he wears bracelets and rings of gold set with agates. He goes barefooted, and the soles of his feet and the palms of his hands are colored red with a red dye. When he goes out, he holds in his hand a golden sword [the Phra Khan, which was said to be a gift from Indra to the ancient kings of Cambodia; on the blade near the guard are figures in relief of Indra, Vishnu, and Shiva].

Among the common people only the women may color the soles of their feet and palms of their hands. The men would not dare. The chief officers and princes may wear material which is sparsely flowered. Only the palace attendants may wear material with two flower groups. Among the common people only the women may do so. A Chinese who recently arrived wearing such material was not prosecuted as he did not know the custom.

Officials.—In this country there are councilors, generals, and astronomers and below them all sorts of petty employees, who differ from ours only in name. Usually they select princes to hold office; otherwise, those selected offer their daughters as royal concubines. The insignia and the retinue depend also on rank. The highest dignitaries use a palanquin with golden hafts and gold-hafted four-tiered umbrellas. After them come those using a palanquin with golden shafts and a single-tiered parasol with a haft of gold. Then come those who use simply a single-tiered parasol with a golden haft. Next come those who use a single-tiered parasol with a silver haft. There are those also who use a palanquin with silver shafts. The parasols are made of red Chinese taffeta and have fringes falling to the ground. The oiled umbrellas are of green taffeta and have short fringes.

The three religions.—The scholars are called Pan-k'i. The monks are called Tch'ou-kou. The Taoists [Hinduists] are called Pa-sseu-wei. I do not know whom the Pan-k'i worship. [The Pan-k'i are the Brahman pandits or *purohita* who officiate in palace ceremonies and guard the sacred sword, the Phra Khan.] They have nothing which resembles a school or a place for instruction. It is difficult to learn what books they read. One sees them dressed like the rest of the men with the exception of a cord of white thread which they fasten at their necks and which is the distinctive mark of the man of letters.

The Tch'ou-kou [Buddhist monks] shave their heads, wear yellow garments, leave their right shoulders uncovered, tie on a yellow linen skirt, and go barefooted. Their temples may be tiled. Inside is nothing but an image which exactly resembles Buddha Sakyamuni and which they call Po-lai [Phra]. It is dressed in red. It is made of clay and is decorated in red and blue colors. These are the only images in the temples. The Buddhas in the towers on the contrary are different and are all of cast bronze. There is neither bell, nor drum, nor cymbals, nor hanging votive offerings of silk, nor dais. All the monks eat fish and meat but do not drink wine. In their offerings to Buddha they also use fish and meat. They eat one meal a day which is prepared in the home of a host, for there is no kitchen in the temples. They recite numerous texts, all composed on palm leaves which are piled on top of one another in regular order. On these leaves they write black characters, but, as they use neither brush nor ink, I do not know what they write with. Certain monks also have the right to a palanquin with gold or silver shafts and to a parasol with a gold or silver haft. The king consults them in serious matters. There are no Buddhist nuns.

The Pa-sseu-wei [probably Shivaites] are dressed like everyone else with the exception of a bit of red or white cloth which they wear on their heads in the style of the *kou-kou* of the Tartar women, but a little lower. They also have temples, but these are smaller than the Buddhist ones. This is because Taoism [Hinduism] has not prospered as much as Buddhism. They worship only a block of stone which is somewhat similar to the stone of the altar of the god of the soil in China [probably a *linga*]. I do not know, as regards them either, whom they worship. There are Taoist nuns, and the Taoist temples may be tiled. The Pa-sseu-wei do not share the food of other men and do not eat in public. They do not drink wine. I have not seen them reciting prayers or performing meritorious deeds for others. Such children of the laity as go to school attach themselves to the monks who instruct them. When they grow up, they return to lay life. I was unable to learn all the details.

The people.—The people are boorish and very dark. Whether they live in distant villages on the isles of the sea or in the most frequented streets, there is no difference. It is only among the people of the palace of the women of the noble houses that one finds many as light as jade. This must be because they never see the sun's rays. In general, both men and women wear only a bit of cloth about their loins, leaving their chests, white as milk, uncovered. They wear the chignon and go barefooted. This is so even of the wives of the king. The king has five wives: one for the private apartment, properly speaking, and four for the four cardinal points. As for concubines and palace girls, I have heard it said that they number from 3,000 to 5,000. These are divided into several classes. They rarely cross the threshold to go out. Each time that I got into the palace I saw the king with his first wife go and sit at the golden window of the private apartment. The palace attendants lined up under the window on both sides of the veranda and passed one after the other to see them. I was able to get a glimpse. No family which has a beautiful daughter fails to bring her to the palace. Below them are the women who are palace servants. There are not less than one or two thousand. They are married and live almost anywhere. They shave their hair at the top of their foreheads after the fashion of the northern people. They then mark the spot with red and also mark the two temples with red. This is the distinguishing mark of the palace servant women. They alone are permitted to enter the palace. None of those below them may do so. These palace servants are always numerous on the roads around the palace.

The women of the common people wear the chignon but have neither hairpin, comb, nor any hair ornament. On their arms they wear golden bracelets and on their fingers golden rings. The palace women wear all these things. The men and the women anoint themselves with perfumes made of sandal, musk, and other essences.

They all worship Buddha.

In this country there are many effeminate fellows who daily rove in groups of more than ten in the market place seeking to lure Chinese with rich gifts. It is shocking. It is shameful.

Childbirth.—After giving birth to a child, a woman cooks rice, rolls it in salt, and applies it to the sexual parts. After a day and a night she removes it. Thereby the pregnancy has no unfortunate aftereffects, and the woman keeps the appearance of a young girl. When I heard of this the first time, I was astonished and I could hardly believe it. But in the family where I was lodging, a girl bore a child, and I was able thus to inform myself. The next day, bearing her child in her arms, she went with him to bathe in the river. It is really extraordinary. It is said also that the women of this country are very lustful. One or two days after giving birth, they have intercourse with their husbands. If the husband does not satisfy their desire, he is abandoned. If the husband is called away on distant business, things go well for a few nights. But after a dozen nights the woman does not fail to say: "I am not a spirit; how can I sleep alone?" That is how far their depravity goes. The women age very quickly without doubt because they marry and bear children too early. At twenty or thirty they resemble Chinese of forty or fifty.

Young girls.—Parents who have a daughter generally offer this prayer: "May you be desired by men. May a hundred or a thousand ask for you in marriage." A Buddhist or Taoist priest is given the task of deflowering girls: between seven and nine years of age for rich girls but sometimes not before eleven years for poor ones. Each year the mandarin chooses a day in the month which corresponds to the fourth Chinese month and announces it throughout the land. Every family in which a girl is to undergo the defloration ceremony informs the mandarin. The mandarin gives them a candle on which he has made a mark. On the appointed day, when night falls, the candle is lighted, and, when it has burned down to the mark, the moment for the ceremony has come.

A month, a fortnight, or ten days before that date, the parents choose a Buddhist or Taoist priest according to whether they are near a Buddhist or Taoist temple. Certain ones have a regular clientele. Monks of some reputation are preferred by the officials and the wealthy. The poor have no choice. The officials and the wealthy make gifts of wine, rice, cloth, silk, areca nut, and silver articles weighing as much as a hundred piculs and worth from two to three hundred taels of Chinese money. The gifts of the less fortunate amount to from thirty to forty or from ten to twenty piculs in weight. It depends on the generosity of the people. Thus, if poor girls reach the age of eleven without going through the ceremony, it is because they are not able to supply the necessary gifts. There are also some priests who refuse the money and perform the ceremony for poor girls as an act of merit. In one year a priest may deflower but one girl. When he has accepted one, he may not promise others. On the chosen evening, they arrange a great feast with music and the relatives and neighbors assemble.

Outside the gate they put up a high platform on which they set clay figurines of men and animals, sometimes more than ten; sometimes three or four. The poor do not place any there. This is an ancient custom. The platform and the figurines are not removed until seven days have passed. On the selected evening they go with palanquins, parasols, and music to bring the priest. With silks of various colors they make two tents: in one sits the young girl and in the other the priest. It is not known what they say. The noise of the music is deafening. That night noise is not forbidden. I have heard it said that, when the moment has come, the priest enters into the apartment with the young girl, deflowers her with his hand, and then dips his hand into wine. It is said that the father and the mother, the relatives and the neighbors, all put a mark on their foreheads. It is also said that they enjoy it. Some claim that the priest really has intercourse with the young girl, others say not. It is not easy for the Chinese to witness these things, so the exact truth is not known.

Just before dawn they take the priest back with palanquins, parasols, and music. The young girl must then be ransomed from the priest with presents of cloth and silk; otherwise she would be his property forever and would never be able to marry another. What I saw took place on the sixth night of the fourth month of the year 1297.

Before the ceremony the parents sleep beside their daughter; after it she is excluded from the apartment and goes where she wishes without restraint or supervision. For weddings they have the custom of giving presents of cloth, but that is a formality without great importance. Many marry women whom they have had first as mistresses. This practice is not a subject of shame or of astonishment. On the night of defloration there are some times more than ten families on a single street which carry out the ceremony. In the city those who are going before the Buddhist or Taoist priests pass one another constantly in the streets; there is no place where the sound of the music is not heard.

Slaves.—For servants they buy savages to do this work. Those who have many have more than a hundred while those who have but a few have from ten to twenty. Only the very poor do not have any at all. The savages are people from the mountains. They constitute a race apart which is called the *Tchouang* thieves. After they are brought into the town, they do not dare to show themselves outside. If in a dispute someone calls his adversary a *Tchouang*, he feels hatred penetrate to the marrow of his bones, so subhuman are these people considered.

When they are young and strong, they are worth 100 *pou* apiece. When they are old and feeble, they are worth from 30 to 40 *pou*. They may sit and sleep only beneath the floor of the house [the houses are built on stilts]. For their work they may ascend to the floor of the house, but then they kneel, salute with their hands, prostrate themselves, and then they may approach. They call their master *pa-t'o* and their mistress *mi*. The former signifies father and the latter mother. If they commit a fault and are beaten, they bow their heads and dare not make the least movement. The males and females copulate among themselves, but the master would never want to have sexual relations with them. When a Chinese has been there alone for a long time and has commerce once with one of these women, if the master learns of it, he refuses on the following day to sit down with him because he has had relations with a savage. If one of them becomes pregnant through some stranger and gives birth to a child, the master does not trouble to find out who the father is, as he does not count, and the master profits on the contrary from the fact that his slaves bear children, as these are more servants for the future. If slaves run away, their faces are marked with blue after they are apprehended. Sometimes they fasten an iron ring around their necks so as to keep them; others have rings on their arms and legs.

The New Year and the seasons.—They always select their first month in the tenth Chinese month. This first month is called *kia-to* [October–November; but in modern times the first Cambodian month is March–April]. In front of the palace they erect a great platform capable of holding more than a thousand persons. This they cover with lanterns and flowers. Facing it about 20 chang away they collect wooden posts and fasten them together to form high scaffoldings, similar to the poles for the construction of stupas, and more than 20 chang high. Each night they build three or four or five or six. At the summits they place rockets and firecrackers. The expenses are borne by the provinces and the noble houses. When night falls, they invite the king to come out and attend the celebration. They set off the rockets and the firecrackers. The rockets may be seen for more than 100 li. The firecrackers are as large as swivel guns, and their explosions shake the whole city. Mandarins and nobles take part in the festival with candles and areca nuts; their expenditures are great. The king also invites foreign ambassadors to the celebration. This goes on for a fortnight.

Each month there is a festival. In the fourth month they "throw the ball." In the ninth month there is the *ya-lie*. The *ya-lie* consists in assembling in the city the population of the whole kingdom and passing it in review before the palace. The fifth month they "go to fetch the water of the Buddhas." They collect the Buddhas from all parts of the kingdom; they bring water, and in the presence of the king they bathe them. They "make boats sail on dry land." The king ascends a belvedere to be present at the festival. In the seventh month they "burn the rice." At this time the new rice is ripe. They go to get it outside the south gate, and they burn it in honor of Buddha. Innumerable women go to this ceremony in carts or on elephants; but the king does not go. In the eighth month there is the *ngai-lan*. *Ngai-lan* means "to dance." They select talented musicians who come to the palace each day to perform the *ngai-lan*. There are also pig and elephant fights. The king invites foreign ambassadors to attend. The festival lasts for ten days. I no longer recall very well what ceremonies there are in the other months.

In this country there are people who understand astronomy and are able to calculate the eclipses of the sun and moon. For the long and short months, however, they have a system very different from ours. They too are obliged to have an intercalated year, but they intercalate only the ninth month. I do not know why. Each night is divided into only four watches, and seven days make a cycle. . . . These barbarians have neither a family name nor a personal name and do not take into consideration the day of birth. Many, however, make a personal name of the day on which they were born. They have a tradition that the second day is very lucky, the third neither lucky nor unlucky, the fourth inauspicious; that on certain days one may go east and on certain ones west. Even the women know how to calculate these things. The twelve animals of the time cycle correspond to those of China, but the names are different. . . .

Justice.—Disputes among the people, even insignificant ones, always reach the king. Formerly they did not have the punishment of the bastinado, but only, as they told me, fines. In extreme cases they neither behead nor strangle. Outside the west gate they dig a ditch where they put the criminal and then fill it with earth and stones piled high. Next in severity comes the removal of toes and hands or the amputation of an arm. Debauchery and gambling are not forbidden. But if the husband of an adulterous woman catches her in the act, he squeezes the feet of the lover in a split piece of wood. He, being unable to endure the pain, gives up to him all his property to recover his liberty. There are also deceivers and swindlers.

If a corpse is found at the door of a house, they drag it with ropes outside the city to some vacant lot. But there is nothing that can be called a serious inquest. Any one who catches a thief may shut him up and do violence to him.

They have another excellent practice. When someone loses an object and suspects another of having stolen it, who denies the theft, they boil oil in a pot in which the suspected person plunges his hand. If he is guilty, his hand is burned, if not, then the flesh and skin retain their former appearance. Such is the practice of the barbarians.

Supposing there are two families in a dispute and no one knows who is right or wrong. In front of the palace there are twelve small towers of stone. Each of the two adversaries seats himself on one of these towers. At the foot of the two towers the two families keep watch on each other. After one, two, three, or four days, he who is in the wrong shows it in some fashion: i.e., by developing ulcers, or boils, or catching a cold or a malignant fever. He who is in the right has not the least discomfort. Thus they decide between right and wrong. This is what they call heavenly judgment. Such are the supernatural interventions in the country.

The dead.—For their dead they do not have coffins but only a sort of matting. They cover them with a cloth. In the funeral procession they too use flags, banners, and musical instruments. Along the way they scatter roasted rice. When they have readied some distant and uninhabited place outside the city, they abandon the body and withdraw. They wait until vultures and dogs come to devour it. If everything is eagerly eaten up, they say that their kinsmen [*sic*] had merit and so have obtained this reward. If the animals do not eat them or eat them only partially, they say that their kinsmen have brought this about through some sin. Now there are also a few people who are beginning to burn their dead. These are all of Chinese descent. At the time of the death of their parents, the children do not wear mourning, but the sons shave their heads and the daughters cut the hair at the top of their foreheads from a spot almost as big as a sapek, and this is their mark of filial piety. The king is buried in a tower, but I do not known whether they bury his body or only his bones. [Cremation of a sovereign was a grand ceremony; the bones were kept in a golden urn in the palace, were honored by the sons on certain stated occasions, and were finally interred in one of the pyramids. Cremation of the common people is the rule in modern times and was regularly practiced in the thirteenth century as was the practice of giving the flesh to the animals in the mountains or to the crocodiles of the rivers as an act of piety. As late as 1859 the Cambodian king Ang-Duong had his flesh fed in morsels to birds of prey as an evidence of his Buddhist faith.]

Villages.—Each village has a temple or a stupa. However few may be the villagers, they have a police officer. Along the highways there are places of rest similar to our stage stations. . . . In the recent war with the Siamese the country has been completely devastated.

The collection of gall.—In olden times, in the eighth month, they gathered gall. Every year the king of Champa demanded a jar of human gall, which contained the gall of thousands. At night they posted men in many parts of the towns and villages. When they met people abroad during the night, they covered their heads with hoods which were tightened by a cord, and with a small knife removed their gall on the lower right side. They waited until they had a sufficient number to offer to the king of Champa. They did not take the gall of Chinese. It happened that one year they did take the gall of a Chinese and put it with the others, after which all the gall in the jar rotted, and they were not able to use it. Recently this custom has been abolished, but there is still the official for the collection of gall who lives in the city near the north gate.

Royal appearances.—I have heard that formerly the king never left footprints outside his palace. This was the custom in order to avoid accidents. The new king is the son-in-law of the old one. He chose the military for his career. The father-in-law loved his daughter. The daughter stole from him the golden sword [the Phra Khan, symbol of the power of majesty] and took it to her husband. So the son, robbed of the succession, plotted to raise troops. The new king learned of it, cut off his toes, and confined him in a dark room. The new king had his body so barbed with iron that even knives and arrows striking against him could not wound him. Thanks to this precaution, he dared go out. I have been in the country more than a year, and I have seen him go out four or five times. When the king comes out, the cavalry leads his escort. Then follow the standards, the banners, and the music. Palace girls numbering three to five hundred and dressed in flowered stuff with flowers in their hair and holding tall torches in their hands form a troop; even in daylight their torches are lighted. Then come palace girls bearing the royal silver and gold ware and all the ornaments, all of very different styles, whose use is unknown to me. Next come palace girls bearing the lance and the shield. These are the private guard of the king, and they also form a troop. Then follow the goat carriages and the horse carriages, all ornamented with gold. The ministers and the princes are mounted on elephants and, as they go forward, look afar; their red parasols are innumerable. After them come the wives and concubines of the king in palanquins, in carriages, or on elephants. They have, I am sure, more than a hundred parasols decorated with gold. Behind them is the king, standing on an elephant and holding in his hand the precious sword. The tusks of the elephant are wrapped with gold. There are more than twenty white parasols decorated with gold and with golden hafts. A large number of elephants press about him, and cavalry protects him. If the king is going to a place near by, he uses only a golden palanquin carried by four palace girls. Usually, when he goes out, the king visits a small golden pagoda before which is a golden Buddha. Those who behold the king must prostrate themselves and touch the ground with their foreheads. Otherwise they are seized by the masters of ceremonies who do not release them without making them pay for it.

Daily the king holds audience twice for the affairs of government. There is no fixed list. Those of the officials or of the people who desire to see the king sit on the ground to await him. After some time distant music is heard in the palace. Outside they blow conch shells to welcome the king. I have heard that he uses only a golden palanquin, as he does not come from far away. A moment later one sees two palace girls lifting the curtain with their slim fingers, and the king, holding the sword in his hand, appears at the golden window. Ministers and common people put their hands together and strike the earth with their foreheads. When the sound of the conch shells has ceased, they may raise their heads. According to the pleasure of the king, they draw near to seat themselves. At the place where one sits down for audience there is a lionskin which is regarded as a royal object. When the business is ended, the king turns around, the two palace girls let the curtain fall, and everyone stands up.[9]

9. P. Pelliot. "Mémoires sur les coutumes du Cambodge," *Bulletin de l'École Française d'Extrême-Orient*, II (1902), 141–77. The translation of the foregoing selected sections is the writer's. The comments in brackets are drawn from Pelliot's extensive footnotes.

IV

SIAM, A HINDUIZED NATION

THE story of Siam as a nation in its present geographic setting goes back about only seven centuries. The Siamese believe that they can trace their history to the beginning of the Christian Era and assert that they have never been anything but a free people. For this reason they call themselves "free," or Thai. It seems certain that in about the seventh century of the Christian Era the Thai formed a powerful kingdom in southwestern Yunnan known to the Chinese as Nanchao. For six centuries Nanchao was an important military and political factor in the developing events in Southeast Asia. It fought with Tibet against China; it sent political and economic missions to China; and it engaged in warfare with the peoples then resident in the areas now known as Burma, Annam, and Cambodia.

During that early period commercial and cultural intercourse between India and China flowed across the kingdom of Nanchao. Trans-Asian routes were established at that time which are still in use to this day. When World War II began, I was asked to supply information on possible routes between India and China. That was not difficult for a student in the history of religions. It was even possible to estimate the probable width of certain routes because it was known that over them persons were carried in chairs by coolies. Along these routes Indian Buddhist missionaries to China passed as early as the second century. Spotty records of missionary expeditions indicate that on occasion Chinese pilgrims to the number of three hundred went to India to secure sacred texts. There are still many evidences of the movement of Indian cultural influence across the kingdom of Nanchao. For instance, two bells have been found there on which appear Buddhist inscriptions in Chinese and Sanskrit that have been dated about the eleventh century. It is thus evident that the Thai people were exposed to Indian influences centuries before they moved southward into their modern home in Siam. In their folk tales they mention Brahmans who settled among them and became advisers to the king in matters of government. The Buddhism to which they were exposed was Mahayana Buddhism. However, Indian culture made no deep impression on them in those early centuries.

In the thirteenth century Nanchao was crushed by the war machine of Kublai Khan, who was trying to subdue southern China by executing a dashing pincer movement over the snow-capped mountains which lay between China and Tibet. In reaching their objective, the Khan's armies rolled over Nanchao. The fall of the Thai capital at Talifu accelerated the southward migration of the Thai which had been going on for several centuries.

Settling in the northern part of Siam, the Thai became a dependent nation attached to the brilliant court at Angkor. One of the friezes at Angkor Wat shows the Cambodian monarch in procession with some twenty dependent princes, each under a state umbrella with the appropriate number of tiers and surrounded by a number of generals. The Thai were shown as fierce warriors dressed in kilts. They had feathers in their hair to add color to their costume. According to Cambodian history, the Thai were used as shock troops in Cambodian campaigns against Tonkin.

It is not difficult to imagine how profoundly disturbed the Thai were when they came upon the highly sophisticated kingdom of Cambodia. It was completely different from anything they had ever seen before. They were as dazed and delighted as backwoodsmen seeing "Radio City" for the first time. It was an experience like stumbling from darkness into a brilliantly lighted room.

Even their previous contacts with samples of Cambodian civilization did not prepare them for Angkor itself. As early as the eleventh century, Suryavarman I, native of Nakhon Sritammarat and later monarch of Cambodia, extended his control westward in the Chao Phya River Basin and northward to the city of Lampoon, or Haripunjaya as it was known in those days. There the Siamese were strongly intrenched even at that early period, and there they had their first taste of what Cambodia had to offer. A number of Cambodian inscriptions were set up at Lopburi in what is now central Siam. Local history relates that the Cambodians drove northward as far as Chiengsen. But Cambodian architecture was not erected farther north than Luang Prabang on the east bank of the Mekong River, or above Sukhothai and Sawankhalok in the Chao Phya River Basin in north-central Siam.

An inscription at Lopburi in central Siam indicates that monks of two schools lived there simultaneously: one school of Mahayana Buddhism and one of Brahmanism, the latter devoted to yoga exercises. Another inscription reveals that the various religions current in Cambodia were also represented in a mild form at Lopburi. The proportion of Buddhist and Brahman monuments discloses that Buddhism was much stronger among the Siamese.

While the Siamese were becoming familiar with the sophistication of the Cambodians, they were also learning about Hinayana Buddhism, using the Pali language, from Mon kingdoms south of them in the peninsula, from Burma to the west of them, and from Ceylon as a result of an exchange of missions.

The principal Mon city in the peninsula was that of Thaton located at the mouth of the Sittang River, where, according to local legend, Buddhaghosa, the celebrated father of the Singhalese church of the fifth century, was born. Other Mon cities in the Chao Phya River Basin which were established as early as the middle of the sixth century were Sri Thep, Phra Phatom, and Phong Tuk. The Siamese first became familiar with Hinayana Buddhism through the latter three cities.

Before the Siamese were in a position to establish direct contact with Thaton, the city had been occupied by the Burmese. As the story goes, a Thaton Brahman named Shin Arahan went north to the Burmese city of Pagan in 1056. He was a Mon monk of the Theravada school of southern Buddhism. He informed the Burmese king of the wealth of Buddhism in Thaton and aroused the king's cupidity. The king sent a message to Thaton, asking for a set of the *Tripitaka*, since Shin Arahan had told him that there were thirty complete sets there. His request was rejected, and so he set out with his army to occupy Thaton, which he succeeded in doing after a three-month siege and after exhuming the remains of an Indian, whose spirit was supposed to be guarding the impregnable city, and casting them into the sea.

The king took back to Pagan with him the king of Thaton and the members of his court, all the monks, and thirty-two white elephants loaded with sets of the *Tripitaka*. As a result of this expedition, Pali superseded Sanskrit as the sacred language and Hinayana replaced Mahayana Buddhism in Burma.

Subsequently the Siamese experienced the richness of the Hinayana Buddhism of Thaton when they swept across Burma in the thirteenth century at the same time that they revolted against Cambodia and consolidated their kingdom in the Chao Phya River Valley with their capital at Sukhothai. The Siamese fell in love with Hinayana Buddhism and held it as a prized possession.

Intercourse with Ceylon sprang up after the foundation of the Sukhothai state in Siam. The Siamese desired to get the best instruction they could in their new religion of Hinayana Buddhism and so invited the patriarch of Ceylon to come and teach in Siam. A special monastery was built to provide him with a university. As a result of this and subsequent exchanges, Siam was thoroughly converted to the forms of Hinayana Buddhism.

One of the oldest inscriptions in the Siamese language gives a brief characterization of Buddhism at Sukhothai during the reign of the famous Rama Kamheng in the latter part of the thirteenth century. It reads, in part, as follows:

"King Rama Kamheng, sovereign of Muang Sukhothai, as

well as the princes and princesses, the men as well as the women, the nobles and the chiefs, all without exception, without distinction of rank or of sex, practice with devotion the religion of Buddha and the observance of the precepts during the period of retirement in the rainy season. At the end of this season there take place the Kathin ceremonies, which extend over a whole month.

"At these Kathin ceremonies, offerings are made up in heaps of cowry shells, and the same with regard to areca nuts, flowers, cushions, and pillows.

"The various articles that go to make up the Kathin gift-offering each year amount to two millions. These Kathin ceremonies are carried out as far as the monastery of the Aranikas, and, when a return is made to the city, the procession forms up from the monastery and advances up to the entrance to the plain. Everybody prostrates himself to the accompaniment of lutes and guitars, hymns and chants: whosoever wishes to play, plays; whosoever wishes to laugh, laughs; whosoever wishes to sing, sings. This Muang Sukhothai possesses four gates: an immense crowd presses there to gain an entrance and see the King light the big candles and play with the fire, and this Muang Sukhothai is full of people bent on enjoying themselves.

"In the middle of the town of Sukhothai there are sanctuaries; there are statues in gold of Buddha; there is one statue of Buddha which measures eighteen coudees [900 cm.]; there are some statues of Buddha which are great, and there are lesser ones; there are great sanctuaries, and there are medium-sized ones; there are ordinary monks, and monks who have taken the vow of celibacy, both of the lower and higher degree.

"To the west of Sukhothai lies the monastery of Aranikas. King Rama Kamheng founded it and offered it to the Patriarch, to a sage who has studied completely the Three Baskets, who is more learned than all the other monks of the country, and who has come from Nakhon Sritammarat. [This city was an ancient repository of Buddhist learning and is located in the peninsula on the east coast.]

"On the day of the new moon . . . the chaplain of the monks and of the lower and higher order of the celibates, mounts and takes his seat on the stone slab, and there recites the law to the laity and to the assembly of the faithful who observe the precepts. Apart from the days of the recitation of the law, Prince Rama Kamheng, Lord of Sri Sachanalai and Sukhothai, ascends and seats himself on the slab of stone and presides over the assembly of nobles and dignitaries, discussing with them the affairs of the country. . . ."

The inscription gives a picture of a monarch who was the father of his nation, who was simple and easy to meet, who sponsored a religion which made no distinction between high and low, rich and poor, male and female. There was scarcely a hint here of the grandeur to come with the assimilation of the practices found in Cambodia at Angkor.

The Siamese captured Angkor four times: in 1352, in 1393, in 1431, and again conclusively in 1460. On each occasion the Siamese swept the area of its population or caused the people to flee. It was not until 1431, on the third occasion of victory, that the Siamese king, Paramaraja II, brought back to his capital Ayuthia a large number of Cambodian statesmen and Brahmans. Such highly placed persons had on previous defeats escaped southward. The succeeding Siamese monarch took advantage of the learning of these Cambodian statesmen and Brahmans and reorganized the administration of the nation and the ceremonial of the court according to Cambodian practices with a view to establishing himself as a divine king.

In a few years the monarchy was autocratically absolute in character, requiring the complete subjection of the people not only to every decree issued by the king but to his lightest whim or caprice. The power of the king was maintained by the utmost severity in order to convince the people of their need to obey the royal mandate. A softening of this attitude began to be evident under King Mongkut toward the end of the nineteenth century. Severities were continued, however, under his enlightened son, Chulalongkorn, who felt impelled to go slowly in abolishing traditional practices.

An eyewitness of one severity which occurred as recently as the first decade of the twentieth century relates that, while His Majesty was riding in the royal barge on the river, he heard the slapping of water against the side of the barge indicating that another boat was passing. It was contrary to royal law for another boat to pass the royal barge, and the penalty was immediate decapitation. His Majesty was a gentle man, a Buddhist, but he was also a direct heir of a dynasty of divine kings. With only a moment's hesitation he ordered the offending craft pursued and the boatman in charge decapitated. The order was immediately carried out. This was not the act of a mild Buddhist monarch but of a *devaraja* of the old order.

After Chulalongkorn's reign ended in 1910, a progressive softening of the old forms went on with a constant increasing of Buddhist elements in state ceremonial and in the administration. The absolute monarchy was formally ended in 1932 by a revolution, and King Prajadhipok, the last of the absolute monarchs, abdicated in 1935. His widow, Queen Rambaibarni, a lovely women in her early forties in 1947, is living in England. While talking with her after dinner in my home in Washington recently, I found it difficult to imagine such a friendly, unaffected person in the midst of the ceremonial which I will describe shortly, in which she participated as the queen of the last absolute monarch of Siam.

The nation that I will describe is, then, a nation which is no more. Constitutional government, political parties, elections, graft, and inflation qualify Siam to take her place among the modern nations of the world.

The royal family of the absolute monarchy was graded, so that by the fifth generation any particular branch of the royal family automatically returned to commoner status. The sons and daughters of the king and queen were known as *Chao Fa;*

those of the king and concubines were *Phraong Chao*. The children of these two classes were known as *Mom Chao*, and they formed the lowest rank of real princes. The children of *Mom Chao* were known as *Mom Rachawong*, and their children in turn were known as *Mom Luang*. The children of *Mom Luang* were commoners. Assimilation to commonership in Siam followed the practice customary in the royal Cambodian family.

Under the royal command there were both royalty and commoners. First of all was a royal person known to Europeans as the Second King and called by the Siamese *Wang Na*, commander of the advance guard. He was in fact a monarch inferior only to the First King and was either the eldest son or a brother, carefully selected for compatability. He was entitled to a five-tiered umbrella and had a magnificent palace near the Grand Palace. He had his own court and a free use of state funds. He was actually the heir apparent if anything happened to the king. He was the only person with whom the king could talk as to an equal and was usually sent to lead military expeditions or was established in the Grand Palace if the king was away fighting so that the king might feel certain that he would still be king upon his return. The office was one common in all the Hinduized states and so apparently stemmed from India. The position was discontinued by King Chulalongkorn on the death of the then *Wang Na*. His palace was given over to the Department of Fine Arts and is today a royal museum.

Next to the *Wang Na* and far inferior in influence was the *Wang Lang*, commander of the rear guard and also a person of the royal family. The government was conducted by six ministers of state. Civil officials on down the line were given nonhereditary ranks of *Somdet Chao Phya*, *Chao Phya*, *Phya*, *Phra*, *Luang*, *Khun*, and *Moen*.

When I first went to Siam, I asked a Siamese why all the walks were so narrow that no two people could walk side by side. He replied humorously that that was an expression of the social system in which no two people were equals and in which each person was busy grinding down the one beneath him while serving the one above him. This was a caricature but true enough to give an idea of the old system of absolutism under the *devaraja* or divine king.

In Cambodia the divine king was usually identified with Siva or Vishnu. However, Jayavarman VII, who was influential at the end of the twelfth and the beginning of the thirteenth century, arbitrarily discarded this concept and made himself the *Buddharaja*, divine nonetheless. The Siamese were aware of this development in Cambodia and saw possibilities in it for themselves, for they were Buddhists. They established a cult in which the Hindu deities ministered to the Buddha who was supreme. According to the Siamese idea, the king was a bodhisattva, a Buddha-to-be. Or he might be regarded as a *chakravartin* or a universal monarch. Indian Jataka tales gave support for this conception of the Buddhist divine king.

The Hinduized Cambodian monarch who was regarded as the receptacle of the divine essence of Siva or Vishnu was no superior in the eyes of a Buddhist to a bodhisattva. Some of these *buddharajas* took their position so seriously that they regarded themselves as the coming Buddha, Maitreya. And, although some of their subjects yielded that honor to them, the career monks in their monasteries in many instances reserved their opinion.

Various ceremonies and taboos were developed around the person of the king and his consorts which were aimed to make them mysterious and godlike creatures in the eyes of the common people. This was a great development over the early simplicity of King Rama Kamheng of the thirteenth century. The inscription relating to that monarch recorded:

"In the porch outside the door of the palace there is a gong suspended: if any inhabitant of the Kingdom has any grief or any matter which 'ulcerates his bowels and torments his soul,' and which he wishes to lay before the prince, it is not difficult of accomplishment: he has only to beat the gong which is hanging there. Every time that King Rama Kamheng hears an appeal, he questions the plaintiff about the case, and decides thereon in accordance with equity."

Such a procedure was very shortly inconceivable, and not even foreign ambassadors could approach informally the royal person. It was not until the twentieth century that access could be had with any ease to majesty, and then only by those in favored position. King Vajiravudhi, who reigned from 1910 to 1920, loved to act in his own plays and so brought himself into more common touch with many of his subjects. But he shocked not only the Siamese but the foreign community by his daring conduct. His successor, King Prajadhipok, the last of the absolute monarchs, was very democratic in spirit and made it possible for all classes to meet him on occasion. He traveled about the country, and vast numbers of his subjects watched him pass. When he came to New York in 1931 and insisted on shaking hands with Siamese students in this country, some of them, I have been told, almost fainted away with their own daring.

The young King Ananda who died tragically in Bangkok in 1946 was a friendly person who liked to do the things that young men his age were doing all over the world. He played a saxaphone and drove a jeep. He entertained me at dinner in Bangkok in the most complete informality in a manner inconceivable in previous reigns. Times have changed and are continuing to change.

The divine kingship carried with it the idea that the king's person was too sacred to be touched.[1] Nothing was ever handed to the king from hand to hand but was placed on a golden plate or in a bowl and then extended to the king. It was forbidden on pain of death to sieze hold of royalty even to save them from drowning. This taboo led to the tragic death of the first queen of King Rama V who was drowned in full view of a number of persons, none of whom dared help her. Bundles of coconuts were usually carried on royal barges which were to

1. On the subject of taboos connected with the king, the best summary is found in H. G. Quaritch Wales, *Siamese State Ceremonies* (London: Bernard Quaritch, Ltd., 1931), pp. 32 ff.

be thrown to a royal person drowning. This prohibition of touching the body was especially regarded in reference to touching the head. This applied strongly to royal heads but was true to a degree in all classes of society.

Respect for the head has led inferiors to make a point of lowering their heads beneath the level of their superior's head. When royalty was passing by in the street, lesser persons came down from the upper stories of their buildings. A member of the royal family was disappointed in not being able to view the first printing press ever taken to Siam in the nineteenth century because it was located under a building in which there were people living. Commoners of approximately equal rank have continued even in modern times to show courtesy by lowering their heads beneath the level of the heads of their friends. I caused great inconvenience to many people attending a wedding in 1930 by sitting on the floor. Those who passed me, even including the governor of the province and his wife, crawled past on hands and knees. According to Siamese custom, they would have been rude if they had towered above me. I solved the difficulty by standing up in a corner.

The idea seems to be that a guardian spirit or *khwan* resides in the head who might be offended and cause harm to the owner of the head. Certain it is that, when men address each other politely, they say *phom* or "hair" for "I," indicating that the most noble part of the speaker is addressing the other person.

Another taboo which also influenced the development of the practice of prostration was that forbidding one to look upon the face of the king. A Siamese having audience with the king had to prostrate himself. Until the reign of King Mongkut fences were erected along any route which the king expected to follow to prevent people from viewing his person. The practice of prostration was abolished dramatically by King Chulalongkorn. However, persons who wished to show great respect for others voluntarily continued the practice in a modified form.

As the king was not supposed to touch the ground, he wore sandals or rode in a palanquin wherever he went. As royal blood should never be shed, it was usual to destroy a royal victim by beating him on the back of the neck with a sandalwood club or by putting him in a sack and beating him. The name of the king was also taboo, and he was always referred to by titles or by some indirection. Sometimes a king's real name was not even known to his chroniclers. The first three kings of the present dynasty were given posthumous Buddhist names by King Mongkut, and he selected names for them which indicated that they were bodhisattvas.

These taboos and others maintained an air of mystery about the person of the king. Some of them were actually very practical because they tended to protect the life of the king from a potential murderer.

It was the business of the court Brahmans to glorify the king. The more they magnified his position, the surer they made their own. The first Brahmans in Siam were brought over from Angkor, and their responsibility was to initiate the ceremonial necessary to establish the cult of the divine king. They were of two sects, Siva and Vishnu, with the cult of Siva dominant. They brought with them their images and sacred books, as many as were necessary. So strong was their influence in those early days that one Siamese monarch renamed his city of residence Pitsanuloke or actually *Vishnuloke*, "the world of Vishnu." During the centuries with the increasing influence of Buddhist monks and the vital interest of all classes in having sons become Buddhist monks, the Brahman priesthood deteriorated. In fact, no powerful Brahmanic caste was ever developed in Siam to offset the power of the king and to intermarry with the royal family, as in Cambodia. This was because the Hindu gods were regarded as satellites or servants of Buddha. The king's chaplain was not a Brahman but was the Buddhist Prince Patriarch, a member of the royal family and frequently a brother of the king.

Modern Brahmans, strange to say, are also Hinayana Buddhists. They do not understand Sanskrit but have memorized certain Pali texts which they use in their ceremonies. They have few written texts because one of the most influential Brahman families withdrew from court life and took their manuscripts with them. The remaining Brahmans carry out their duties when called upon by depending on their memory of previous ceremonies in the days when the Brahmans in Siam did read Sanskrit and had all the necessary texts.

It is probable that the strength of Brahman influence in Siam continued at a high level until the fall of Ayuthia at the hands of the Burmese in 1767. Many of the Brahmans fled at that time to Nakhon Sritammarat and only a few returned. Those few continued to officiate at state ceremonial.

The Brahmans in Siam developed ceremonies of coronation, tonsure, cremation, and lesser rites connected with agriculture. They did not become court astrologers and soothsayers as many believe. These were activites which were monopolized by non-Brahmans.

The first problem in connection with the coronation of a king was that of succession. In theory the eldest son of the chief queen succeeded to the throne. This would seem to indicate a matriarchy. In fact, however, a brother might succeed if there was no son of a queen available. Or there might be a selection from among quite a few eligible persons. During the Bangkok period on a number of occasions the eldest son of the queen did actually succeed. The cult of the divine king put women of the upper classes in an inferior position and so tended to minimize the matriarchal influence which stemmed from ancient practice. The maternal line of inheritance was common in Southeast Asia.

After the succession was decided, the next step was that of coronation.[2] For three days before the day of coronation the Brahmans performed sacrifices of fire before Hindu deities. A circle of eight basins of water around a central basin were

2. *Ibid.*, pp. 67–121. See also the published descriptions in Siamese of the actual coronation ceremonies of King Prajadhipok. These volumes in Siamese are rich with pictures taken during the ceremonies, thus admirably helping one's imagination.

heated on a stone for the steeping of leaves which were supposed to have purifying powers. At the same time offerings were made in Brahman temples to the Hindu deities, before the royal white umbrellas, which were supposed to have guardian spirits, and before the guardian spirits of the city. A Buddhist element was carried on simultaneously with three days of Buddhist services in the chief residence. Each evening a Buddhist monk delivered a sermon, and each morning the king presented food to the monks and sent offerings to the Hindu deities. At the beginning of these ceremonies the Candle of Victory was lighted, which was the equivalent of the Hindu sacred fire. At the end of the Buddhist ceremonies mentioned the candle was put out. This occurred on the morning of coronation day.

On coronation day, at the auspicious moment selected by an astrologer, the high priest of Siva invited the king to don white garments and receive a purifying bath. Before taking the bath the king made offerings to the Hindu deities. Consecrated water brought from all the principal streams of the kingdom was used.

The king took his seat in a ceremonial pavilion, and the Brahman handed him a small golden bowl of the sacred water. The king dipped his hand in and rubbed some on the top of his head. The Brahman then pulled a rope and released a shower of water from a tank over the king's head. Various honored persons then approached and offered sacred water for the king to pour on himself. At that moment guns were fired, drums were beaten, and trumpets sounded. The Brahmans played ceremonial music, and a great number of Buddhist monks chanted.

The king withdrew and returned in dry regal robes in a processional led by the Brahmans. In the procession both the Buddha and the Hindu gods were carried, showing the fusion of the two religions in the ceremony. The king then seated himself on an octagonal throne of fig wood beneath the seven-tiered white umbrella of state. The king sat facing the east first, and a nobleman invited him to rule the east and handed him a conch shell of water, probably drawn from an eastern stream. The king was addressed and spoke in reply in Pali and agreed to rule the east. This was repeated all around the compass, with different noblemen inviting him to rule the various directions. In every instance the king promised to protect his people and the Buddhist religion. No mention was made of the Hindu deities.

The king then went to another throne of fig wood followed by pages carrying the royal regalia. This included the white umbrella of state, the crown and the sword of victory, the slippers, the fan, the whisk of yak's tail, the scepter and stick, the personal sword, the Brahman girdle, other girdles and rings, the spittoon, the betel set, the water urn, the libation cup, the golden tablet, and the eight weapons of sovereignty.

The white umbrella was an ancient symbol of authority. The umbrella had seven tiers before the king was crowned and nine after. Such umbrellas were common in all parts of Southeast Asia. They were shown in the reliefs of Borobudur in Java. They were used by royalty in Champa. They were included in the reliefs at Pagan, Burma. And Angkor Wat showed a profusion of umbrellas in processionals. There were umbrellas single tiered, three tiered, five tiered, seven tiered, and nine tiered. Puranic literature of India mentions the white umbrella also. To this day, when the king of Siam goes walking in processional, he is covered with a single-tiered white umbrella.

The crown of victory looked like a pagoda and was a cone of several stages terminating in a spire. Perhaps it took that shape to symbolize Mount Meru.

The sword of victory, which may have dated back to the tenth century, was brought from Cambodia in 1783 and was the emblem of sovereignty of the ancient Cambodian kingdom. A similar sword is still kept at the modern capital of Cambodia which is supposed to be the sword of Jayavarman II, of the ninth century. An inscription at Wat Mahatat claims that the founder of the original Siamese kingdom in the thirteenth century received such a sword from the king of Angkor.

The slippers were the prerogative of royalty, since the common people did not wear them and, if occasionally they did, had to remove them in the presence of superiors. The slippers of royalty were mentioned in the *Ramayana* when Rama sent his slippers to govern in his place.

The fan was made of a palm leaf bent at right angles to the stalk. Such fans figured prominently in the friezes of Angkor and were associated with divine kings who could stay cool in hot climates.

There is not space enough here to describe in detail the other items completing the royal regalia. Each one of them originally had a practical function and by the extension of royal power was given a special significance.

The king seated himself on a throne under a seven-tiered umbrella while the pages stood holding the royal regalia until the appropriate moment had come to present the various items to the king. The high priest of Siva approached and pronounced the Tamil mantra known as "Opening the Portals of Kailasa," which was an invitation for the gods to descend on earth. The Brahman then spoke in Pali and presented the king with a golden tablet, resting in a gold bowl, and bearing the new formal name and title of the king. The king replied in Pali and agreed to rule. The Brahman then took the Crown of Victory and handed it to the king on a gold platter. The king put it on his own head. This was the supreme moment and was accompanied by Brahmanic music and the ringing of Buddhist monastery bells. Buddhist monks began to chant also.

The Brahman then handed the king's regalia to him one by one, and the king put the various objects on small stands or tables near at hand. And, finally, the great nine-tiered white umbrella of a reigning monarch was placed instead of the seven-tiered one. The symbolism of the ceremony was to imply that the gods descended and merged in the person of the king. After being fully crowned, the king scattered gold and silver flowers and coins among the Brahmans. This was reminiscent of the scattering of gold flowers in the *Ramayana* at the coronation of Rama.

Later in the day the king held a general audience, which is all that most Europeans have ever seen of the coronation ceremony. At this the king sat in full state robes. In the late afternoon the king proceeded to the Chapel Royal and made offerings of gold and silver flowers and lit candles before the Emerald Buddha and before the images of Buddha representing the earlier kings of the dynasty. Then before the chief clergy of the Buddhist church he declared his religious faith and acknowledged himself "Defender of the Faith." Interestingly enough the most modern constitution gives religious liberty to everyone in the kingdom but to the king, who must be a Buddhist.

The close of the ceremony included homage to ancestors in the Dusit Mahaprasat, where the urns containing the relics of the king's predecessors had been brought. This was a ceremony left over from earlier days of ancestor cult.

Closely connected with coronation was cremation, since it was in fact a coronation of the spirit for the world to come and was aimed to put the spirit of the departed into such a happy frame of mind that he would work for the good and not for the harm of the nation. The departed was a bodhisattva whose primary function would be to use his merit for the salvation of those without merit. The royal cremation has continued essentially unchanged through many centuries and took on its general form in about the fourteenth century.

Cremation[3] was ordinarily a Buddhist practice in Siam, but for royalty it was Buddhist plus gorgeous Brahmanical ritual. Everyone in Siam was cremated except criminals and persons who died violently. Such persons had dangerous spirits and required special treatment. It was the custom to store the bodies of the dead to be cremated for a period of time in order to show honor. The earliest possible moment for the

3. *Ibid.*, pp. 137–69. See also the published descriptions in Siamese of cremation ceremonies of royal persons.

cremation of a royal monarch would be after the hundredth-day rites. The body might be kept for a longer period.

As soon as the king had died, princes placed him on his back, closed his eyelids and mouth, covered his body with a golden shroud, and lighted two candles. Persons of authority in the kingdom then met promptly to select the successor. As soon as this was done, the body of the dead king was bathed with scented water and dressed. The clothing was remarkable and worthy of a god. There were silk drawers embroidered with gold and a cloth-of-gold panung to cover the lower part of his body. He was dressed in an embroidered yellow silk vest and silk gloves and socks. Golden plaques were put on his chest and sides, and baldricks studded with diamonds were crossed over his chest. Gold shoes and epaulets, gold bracelets, anklets, and rings were used and a golden mask to give him the face of a god. In his hands were placed a pair of gilt candles, a lotus, and a pair of gold horns containing areca nut in betel leaf. A silk hat was placed on his head.

He was then put in the urns, of which there were an inner and an outer. The inner one was of silver and could be sealed. The outer one was of gold ornamented with the nine gems and capped with a spire. This design appears on a great deal of the most valuable jewelry. The inner urn was about four feet high and less than three feet wide—just large enough to sit in.

The king was then made to sit up, and a gold ring was placed in his mouth, the equivalent of the coin that was put in the mouth of the commoner. This was supposed to be used to pay the toll at the gates of paradise and is an ancient concept which goes back beyond the Hinduization of Southeast Asia.

The palms of the king's hands were then joined opposite his face with a clamp to hold them in the posture of respect to Buddha. The knees were lifted to the level of the hands and tied in a sitting position. The king was then seated on long strips of cotton the ends of which were tied over the top of his head. The king-elect then approached and set the Kathin crown on the dead king's head and hung a gold chain studded with diamonds about his neck. Everyone then venerated the dead king before he was placed in the inner urn. Up to this point the Brahmans took no part in the ceremony.

The royal urn was then conducted in processional to the Dusit Mahaprasat and elevated on a catafalque where it lay in state. The model of this catafalque was supposed to be a Cambodian shrine at Angkor Thom. Every day offerings of food and flowers were placed before it. From the base of the urn three ribbons each six inches wide stretched out to golden trays on the east, north, and south.

Day and night Buddhist monks kept up ceaseless chanting, and on occasion persons came in to show their respect. Even in the most modern times these persons bow low or even prostrate themselves according to ancient custom in order to show the most profound respect. On the seventh, fiftieth, and hundredth days special Buddhist services were conducted. This ended the official period of mourning, and people could discard their white clothing, a sign of mourning, and resume their social lives.

The funeral pyre, called Phra Meru because it was supposed to represent Mount Meru, the home of Vishnu and Indra, was erected near the Grand Palace. I was fortunate to receive from a friend in Bangkok an architect's drawing showing the design of the Phra Meru to be used in the cremation of King Ananda Mahidol, who died in 1946. It seems to be as magnificent as any in the past. The funeral pyre was a costly structure because all the materials were new and were not supposed to be used again for such a purpose. The pyre was built like a pyramid with a spire at the top. At each of the four corners there were towers in which monks chanted ceaselessly. On the floor of the Phra Meru was an iron plate on which the fire would be built. High above hung the traditional white umbrella of nine tiers. Each of the four entrances to the pyre were gated with doors of silk embroidered with designs of mythical creatures. The engineer who had charge of the lighting of the pyre for the cremation of King Chulalongkorn showed me pictures which he had taken illustrating the details of this magnificent structure and the gorgeous handwork on the silken doors. The whole structure blazed like a jewel by day under the tropical sun and by night under special lighting arrangements.

Near by was a pavilion where the living king would stand on the day of cremation and distribute wooden limes from a golden bowl to nobles and high officials and to the common people as well. Each lime contained a coin or a promise to give a house or a garden or a boat or some other thing of value.

On cremation day the Brahmans came into prominence in the ceremony, and their music filled the air as the body of the dead king was taken from the inner urn. The crown and the ornaments were removed, and the body or, rather, the bones that were left were arranged in the form of a skeleton over which the nobles poured coconut water before wrapping the bones up and replacing them in the inner urn. This was then escorted to the funeral pyre in a grand processional identical with the coronation processional, in which representatives of Indra and Brahma and Buddha marched. The cremation processional did not differ materially from the coronation processional, because the general purpose was the same. The cremation was the coronation of the spirit for the world to come when the king would function as a bodhisattva. In the parade there were fabulous mythical animals represented that were supposed to inhabit the fairyland of the Hindus.

Upon arriving at the funeral pyre, a part of the processional circled the pyre three times, with their right shoulders toward the pyre, while the Brahman conch-blowers sounded their instruments. Then the inner urn was hoisted up on the Phra Meru. The living king ascended also, did homage, and lit candles.

For the actual cremation the inner urn was replaced with one of sandalwood. This was set on cross-layers of fragrant wood. The Prince Patriarch of the Buddhist church preached a sermon, the monks chanted, and then the living king applied the fire at sunset. This was the supreme moment when the drums were beaten, cannons were fired, and the national anthem was played while everyone showed veneration. Other high nobles then added candles or sandalwood to the blaze to show respect. The fire was kept going all night.

In the morning the ashes were given the form of a human figure, with the head toward the east, and then re-formed with the head toward the west. Gifts and robes were distributed to the monks, and a search for relics began in which royalty took part. Fragments of burned bone were collected; some were retained to be put in gold lockets and some in a small golden urn which would be kept in the Grand Palace and would be brought out on occasion for veneration. The ashes of the wood were kept for veneration at some one of the royal temples. In ancient times they were tied up in a white cloth and tossed into the river.

The Siamese kings imitated the ritual of the Buddhist kings of Ceylon, but, as the Siamese kings were also affected by the Cambodian cult of the divine king, there was a strong element of Cambodian Brahmanism involved. The essential Buddhist elements were the chanting of the monks, the preaching, and the giving of robes to the monks. Chief among the Brahman elements was the coronation processional. The underlying purpose of the ceremony was Brahmanistic in that the object was to impress upon the people the fact of the deification of the king. The pomp and ceremony of cremation tended thus to exceed even that of coronation because it represented the supreme elevation, the final victory, of the chakravartin. By his religion the king thus gained victory over the flesh and over death.

Since the people should not be permitted to get the idea that the king was a mere mortal, it is obvious that the greatest hazard to the concept of divine kingship was death. When he was taken ill, the physicians had to prescribe for him sight unseen. Early missionary doctors who were called in to prescribe for majesty had the experience of being required to diagnose a case from the excited descriptions of the symptoms by pages. The king could not be touched or too closely observed. The king was immortal, and the victorious cremation ceremony of the divine king was aimed to impress the idea of victory upon the common people. The people expected such a monarch to continue to take an interest in the nation, and it was for this reason that regular periods for the veneration of previous monarchs were set aside. The king had merely migrated to another plane to function as a bodhisattva for the good of humanity. Incidentally, this was an expression of the ancestor cult in a most glorified form.

There were both a Hindu and a Buddhist method of ancestor worship in Siam. According to the Hindu method, the reigning king and his court and the common people lit candles and made obeisance before golden life-sized statues of previous monarchs located in the precincts of the Grand Palace. The statues of the Bangkok monarchs were as nearly portraits as possible and so differed from the statues of the Cambodian monarchs, which represented the features of the kings together with the attributes of the god they had patronized. The purpose was the same in both cases.

The Buddhist method of showing respect to the ancestors was to place the urned relics under a nine-tiered umbrella of state where royalty lit candles and showed respect while Buddhist monks chanted and a sermon was preached. Such Buddhist and Hindu ceremonial was carried out two or three times a year and kept alive in the minds of the people the divinity of the kings and the fact that the monarchs were still interested in the kingdom.

Two other factors should be mentioned which were aimed at glorifying the divine king and assuring his position. The first was the oath of allegiance, known as drinking the water of allegiance, which was celebrated in a manner similar to Cambodian practice. After the Siamese revolution of 1932 the oath of allegiance was replaced by a government-sponsored New Year's celebration during which hundreds of Buddhist monks were offered food.

The ceremony of the oath of allegiance occurred twice a

year in the royal chapel in Bangkok and in a Buddhist temple in each province. The water was first made sacred by Buddhist monks who chanted and by Brahmans who dipped into the water the State Sword and other royal weapons. The idea was that, by magic, any official plotting rebellion would die shortly after drinking. On the appointed day a Brahman read the oath, and each official had to drink a small cup of the water. Any choking or sputtering was a clear sign of treasonable thoughts. This was an ancient Cambodian practice, and instances of the ceremonial were depicted in friezes in temples. Probably the underlying concept was ordeal by water. The oath was of a nature to show clearly that the Siamese people lived in the daily presence of countless spirits and felt the need to propitiate them. I quote one significant section from a translation made by M. L. Cort during the fourth reign:

"We, the slaves of the Lord Buddh, beg to offer to His Majesty, the King, this our personal oath, pledging our loyalty, in the immediate presence of the God Buddh, the sacred teachings and the sacred priests. . . . We pray the deities of lands and forests; the guardian deities; the atmospheric deities; the goddesses who care for the earth, especially the powerful deities who are located where is the great white Umbrella, emblem of royalty, may plague us with evil, destroy our lives, effect our destruction and death by breakage, by severance; cause our death by lighting and thunderbolts, by royal weapons, the powerful royal sword, by poison and the power of land and water animals; let there be some opportunity for the destruction of the perfidious ones; let swift destruction come; let us not escape all great disasters and consequences of all localities, which those who have the power can inflict for all offenses. We beseech the power of the deities to plague with poisonous boils, rapidly fatal, and all manner of diseases the dishonorable, perverse, and treacherous, plague with untimely, wretched and appalling deaths, manifest to the eyes of the world; when we shall have departed this life from earth, cause us to be sent and all to be born in the great hell, where we shall burn with quenchless fire for tens and hundreds of thousands of ages and limitless transmigrations; and when we have expiated our penalty there, and are again born in any world, we pray we may fail to find the least happiness in worlds of pleasurable enjoyments; let us not meet the God Buddh, the sacred teachings, the sacred priests, who come to be gracious to animals, helping them escape misery, reach heaven and attain a cessation of births and deaths; should we meet them let them grant us no gracious assistance."[4]

At the end of the long oath the idea was added that if the person taking the oath was faithful, he might escape rebirth and the wheel of existences. The major part of the oath was aimed to scare the wits out of anyone who contemplated rebellion against the divine king. The oath is a revelation of those supernatural powers which the Siamese regarded as valid.

Incidentally, the oath was a commentary on the theory of government under the divine king, in which the king was all and the people were nothing. This theory of government was illustrated by the behavior of the missions which the divine king sent to foreign nations. The persons in such a mission were of no consequence as compared to the royal letter which they bore expressing the royal will. They were merely messengers. This led to great misunderstanding with European missions to Siam whose documents were merely to identify them and who were important as persons. Two radically different theories of government met headlong in such an exchange of missions.

Another factor which enhanced the divinity of the king and which played an important part in his administration of the nation was the royal harem. This was one aspect of government which the Siamese monarchs took over wholeheartedly from Cambodia. According to the Chinese observer Tcheou Ta-kouan, the Cambodian king had a city of several thousand women. Mrs. Anna Leonowens described the

4. Mary Lavina Cort, *Siam* (New York: Randolph & Co., 1886), p. 123.

harem city of King Mongkut as consisting of almost ten thousand women. However, few of these were actually consorts of the king. Dr. Dan Beach Bradley in his Bangkok Calender for 1863 described the family of King Mongkut which was a small one as such things went. He had been handicapped by having been a Buddhist monk for about twenty years while his brother held the throne. King Mongkut's family was as follows:

"There have been altogether 27 royal mothers in the king's family: one of them had 7 children, two of them each five, another 4, two of them 3 each, four of them 2 each, and all the others but one each. His Majesty has at the present time 34 concubines. Each of these receives a government salary designed for the support of her own person, not including her children. . . . Besides these 34 concubines, there are 74 daughters of noblemen, who have been presented to the king by their fathers, with the view to serve as maids of honor. . . . When any of them desire to exchange their situation for one out of the palace, with freedom to marry or otherwise, they may obtain the privilege by requesting it of the king."

No man ever entered the city of women, and, consequently, all the services had to be performed by women. There were women judges, women police, women teachers, and a great host of servants. There were shops and gardens with women shopkeepers and gardeners. It was a city in which the only way a woman's ambition could be expressed was by winning the favor of the Lord of Life at the expense of her fellow-creatures. To be a favorite was to be in an earthly paradise.

One of the functions of the harem was to dignify the position of royalty. An even more important function was administrative in nature. The loyalty of the nobility was secured to the throne by the practice of having a daughter of each important family in the city of women. These concubines were hostages to guarantee the support of the girl's family. The girl was expected to maintain contact with her family and to act as the king's reporter on current events.

According to Dr. Bradley in his Calendar for 1864, when a

new king ascended the throne, all nobles and lords even down to the lowest ranks presented to the king his most beautiful daughter or niece to serve as his concubine. That would provide him with hundreds to begin with. But this number was further augmented by persons of former noble stock who offered their daughters in the hope that, by becoming a son-in-law, the family head might prosper. And then the king himself frequently caught sight of a beauty who pleased him and asked for her. This system was common in all the states in Southeast Asia affected by Hindu civilization. The implications of the system for the administration of the nation are obvious.

The form of administration was indicated in the Law of the Civil Hierarchy promulgated in 1454, according to which the feudal nobles were transformed into government officials. The whole population was divided into two categories: civil and military; and the ranks, duties, and privileges of every official were strictly ordained.

Every official was given four designations to describe his status.[5] The first was his *saktina*, which was a number starting with 10,000 for ministers down to 400 for lesser officials directly appointed by the king. The importance of the *Wang Na*, or second king, was shown by the fact that his *saktina* was 40,000, or four times that of a minister of state. Those with a grade below 400 were appointed by high officials and were petty functionaries. Persons in this latter category were little better than nonofficials. Originally the *saktina* number referred to the amount of land over which a person had jurisdiction. Thus a person with a *saktina* of 10,000 had jurisdiction over 10,000 rai of land and all the serfs occupying it. Gradually this shifted from a territorial to a personal basis, so that the *saktina* number became a personal and not a territorial designation and was supposed to indicate an individual's personal status in the hierarchy of government.

The second designation was that of *yot*, which were honor-

5. H. G. Quaritch Wales, *Ancient Siamese Government and Administration* (London: Bernard Quaritch, Ltd., 1934), pp. 35 ff.

ific titles such as Chao Phya, Phya, Phra, Luang, and Khun.

The third designation was *rachathinnam*, or royal name granted by the king.

The fourth designation was the *tamnaeng*, or grade of position in a particular administrative department.

The most important of all these was the *saktina* because that determined the salary and power. For instance, my friend Phya Sritammarat had the *saktina* of 8,000, his *tamnaeng* was that of lord lieutenant over several provinces, his *yot* was that of Phya, and his *rachathinnam* was Sritammarat. All officials were graded in this way, and one could just about place a man, his power, and his salary when introduced to him. When meeting him, one was not meeting a person but an office. If he changed his office, everything else about him changed also. If a person was on the upward path in government, one might know him as Khun Chang in one job, Luang Thamrong in the next, Phra Dhun in the next, and Phya Trang in the next. And all the time his personal name might be Charoen, and one might never find it out.

An official would therefore be referred to by the title of his position. When one man stepped out of the position and another took over, the reference to the position was the same, only another man sat in the place of authority. This practice made all civil officials except the king anonymous, and no man could build for himself a name of fame. If a man known as Chao Phya Yomarat became famed in the kingdom and then died suddenly and his position and title were taken by another, it did that other no good. The fame attached to the title was an impersonal one. There was thus no possible competition with the divine king, who remained changeless and eternal before his people.

There was no lasting advantage in being of royal birth because one could not hope to build up a competing royal family. By law a son was automatically one grade down from his father, and in five generations a family which began with the highest possible birth was at commoner level. Everything was aimed to insure the position of the divine king and his alone.

The officials were dependent on the people under their authority for their living. They received no salaries. The commoners gave of their labor and of their rice. If officials collected funds from the people for any reason, a portion of the amount was theirs to keep. Higher officials or officials who rendered some special service to the king were sometimes rewarded with houses, lands, boats, servants, or other things of value. All these could be recalled arbitrarily by the king at any time. To recall them, all he had to do was to admire them, and the official perforce had to offer them to the king, who then accepted them if he chose. For instance, one king in modern times who desired to strip a noble of his wealth made a visit to his palace and went about admiring everything, and, when things were offered to him, he accepted them.

No person could be without a patron, because, if he had no patron, he had no one to protect him. All persons chose their own patrons within the limits of their division, civil or military. If one were interested in literature, dancing, or handcraft, he tried to choose a patron who could promote that interest.

A young man at the age of eighteen had to choose his patron and begin his lifework. When skilled in his trade, he was supposed to become a king's man and be available for the king's service. This might require him to serve the Lord of Life six months out of the year free of charge, and during this service he might not even receive his food, for his wife was expected to bring it to him. By this system the whole nation was brought into servitude to the divine king and made to bow before his every whim. It was not to a man's personal advantage to show outstanding ability. He might be required to devote all his time to the Lord of Life. He who was too clever might be too clever for his own good. Abuse of this system finally led to the possibility for skilled persons to pay money to get themselves released so that they could continue in business for themselves. But this was a later development.

This system of absolute control over the lives of the people developed a class of slaves, chiefly debt slaves, who in the middle of the nineteenth century amounted to about a quarter of the total population. There were redeemable slaves and nonredeemable slaves. The former were the debt slaves; the latter, persons who had been sold for their full value and over whom their masters held the power of life. They could sell them as they sold goods. This was what Hinduization did to a formerly free people, who according to their monarch Rama Kamheng, played when they wanted to play, sang when they wanted to sing, and freely selected the work they liked to do.

As all these areas in Southeast Asia were underpopulated and as there were never enough slaves, the dry seasons became the time for making wars which were little more than slave drives. The conquered were driven off to the land of the victorious. These war slaves all belonged to the king for his disposition and were used to enhance further his exalted position as divine monarch.

In such a state how could a person in authority keep track of the people under him? The system was to tattoo the people. In one reign the mark was put on the outer part of the arm or wrist, and in the next reign it was put on the inner part. Nonredeemable slaves were given special marks by their private masters. Monks and women were not required to perform government work, but the monks were recorded because they might leave the temple at any time and become available for royal service. By these means the manpower of the nation was thoroughly organized and controlled for the exaltation of the divine monarch.

In the definition of a Hinduized state it was mentioned that it was an extension of organized Hindu culture; that it was an acceptance of the Hindu conception of royalty, the divine king; that it included the Hindu idea of administration according to which the administration was as completely swallowed up by the king as the footprints of all other creatures were swallowed up by the footprints of an elephant; and that it included the acceptance of the Hindu or Buddhist religions and of the mythology of the puranas, the observance of the dharmashastras, which contained the canonized common law, and the use of the Sanskrit language.

On these latter four points we have the following observations to make: Siam is a land in which the Pali language has been chiefly used as the classical language. The language of the monks is Pali. They chant in it and preach in it. Their sermon notes are jotted down on palm leaves in Pali. Their sacred books, the *Tripitaka*, are in Pali, and by their efforts they put the canon in excellent shape.

The Ninth Buddhist Council was held in Bangkok in 1788 with the purpose of producing a revised edition of the *Tripitaka*.[6] After five months they had on hand 3,568 packets of palm leaves consisting of forty books of the Vinaya, one hundred and fifty-seven books of the Suttanta, fifty-six of the Abhidharma, and thirty-five of the Saddavises, the latter being a dictionary of Pali terms. Subsequent efforts at revision were made, and about a hundred years later during the reign of Chulalongkorn the complete *Tripitaka* using Siamese characters for the Pali words was published in 1893. This was the first complete edition of the *Tripitaka* in Pali. Other editions have followed. Pali is not Sanskrit, true enough, but it is supposed to be a dialect of Sanskrit or at least a brother descended from the same stem. And there can be no denial that it migrated from India.

Nevertheless, the Siamese have also made wide use of Sanskrit. Such works as the *Ramayana*, the *Mahabharata*, and the *Sakuntala* were famous epic and dramatic literature in the Sanskrit language. All these works are well known in Siam and form the basis of some of the outstanding productions of Siamese literature. The *Ramayana*, known in Siam as the *Ramakien*, is a Siamese classic. Well-educated Siamese

6. Kenneth E. Wells, *Thai Buddhism, Its Rites and Activities* (Bangkok: Bangkok Times Press, 1939), pp. 223–27.

know it as well as cultured Americans know their Shakespeare. The *Ramayana* has been recited by Siamese minstrels for at least nine hundred years. The earliest complete version in the Siamese language extant is that of Phya Tak Sin, who delivered Siam from its Burmese conquerors after its fall in 1767. This edition is in the Bangkok National Library and consists of four volumes written in gold script. The monarch who succeeded him purified the translation to such a degree of perfection that Siamese scholars say that the reader "will catch no smell of Indian butter."

In connection with Siamese literature we should also notice that Siam qualified in another respect as a Hinduized nation in that it made extensive use of the mythology of the puranas. This was a class of Sanskrit literature dealing with the creation, destruction, and renovations of the worlds, the genealogy and deeds of the gods and of great heroes. Among the best known of the secondary puranas are the *Mahabharata* and the *Ramayana*, which have previously been mentioned. G. Coedes regarded the puranas as the principal if not the unique source of literary inspiration throughout Southeast Asia during the period of Hinduization. This epic and legendary literature provided the themes for the classical theater, the dance, the shadow theater, and the marionette shows. Especially the characters of Rama and Sita were known everywhere and by all classes of people.

A casual examination of the royal parades at coronation or cremation reveals the emphasis placed on mythological beings. In the royal cremation processional on one occasion more than sixty effigies of mythical animals were represented. It was reminiscent of a Macy's parade in New York. The animals included such figures as the garuda bird, the elephant bird, the woman lion, the winged tiger, the elephant lion, and the swan horse. A survey of the history of Siamese literature, especially of the second reign of the Chakri Dynasty, is convincing as to the profound effect the puranas had on that literature. This golden age was described by one of the poets of the day as follows:

The dance halls were gay and merry	Boisterous.
The tunes were melodious, resounding, captivating,	Instrumental music reverberating.
Prosperous and happy was the city	And the royal palace.
There was carefree dancing and song	Ceaselessly.

This was a characterization of the court and not of the nation in general because the poets and the dance halls were in a cluster about the royal palace and catered to the whims and fancies of the royal family. The chief poet of the period, Sunthon Phu, died in poverty, an outcast from the court, which was the only source of income for a poet. He made the fatal mistake of correcting the verses of His Majesty in a version of the *Ramayana* and of praising those verses privately and then in a moment of drunkenness of ridiculing them publicly because he knew that, even with his corrections, they were bad poetry.

Siam qualified in another respect as a Hinduized nation, as its legal system was directly dependent on the Hindu dharmashastras. The divine king, in issuing royal edicts, depended on the dharmashastras, which were known in Siam as early as the fourteenth century. The dharmashastras provided the skeleton on which the body of Siamese justice was built and by which the divine king justified his system in the eyes of the people. He found authority in it for doing what he was doing to the nation.

The destruction of Ayuthia in 1767 by the Burmese scattered or burned nine-tenths of the collected manuscripts in the royal library. With the establishment of the Chakri Dynasty, efforts were made to recall the scattered pieces from all parts of the nation, even from so far away as Nakhon Sritammarat some six hundred miles south in the peninsula. The earliest available legal corpus is accordingly as late as 1805 and was produced after the *Tripitaka* already mentioned which had been completed fifteen years earlier. Three identical sets, each comprising forty-one manuscripts, were produced and sealed authoritatively with three seals, the lion, the elephant, and the crystal lotus, the seals of the War Department, the Department of Interior, and the Treasury Department.

The first volume listed in this famous work was appropriately the *Phra Dharmashastra*, or the sacred Code of Manu. Through this item the legal system of Siam was directly linked with the legal system of India. The Code of Manu was the most authoritative of the Hindu lawbooks and is supposed to date back at least to the first or second century of the Christian Era. It discussed the creation of the world, the state of the soul after death, the duties of caste and of religion, and all that pertained to custom and society. The divine king of Siam was no dullard and did not miss the opportunity to consolidate his position with the authority of such a code.

Other volumes in the Siamese Code bear such titles as the *Words of Indra*, whose word, of course, would be unquestioned in Siam; the *Law of Quarrels;* the *Law of the Civil Hierarchy;* the *Law of Slavery;* and many others.

Siam further qualified as a Hinduized nation in that it sanctioned and made use of both Hindu and Buddhist religious cults. Buddhism was regarded as the national religion, and the king was the layman sponsor or protector of the religion. The Hindu deities were utilized for the enlargement of the position of the divine king, and, as they had little relation to the life of the common people, they never achieved any popularity except in seasonal pageantry when the Hindu gods were represented in a plowing or a swing ceremony. Hinayana Buddhism was held by all the people to make provision for the life to come. The activities of the church were strictly religious and cultural and never were permitted to have a political reference. The church achieved no temporal power, because a divine king could permit no opposition to his authority.

The church hierarchy which is current in modern times was unknown during the period of ascendancy of the divine king. When King Mongkut inaugurated his enlightened policies, the church was reorganized in the direction of an episcopal hierarchy. Before that time the only attention paid to church organization was the division into northern and southern branches in 1577. A highly organized religious body might have been a challenge to a king. The church itself played into the hands of the absolute monarch because only a few monks entered the church to make it a life-career. The majority became monks for a few months to make merit and to acquire what little education was available in those days. Education was a monkish monopoly and consisted of the most rudimentary information about the national religion. The only religious examination of a scholarly sort was held by order of the king, not with a view to furthering education, but to show up the ignorance of vast numbers of monks who sought immunity from the annual period of military or civil service. Those who failed in the examination were obliged to leave the temples and become available for the service of the king.

With the advent of King Mongkut and the beginning of a trend away from the idea of the divine king, the organization of the church was progressively improved, and the scholarship of the monks was raised so that there were many fine scholars in the church.

During the period of ascendancy of Hinduization in Siam, we have seen, then, that there was a drift away from the pristine Thai way of life in which the king was the father of his people and the people led comparatively free lives. With the passing of the absolute monarchy—a passing which was accelerated and apparently planned by the last few monarchs—there was a drift toward a democratic way of life more in harmony with the spirit of Siamese life in the pre-Hinduized period. Siamese kings in modern times were aware that their method of administration was unworkable and anachronistic. King Prajadhipok, the last of the absolute monarchs, had two draft constitutions ready for consideration when the revolution of 1932 occurred, dramatically dropping the curtain on the centuries-long drama of Siam, a Hinduized nation.

V

THE ISLAMIZATION OF SOUTHEAST ASIA

ISLAM is the religion of about sixty-five million people in Southeast Asia resident in the southern provinces of Siam, the Malay Peninsula, and the Malay Archipelago. Southeast Asia has more than half the number of Moslems who have been attracting so much attention with their demands for Pakistan in British India. One naturally questions when and how Islam so successfully penetrated and conquered areas which had previously been Hinduized.

Christianity and Islam both strove to win the peoples of these areas to their banners. Neither was very successful in winning souls from the other, but both seemed able to penetrate the Hinduized kingdoms or those in which the native folkways were dominant. Only the small island of Bali in the archipelago was strong enough to resist both Islam and Christianity. Catholic Spain gave Catholicism to the Philippines, and in modern times there is a Catholic church in most villages with the exception of the villages of the Mohammedan Moros. Minahassa, North Celebes, and Amboyna are both nominally Christian.

The sword had little to do with the spread of Islam in the peninsula and islands, nor did Arabs. Moslem traders and teachers came chiefly from southern India, many embarking at Gujarat and Malabar. They came, in general, as others had come in previous centuries from India, seeking profit. They were not zealots prepared to sacrifice themselves for the holy cause, nor were they missionaries sent out by the home church. Even teachers who arrived later from Egypt, Mecca, and Hadramaut came in search of rich patrons.

An example of this practice was the scholar Maulana Sadar Jahan, who secured Sultan Mahmud Shah of Malacca as his patron. The sultan required his son Raja Ahmad also to study.

One evening during a lesson a drunken friend named Sri Rama came in and had a bowl of food with the sultan. When he saw the Moslem scholar there, he invited himself to have a lesson. The teacher realized that Sri Rama was drunk, and so his first observation was that drink was the mother of all beastliness. Sri Rama replied that covetousness was the mother of all beastliness and that the teacher had come in search of profit. The teacher was very angry.

The common language of the early merchants and missionaries was Persian. Their influence is still evidenced by the Malay alphabet, which is Perso-Hindustani in character. They brought books with them, and many of these were translated into Malay from the Indian versions of the Persian originals. Their tactics were much like those of Hindu traders of previous centuries. They had a strange and new learning; they claimed to be able to heal sickness and to drive away spirits; and they married the daughters of communal chiefs and through them influenced such communities.

No religion ever made conversion easier than did Islam. It was possible to become a member of the community without offering any evidence of genuine belief or of knowledge of the law. All one had to do was utter the two words of the confession of faith ("I bear witness that there is no God but Allah and that Mohammed is the Messenger of Allah"), and one was a convert and a member of the community of Mohammed. No one had the right to call another's faith in question.

A popular legend relates that an old Malayan saint who understood his people took charge of converting his own community to Islam. He knew their easy belief in mysterious formulas. His opportunity came when a local cockfighter whose bird was not winning asked him for an incantation to guarantee victory for his bird. The old Malay said that he had an incantation which if carefully studied would make the cock invincible. He taught the cockfighter the Moslem confession of faith which constitutes the first pillar of Islam. The cock won. Other cockowners heard of the incantation and came to learn it.

The original inquirer had lost his advantage and came back for another incantation. The old Malay taught him the ritual prayers to be performed five times a day, the second pillar of Islam. The cock won. The other cockfighters came again to learn this new incantation. The process was repeated until the whole gambling community had learned by heart the pillars of Islam.

Islam was propagated by attaching it to local practices and by making it seem useful in procuring the things the Indonesians wanted. As we shall see later on, many Indonesian customary practices were sanctified by the addition of Islamic ritual. Islam made large concessions to Hinduized elements also as is shown by the fact that the Islamic word for Mohammedan fasts is the Sanskrit *puwasai upavasa*, for teacher is *gurū*, and for disciple is *sisya*. Moslem chiefs bear such Hinduized titles as Maharaja, Mandulika, Lela Perkasa, Lela Wangsa, and Srinara.

The Hinduized wayang show and the gamelang, the native orchestra, were so strongly intrenched that Islam wisely left them alone and did not try to affect them. The gamelang music with its soft beating of drums, which always sounds as though it came from a distance, raises both players and audience into a sphere of relaxed inertia. The hero of the wayang play always wins by craft or by his knowledge of some magic practice. Characteristic Indonesian mysticism is expressed in the wayang and gamelang, and Islam at first did not fight with such mysticism. These things formed such an important element in native life that they took precedence over Islam in the minds of the people. A native chief engaged with his actresses in his wayang-wong troupe in a practice session would not be interrupted in order to fulfil some duty to Islam. To him the dance was a Hindu-Javanese ritual which required the utmost attention and concentration.

Islam did attack boldly the manufacture of images and art objects of a religious nature and as a consequence brought to a sudden halt the budding genius of Indonesian sculptors and architects. Islam produced no art and no structure to compare with Buddhist Borobudur. Artistically it was sterile.

The progress of Islam through the archipelago and the peninsula was slow but relentless. In 1292 Marco Polo visited Sumatra and found Moslem merchants in the small port of Perlak on the north coast. A daughter of the ruler of Mohammedan Perlak married a ruler of Pasai, which was one of the chief trading ports in Sumatran-Malayan waters. As a result of that marriage Islam advanced a step. Mohammedan tombstones dated 1407 are still found at Pasai and are said to have been brought from Cambay in India for sale. It was regular practice in those days to bring tombstones from India. Perhaps the workmanship of the stone was better than local products. Or perhaps traders used them as ballast just as the Chinese did the large stone figures which they sold the Siamese, some of which are still in evidence in Bangkok. Pasai became a strong Moslem community and engaged Moslem teachers for the instruction of the local population.

A Pasai princess married into a Malaccan family and carried her religion with her into Malacca, which then became a focal point for Islam in the fifteenth century. Malacca was important for the spread of Islam because it attracted traders from India, Siam, Sumatra, Java, and other islands and because men of great religious learning were attracted there by the opportunity it offered them to teach wealthy patrons.

The work of Moslem teachers was effective, and many translations of Moslem works were in common use in Malacca when the Portuguese D'Albuquerque conquered the city in 1511. Although he was conquering an Islamized city, he was seizing a dependency of Siam, a Hinduized nation. The Siamese *Kot Monthienban* cited as tributary to Siam in 1360 Johor, Malacca, Malayu, and an unidentified Wurawari. Malayu is the usual name for Jambi in Sumatra. A Ming chronicle supported in part this assertion of the extension of Siamese influence by stating that in 1403 the emperor of China sent the eunuch Yin Ch'ing as envoy to Malacca and that Yin Ch'ing reported that there was no king in the country and that it was not called a kingdom but belonged to Siam, to which it paid an annual tribute of forty taels of gold.

After the fall of Malacca the Moslem stronghold became Acheh in Sumatra. It, too, was a trade center and was prominent in the dissemination of Islamic thought in the sixteenth and seventeenth centuries. From Acheh, Islam spread to Ulakan and on to Minangkabau in the center of Sumatra. In the seventeenth century the people along the coast of the Lampong district turned to Islam. The spread of Islam in the islands actually took several centuries. The Bataks, in fact, opposed the entrance of Islam and only welcomed it as late as the nineteenth and twentieth centuries. A large percentage of Bataks are nominally Christians.

Early centers of influence in Java in the first quarter of the fifteenth century were Grisek, Madura off the Java coast, and Surabaya. Islam spread slowly to neighboring principalities until in 1478 the Mohammedan princes of Java united to overthrow the old Hindu kingdom of Majapahit. This formally brought to an end the last of the Hinduized states in Java. The Hindu princes then took refuge in Bali and carried their literature and their gods with them.

When Majapahit fell, a Moslem at Cheribon took over the administration of that district. Two of his sons later assumed the administration of the areas of Batavia and Bantam. In this way strong Mohammedan families developed.

In the sixteenth century Palembang, which had previously been famed as a Buddhist center for the dissemination of knowledge, sent Moslem teachers to Borneo to initiate the people there in the new faith. In the seventeenth century a Minangkabau trader from central Sumatra converted a Hindu Raja in Celebes to Islam, and most of these islands then came under Moslem domination. Islam did not win a quick victory but pressed its way slowly for at least five centuries before it was securely established in most of the islands.

Islam appealed to the Indonesians because in their spirit

worship and ancestor cult they were essentially mystics, and the brand of Islam which was first introduced was mystic in character. It was easy for Indonesians to understand it, appreciate it, and use it.

Early Islam was infected with Shiah heresies which had come to India from Persia. The main items of interest to the Indonesians were Sufi pantheism, the veneration of innumerable heroes and saints, and mystic numbers which were miraculous in their effect. They discarded shopworn Hindu magic for Islamic magic. They brightened up their Hindu charms by beginning and ending them with the addition of their new confession of faith in Allah and Mohammed. Moslem teachers stimulated reading in the Koran and in other sacred tales by promising that one who acquired a thorough knowledge would acquire the same merit as warriors who died in holy war.

The Indonesians made magical use of such mystical names and numbers as the four first caliphs, the four Arabic letters that spelled the name of the prophet and of Allah, the twelve signs of the zodiac, the twelve imams of the Shiahs, and others. Hindu teaching of incantations had prepared the Indonesians to accept the Sufi mysteries which were imparted only to the initiated and at a price. They had faith in the exorcist who in exorcising the spirits which caused disease in a man would remind the spirits that the man's belly was God's sea, that his backbone corresponded to the pillar of God's throne, and that therefore the spirit should come out of such a holy place.

An eighteenth-century Malay charm which was supposed to grant one a dominant personality was as follows:

> I sit beneath the Throne of Allah;
> Muhammad my shelter is beside me,
> Gabriel on my right, Michael on my left,
> All the company of Angels about me,
> Vicegerent of Allah!
> Only if Allah suffer harm, can I suffer harm;
> Only if His Prophet suffer harm, can I suffer harm.[1]

1. R. O. Windsted, "Malaysia," in *Islam Today*, ed. Arberry and Landau (London: Faber & Faber, 1943), pp. 214–23.

Raymond Archer described a ceremony which he called the *Suluk* which was typical of the earlier form of Islam in the archipelago.[2] Those who practice the *Suluk* are persons who are discouraged and dissatisfied or persons who want more power and must resort to magic to get it. One seeks out a teacher who is the head of an order capable of imparting the necessary instruction and first bargains with him as to the amount to be paid and the extent of the instruction to be received. The initiate is then washed and wrapped in a white cloth like a corpse. The teacher reads the prayers for the dead, and the novice meditates and repeats a *dhikr* such as the name of Allah slowly. He is supposed to go without food and drink for three days and nights if he is able. To help the novice concentrate, he is told to hold his breath in yoga fashion.

The novice attempts to put out of his mind all the things that hinder or worry him. He drinks holy water and puts his faith in his teacher and Islam. He sleeps with his head pointed toward Mecca and with his left hand above his right. At daybreak he performs his ablutions and worships, saying:

> O Allah, my Lord, complete good works in me.
> O Allah, my Lord, grant that I may be strong to fulfil your commands.
> O Allah, my Lord, grant me strength so that I may recognize what you forbid.
> O Allah, my Lord, bury me in pure Islam.
> O Allah, my Lord, bury me in perfect faith.
> O Allah, my Lord, grant good works on behalf of my teacher.
> O Allah, my Lord, grant that my teacher may have strength to fulfil your commands.
> O Allah, my Lord, grant that strength may be given to my teacher so that he may be able to recognize what you forbid.
> O Allah, my Lord, bury my teacher in pure Islam.
> O Allah, my Lord, bury my teacher in perfect faith.

The novice then repeats the first sura of the Koran. He is considered to be dead. He is bathed, and the burial service is said over him. At this point he surrenders himself completely to the spirit, whereupon the teacher is supposed to enter into

2. Raymond L. Archer, "Muhammedan Mysticism in Sumatra," *Journal of Royal Asiatic Society, Malay Branch*, XV, No. 2 (1937), 1–126.

the person of the pupil. The pupil then expresses thanksgiving and repeats the name of Allah five thousand times while thumbing over the rosary to keep count.

The novice then begins to see visions. He has hallucinations of the most terrible sort. Prophets appear to tell him the secrets of the universe. The climax comes when the novice loses his senses as Allah descends upon him and enters into his inner being. When he becomes conscious again, he is equipped with magical powers by which he can achieve happiness for himself and perhaps for others. One who is familiar with mystic practices in India will doubtless see how extensive was Indian influence on Islam as it migrated to Indonesia.

Another and more hysterial type of ceremony which was an expression of Islam in the earlier period was known as the *dabus*. The word referred to any steel or iron instrument which might injure human flesh. This ceremony involves dangerous practices which must be learned from a guru or from the founder of a spiritual order. The participants learn the mysteries in a yoga-like manner by constant practice in some quiet place until they have achieved real skill as magicians. When they are ready to demonstrate their immunity in Allah, they go to some public square in the evening and beat a drum and praise Allah and Mohammed. The idea is to demonstrate Allah's grace. This is done by going into an ecstasy and by creating a similar condition in the spectators. The climax of the ceremony comes when they turn their weapons on themselves and apparently stab their stomachs or even cut off one another's heads. After such a stabbing and cutting the victim or victims are covered with white cloths, while the others chant praises to Allah and Mohammed and to the saint of their mystic order. The cloths are removed and the wounded leap up unhurt. This makes such an impression on the minds of the credulous observers that some of them may get into the spirit of the thing and really cut themselves seriously, doing actual injury.

As Islam became well established in Southeast Asia and

put down roots, Moslems in other parts of the world became increasingly conscious of the growing Moslem community. Lines of communication were established with Egypt, Mecca, and Hadramaut. Indonesian intellectuals became aware that they were attached to heterodox practices and began to study with orthodox teachers. A sort of orthodoxy developed among the Indonesians. Even those Indonesians who leaned toward heterodox mystic practices came to speak of themselves as Sunnites of the school of al-Shāfiʿī.

Although heterodox mysticism has regularly been opposed by the orthodox, mysticism managed to survive until modern times in such orders as the Shattariyyah, the Kadiriyyah, and the Naqshbandiyyah. These had little energy as separate orders, however. The extreme forms of mysticism tended to pass and to be replaced by a mystic expression of piety which might be engaged in in conjunction with the daily prayers. The worshiper might sit on the ground with his hands on his knees so that the tips of his fingers would not stick over his knees lest the Prophet cut them off. He shut his eyes and listened to Mohammed. He might help himself concentrate by a rosary of a hundred beads which symbolized Allah and his ninety-nine names. Before telling the string over ten times as rapidly as possible, a prayer such as the following might be murmured:

> Pure is the garment,
> Pure the body,
> Pure the place of prayer,
> Sitting in the left unison of the heart,
> Turned toward the West,
> The heart of heart's in view,
> One in perception with the teacher,
> Help me to obey thy law.
> May God slay me in the All Holy,
> In the true faith, in pure Islam,
> Lord God, admit me to Glory.[3]

The mystic was then transported in spirit out of this world as he continued to utter the attributes of Allah, and he became able to look back upon the world as upon a coin.

3. *Ibid.*, p. 94.

The basis of orthodox Islam is supposed to be the five pillars which include the confession of faith, the ritual prayers with the condition of ritual purity, the religious taxation known as *zakat*, the fasts, and the hadj. Probably no Moslem state in the world has a general population which lives up to the five pillars. In the popular view there is a great deal of difference as to the degree of obedience necessary. The tendency is to reduce the indispensable obligations to a minimum. The pandits in all Moslem countries complain that the law which they teach becomes more and more a dead letter and less and less a guide to human action. What they are saying amounts to the fact that the law is everywhere the same but that the practice varies according to the kind of people observing the law.

Although the Indonesians regard themselves as orthodox, they have as a race a tendency toward the mystic and the mysterious. There is not on their part a conscious departure from orthodox doctrine, but nevertheless they do have unorthodox ideas. These ideas and their concomitant practices cannot be regarded as anti-Moslem. They are simply expressions of what they are as human beings. The domain of popular belief has been brought under the skirts of Islam and made safe for Mohammedan society.

Perhaps the best way to test the orthodoxy of the Indonesians is to measure their practice against the five pillars of Islam and then to note what non-Islamic practices are sanctified by inclusion in Islam.

The first pillar, the confession of faith and of orthodox belief and practice, is incompletely fulfilled in Indonesia. When the Indonesians entered the mosque, they carried with them all their religious baggage and left almost nothing behind. All they actually did, in the beginning, was to add to their burden the Moslem confession of faith. It is evident that the Indonesians were not converted to the point of view of Moslems in orthodox communities. The conversion was of the confession of faith in Islam to the uses of Indonesians. Islam provided the Indonesians with one more way to express their usual point of view about their universe. The confession of faith was a new incantation of great efficacy.

The second pillar in Islam is the ritual prayers which are to be celebrated five times a day, once a week on Friday at noon with some additional ritual, and also on certain special occasions. Indonesians generally neglect the daily prayers. And they equally neglect the ritual purification connected with these prayers. G. H. Bousquet in his "Introduction à l'étude de l'Islam indonésien"[4] illustrated the indifference shown by Indonesians by reporting a conversation he had with S. A. Mangkunegara, prince of Surakarta. The *khotba* or Friday sermon was supposedly given in the name of the local sovereign or regent. Bousquet asked Mangkunegara whether the *khotba* was called in his name. He replied that he did not know but that he could find out. He was completely indifferent to the matter.

Indifference of Indonesians to the ritual bath, which is supposedly obligatory when one has been tainted with major impurity, is shown by the fact that many Javanese women wet only the extremities of their hair, making it nothing but a symbolic bath. Like most of the peoples of Southeast Asia, the Indonesians are a clean people and bathe completely once or twice a day. But that has nothing to do with a ceremonial bath which is the religious bathing of the body after ritual impurity.

Only a few Indonesians carry out their prayers faithfully. If a volcano explodes, or if there is an epidemic of cholera, the people suddenly remember their prayers and crowd into the mosques and halls of prayer. But people who have work to do tend to neglect their prayers. If Islam had been introduced from some more orthodox source such as Hadramaut, it is possible that the Indonesians would have taken greater care to observe the ritual prayers and the accompanying purification. But they had an unorthodox beginning which permitted

4. *Revue des études islamiques*, XII (1938), 135–260. Bousquet visited Indonesia and in the light of his wide experience in North Africa made a study comparing Islam in Indonesia with that in North Africa. It is a concise survey of the living situation in Islam in Indonesia in the period shortly before World War II.

them to feel that they were Moslems without paying much attention to the prayers. They had the idea that a man could become united with his creator by mental exercises and that the bodily forms of worship were merely preliminary and could be dispensed with when one achieved the higher mystic level. This was an aspect of Indian yoga which had become attached to Islam in transit across India. For those persons who could not scale the mystic heights there were charms and other formulas which worked by magic. So we may conclude that the second pillar has never been sedulously observed among Moslems in Southeast Asia.

Another pillar is the fast in the month of Ramadhan. The fast is held in high esteem because of the general impression that, by observing the fast, one could make up for all his failures the rest of the year. Many of the details of observance of the fast are difficult to observe, such as the injunction not to swallow one's saliva during the fast in places where spitting is prohibited. Nevertheless, the fast is observed in spirit.

A fourth pillar of Islam is the tax called *zakat*, which in the Indies is called *pitrah*, and amounts almost entirely to an offering of rice. The *pitrah* is offered on festive occasions, and, as the Indonesians love festivity, the tax is popular. Another reason for its popularity is that it is believed that what shortcomings were not equalized by the fast might be paid off by the offering of rice, and God's books balanced for the year. The rice offering is observed faithfully by even the poorest people to an extent out of all proportion to the original intent of the tax, the idea originally being to make it possible for poor people to enjoy the feast. Furthermore, the grain is not fairly distributed according to the law, and, therefore, much of the rice offered should not legally be counted in the tax payment. Tax which should be paid on other things such as on cattle is seldom paid at all. Enthusiasm is shown only for the rice offering. Legally speaking, then, the tax is inadequately observed.

The fifth pillar, the hadj, is believed by Indonesians to be binding on all who have the means to make the journey. According to the school of Shāfi'ī, which is dominant in the archipelago, it is legally not imperative to perform the hadj as soon as one has the price. In fact, the trip can be postponed indefinitely if one leaves provision for a substitute to make the trip. Every year there are many substitutes who make the hadj for wealthy men who kept putting the trip off. But most people who have the money make the trip themselves.

This is one pillar which the Indonesians love to observe not only when they can afford it but even when they cannot. They go to Mecca the way Americans go to Niagara Falls. Some of them go several times. How soon Indonesians began going to Mecca is not known, but they have been going for centuries. While at Mecca they study with advanced teachers in orthodoxy and return to spread orthodoxy in the islands. The hadj has been one of the most important factors in the development of orthodoxy among the Indonesians.

In the nineteenth century the *Jawah* or Indonesian community at Mecca was one of the largest and most active.[5] The Indonesians conduct themselves with great modesty in Mecca because they feel that they are at the center of the religious world. The Meccans operate their end of the pilgrimage as though it were a Cook's tour. Agents are sent to the islands to organize the pilgrims and to exploit concessions such as the selling of scraps of *kiswah* (the covering of the Kaaba, the cubelike building at Mecca which contains the black stone) for amulets. As the covering is changed annually, it can be manufactured into many amulets which sell handsomely.

Indonesians who travel to Mecca go with no thought of money profit, no goods to sell, and, in fact, usually with a bag of money to spend. They go to have a good time and to study religion. They visit about the holy city with guides and discover as much as they can about the various ceremonies in which they participate. They learn prayers and recite the Koran and, if possible, learn some mysteries from some sheik.

5. C. Snouck Hurgronje, *Mekka*, trans. J. H. Monahan (London: Luzac & Co., 1931), pp. 249 ff. Hurgronje gives a very clear picture of the *Jawah* community at Mecca based on firsthand experience.

Indonesians from the various islands tend to get together at Mecca, and this tendency has helped them to find out more about their own island world. During the period that the Achinese were fighting the Dutch there is no doubt that at Mecca the Achinese took the opportunity to stir up other Indonesians against the Dutch as far as possible. It can certainly be said that Islam has been a unifying element in the archipelago and the peninsula and that its effectiveness in this respect is partly due to the hadj.

Snouck Hurgronje in his *Mekka* summarized the matters of importance at Mecca for Indonesians under three main categories: (1) the Indonesians at Mecca had opportunity to be initiated into the mystic societies which flourished there; (2) active intercourse among the Indonesian pilgrims led to exchanges of thought between themselves and with Jawah settled at Mecca and impressed them with the might of Islam radiating from Mecca; and (3) Indonesians first became habituated in Mecca to their daily ritual duties, and many of them returned home as well-disciplined Moslems. The importance of Mecca to the Indonesians is evidenced by the large number of Hadji who have made the pilgrimage and who are a conspicuous feature of street life in every Indonesian town.

It requires little imagination to see what an impact upon the cultural life of the Indonesians throughout Southeast Asia the returning Jawah have had for at least two centuries. They returned home to become the intellectual leaders and in some instances the zealots who stirred the population into religious frenzies.

We have seen how inconsistently the Indonesians have observed the five pillars of Islam, stressing some and ignoring others. The foundations on which the Islam of real life rests are not manufactured entirely from the five main principles on which the Islam of the books is based. Mohammedanism, in the course of its life-stream, has picked up the sediment of the regions through which it has flowed. It has adopted a vast quantity of loose matter which was alien to it but which was swept along by the new current. Its action was reminiscent of the flood freshets of the monsoon which swept down gulleys and through villages carrying everything loose with it. These new elements have come to fill out the body of Islam in Indonesia. Orthodoxy always struggles against such accretions and almost always fails if the people involved regard those elements as essential to their happiness. As we proceed to examine more of the practices of Islam in Southeast Asia, we shall notice many alien elements which have been adopted into the Moslem community of practices. They are nonetheless Moslem by virtue of their adoption, and this we may say even in the face of Moslem law, which does not recognize adoption and does not provide that adopted persons may inherit.

One contribution of Southeast Asia to Islam which no Moslem from North Africa would recognize is the form of the mosque. Most of the mosques were erected in large centers, perhaps in regency or district capitals. The older mosques followed the type of architecture which was common in Southeast Asia for religious structures, having had multiple pitched roofs which rose one above the other. The mosques looked like pagodas with three or five superimposed roofs. Many of the mosques were a wakf or perpetual endowment made by some pious person or persons. The older mosques generally did not have minarets. Later they built minarets beside the mosques. One of the oldest Moslem monuments in Java is the minaret of the mosque of the Koudous, which is a sort of chandi of eastern Java architecture, that is, a tower-like square structure resting on a raised base.

In some places, such as at Medan in Sumatra, they did erect mosques according to the classic style, but these were the exception. In general, the architecture of mosques followed the traditional pattern of religious structures and was not well executed.

At first, mosques were oriented toward the west and later on, after the builders got better maps, toward the west-north-west. It is accordingly not difficult to guess the approximate period of some mosques by the use of a compass. But none of them is worth that much attention.

The call to prayer is carried out by means of a drum known in Java as the *bedoug*. This drum is also used in the month of Ramadhan to mark the period of the fast.

In the western wall of the mosque is the mihrab, or niche, which indicates the direction of Mecca.[6] In many of the Indonesian mosques the pulpit or mimbar is in the form of another niche at the right of the mihrab, and from this pulpit the Friday sermon is preached. One ascends to it by steps cut into the wall. The mosques are also generally fronted by an open hall where justice is dispensed and where sacred repasts called *slametans* are eaten.

The personnel in the average mosque includes the leader of prayers (imam), the clerk (khatib), the one who calls to prayer (muezzin), and the director of the affairs of the mosque who is known as the penghulu. This last is an office which is not met with in other parts of the Moslem world. The penghulu not only is the director of the affairs of the mosque but is also the religious judge and so has status with the government. More will be said of his functions in connection with Moslem law.

In connection with the mosques, or quite independent of the mosques in those villages where there are none, there are schools of Islam known as *pesantren*. A pesantren is made up of a community of students and gurus. They may have a number of buildings for residence and a hall of prayer. Courses of study are laid out which may require as many as ten years to complete. Some pesantrens specialize in certain aspects of Islam, so that students may migrate from one to another, getting the flavor of each school of specialization. In general, they teach the law, the doctrine, and some form of mysticism. Most of the students do not graduate but learn a few elementary things, including some of the Koran, the

6. G. H. Bousquet, "Introduction à l'étude de l'Islam indonésien," *Revue des études islamiques*, XII (1938), 135–260.

prayers, and the ritual ablutions. Those few who complete the course signalize the event with a ritual meal called the slametan, which is a meal of mystic significance. Graduates go out into the world looking for work at some mosque or pesantren and, if this fails, may become village wizards selling amulets, concocting magical formulas, or carrying out religious ritual on occasion for remuneration.

Constant rivalry goes on between the pesantrens and the mosques, each attempting to exert the greater influence on the religious community. The contest is often sharp between a local guru of a pesantren and the penghulu of the mosque, who regards himself as the religious judge of the people.

Another structural manifestation of Islam was developed to meet the simple needs of the villages at a level below the pesantren or mosque. These were village halls of prayer where the villagers could make their daily prayers and where elementary instruction could be given in the Koran. These were wooden buildings, usually square, with the hint of a prayer niche visible from outside and generally with a double roof with a little tower in the middle.

The persons in charge of these elementary institutions have usually attended a pesantren for two or more years and have little more than an elementary education themselves. In spite of their ignorance, they are chiefly responsible for the millions of Moslems because they are in intimate contact with the common people. They act naturally as representatives of their village at the nearest mosque, and conversely they represent the mosque to the village. For instance, they collect the religious tax and remit the part of it due to the higher authorities. They are ever present in the village in an official capacity at all fetes, marriages, funerals, ritual slaughtering, and ritual banquets. If some guru or peripatetic teacher attempts to cut into the village activities and incidentally drain off part of the religious income, there may be serious trouble, especially if religious zeal is aroused.

Generally speaking, these village leaders who are known as *lebe* are especially active in calculating lucky days, in controlling malignant spirits, and in providing *jimats* or charms. A *jimat* may consist of the statement, "Lā ilāha illā 'llāh," written several hundred times on a paper, the paper rolled into a small tin box, and the box tied around a person's neck and worn at all times except when bathing. A *jimat* to make one invulnerable may be a statement of faith in the power of Allah. The person making such a *jimat* has to have magical powers because he makes a small wound, apparently, in the right side or in the right arm of the person buying the charm, inserts the *jimat* in the wound, binds the flesh over it, utters Arabic prayers over it, removes the bandage, and, if there is no sign of scar or wound, the charm is effective and the person invulnerable!

In such practices there is hardly a semblance of orthodoxy, and one comes upon the undefiled folkway of the common people. Nevertheless, Islam has given these practices a Moslem flavor. This is evident in a mystic ceremony known as the *ratib*.

The *ratib* has as its main feature the repetition of a *dhikr* a few hundred times. Such a ceremony may be held during a feast celebrating any event in the life of a Moslem family. Anyone who can pray in Arabic may be the leader. He is usually supported by at least ten men, and there may be many more. Their job is to respond with the ameen during prayers, or they may join in the repetition of the *dhikr*. The occasion may be to celebrate a year of profit and to pray for another good year, asking that the spirits in the graves might also be happy and be lying in a comfortable, dry place. The leader then includes the purpose of their meeting in his prayers, repeats some of the Koran, and then they come to the real business when the ten or more men supporting the service and the leader form a circle, with shoulders touching, and begin to sway in rhythm with their *dhikr* as they shout it louder and louder. Everyone present gets into the spirit of the thing by swaying and beating out the time. The crowd gradually gets into an ecstasy after the *dhikr* has been uttered hundreds of times. The ceremony closes on a quieter note with several prayers by the leader. The evening is concluded by a feast.[7]

A ceremony of this sort may also be used with some variations to ward off sickness of an epidemic nature such as cholera. In such a ceremony the participants carry banners, lights, rice, and incense. They start off with a *dhikr* to warm themselves up and then march around to all the homes in the village, singing and praising Allah and asking for alms. Whenever they come to a road intersection where ominous influences are known to gather, they shout to drive the illness away. When they feel they have covered the area of their responsibility, they gather again at their central meeting place and divide up the alms which they received during their visits to all the homes. They then close the evening's work with the repetition of a *dhikr* several hundred times. They scatter to their homes toward morning feeling secure in Allah.

A variation of the *dabus* type of ceremony referred to previously has survived into modern times in such a cult as the "Gold Needle Invulnerability Cult," which in 1947 was a powerful organization in Johore on the Malay Peninsula. The cult members were sanctified with a *jimat* and at the climax of the Moslem ceremony were pierced in the right side or right arm with a sacred golden needle. Those who successfully became cult members were those who showed no wound after being pierced. This proved that they had supernatural powers. The organization, although religious in nature, was an instrument for co-ordinating Malay opposition to rising Chinese influence. In order to impress the Chinese with their invulnerability, the cult members fearlessly attacked Chinese on occasion.

One orthodox practice which everywhere is thought of highly in connection with Islam is that of circumcision. The original instructions to observe circumcision were no more emphatic than instructions in other particulars, but circumcision is faithfully observed even when more important mat-

7. Archer, *op. cit.*

ters are ignored. Circumcision is not one of the five pillars, but the way the faithful adhere to it one might think it was the first and most important pillar. Perhaps it is popular among the Indonesians because it was practiced either as circumcision or incision of the foreskin in pre-Islamic days. It has become identified with Islam, however, because of the instruction concerning circumcision in the law.

Pre-Islamic practices still cling to the ceremony of circumcision. The act may be preceded by a cold bath and be carried out in a small structure erected in a place determined by magical means. When an important family has a member circumcised, there may also be a wayang show, a gamelang orchestra, and a slametan banquet. When Indonesians began arriving at Mecca only incised and not circumcised, the Meccans saw an opportunity not only to improve Indonesian practice but to make a profit for themselves. They examined all Indonesians as they arrived, and before they gave them the liberty of the city they required them to be properly circumcised.

Abstention from pork is held to be as obligatory as circumcision. Although theoretically the drinking of wine is forbidden with equal strictness, it is not regarded as so grave a transgression as the use of pork. When some villages first learned of the prohibition of pork, they became hysterical and killed all their pigs, thinking that such dreadful creatures were inhabited by evil spirits.

Another prohibition which the Indonesians transgress is the one forbidding the use of silk or of gold and silver ornaments. Gold and silver ornaments are one of the chief ways Indonesians save their money. And the men love nothing more than a silk shirt studded with gold buttons. Yet most of them will not wear neckties because that is an irreligious act —perhaps because the necktie is believed to be symbolic of the cross of Christianity.

An ancient Indonesian custom which has been given sanction by Islam in the minds of most of the people is the practice of polishing down or breaking off the six front teeth of the upper jaw. Prominent white teeth are supposed to resemble the horselike teeth of spirits and might attract spirits to come seeking a friend. The common people think that they destroy these teeth because of Moslem law. The practice is less popular in modern times, but in Mohammedan areas, whenever it is done, it is sanctified by Islamic formula.

Another Indonesian social element which is not in accord with orthodox Islam is the position of women. The high social status of women from the most ancient times has led to a practical modification of the usual form of Moslem divorce whereby, if a husband is absent for six months by land or for a year by sea without communicating with his wife, the marriage is dissolved. This was aimed to protect local girls from itinerant adventurers. The women of the Minangkabaus of both Sumatra and Negri Sembilan, Malaya, are especially favored in their social position. The Minangkabaus are an exogamous people who regard many Moslem marriages as almost incestuous. Nevertheless, Indonesians have never proposed that the Moslem law on marriage be changed. They simply respectfully ignore those injunctions which clash with customary law.

There would be no toleration even among the Minangkabaus for a system under which contracts of marriage were concluded or dissolved under rules other than those which include provision for a man to marry four wives. The practice of marriage, divorce, and the rearing of children is in its main essentials Moslem. The chief open conflict with Islamic law has been with the Minangkabau, among whom the children do not inherit from their fathers but from their mothers, and among whom marriages are forbidden between persons descended from the same woman through the female line.

In general, the position of Indonesian women is not Moslem in character. Official Islam has regarded women as socially inferior to men. But in Indonesia, even in the Moslem sphere of family law, the women retain a position of privilege far above that of women in other Moslem lands. The authorities of the mosques have always been opposed to education for girls and against the entrance of women into world affairs. But in Indonesia the women have succeeded in securing some education, little though it be. And there are women's organizations in connection with the mosques and with nationalist political movements.

Indonesian women do not observe purdah and work openly in the rice fields, give evidence in public courts, dance in the wayang-wong show and remain women of virtue, and vote when they have the opportunity. Islam has not damaged the position of Indonesian women, nor has it handicapped them for modern life. They mingle freely and easily with the men in today's world. In almost every financial deal one of the silent partners who holds the moneybags and who sits in on the final decision is a sharp-eyed old lady who has had a lifetime of experience with profit and loss. Many a mother-in-law knows and makes use of the old saying: "My son-in-law shall be subservient to me: if he is clever, I will cajole him; if he is stupid, I will see that he works: like the buttress of a tree he shall protect me: like thick foliage he shall shelter me."

One customary Indonesian practice which Islam easily accepted was that of the veneration of saints. All Moslem communities in all the world venerate saints. From the most ancient times Indonesians honored ancestors. It put no strain on their imagination to add the Moslem saints to their list. They did not feel that it was necessary to mark off their list the old Hindu saints either. Veneration of ancient statuary of great Hindu and Buddhist figures has continued. The practice is so common that the museum at Batavia has had to forbid people to venerate statuary in the museum. There is no accepted list of Moslem saints against which to match the list which the Indonesians honor. The tombs of the most ancient saints which contain the first propagators of the faith date in Java from the fifteenth century. Persons who desire their aid in solving the problems of life go to their tombs and make a vow that they will do certain things if the saint will cause certain things to come to pass. As an offering the usual things, such as incense, rice, and flowers, are taken to the

these 9 saints, who first promulgated the Islamic relig., are Chinese! (from Champa). ...Slamet Muljana
Mar 10, 1971 arsury

tomb. The person in whose behalf the vow is made usually has his head washed at the sacred spot as a symbol of devotion and purification. Food offered to honor the saint is always eaten by living persons, either by those making the vow or by poor persons who benefit by the offering. To hallow the food, a village teacher of Islam who knows some Arabic is present. This adds the necessary blessing of Islam to lift the ceremony a degree above the ordinary veneration of spirits.

As Indonesians in prominent position often desire to venerate the tombs of famed saints abroad and have no opportunity to visit those tombs, it became the custom to make the vow and offer the food to a local representative of Islam. By the expenditure of a little money a wealthy Indonesian could thus take advantage of the powers of all the leading saints of Islam of all time in all parts of the world.

Another expression of the native folkways which has been accepted under the cloak of Islam are the slametans, or ritual feasts, which form one of the most important religious and social expressions of the Indonesians. Slametans are of almost daily occurrence in some form or other and use up a considerable part of the Indonesian income. One of the common arguments to attempt to persuade Indonesians to be converted to Christianity is that they would not need to continue the slametans and could thus save money. But this to an Indonesian is about as pointless as urging a Christian to give up Christianity in order to abolish Christmas. The Indonesian loves his slametans. They may be banquets in connection with the veneration of the saints. They may be offered to ward off evil. They may be offered before or after a trip or at any other event in the life of an Indonesian which he feels calls for some special recognition. Slametans play a vital part in the religious and social life. In family life they are held at pregnancies, at births, at marriages, and at death. Indonesians are not content to have one for each of these occasions but will have slametans at stages in each event so that there will be as many as four for a marriage, four for a birth, and a great number for a death, as they continue at intervals after death for a considerable period.

The Indonesians studied the religious calendar and picked out all the usual orthodox days for slametan celebrations and then added other days which held religious significance.

On January 31 they celebrate Ruwah 29, which is the Javanese equivalent to the Arabic *Sjaban*.[8] *Ruwah* means "soul" and is the Moslem all-souls month. During this month burial places are cleaned up and venerated and slametans held. Ruwah is succeeded by Puasa. *Puasa* means fasting, and preparation is made for it in Indonesia by a day of bathing and cleansing which is more a day of festivity than of ritual bathing. During Puasa there are a number of occasions for ritual feasts which in this instance are called *maleman*, which means "night," and are so named because the feasts are held at night. Puasa is closed by Lebaran Puasa on March 1, 2, and 3, which is a period of feasting to indicate the end of the fast. Slametans are held everywhere, and even the poorest people take part in them and visit all their relatives and friends with the idea of making a new start on another year with Allah's bookkeeping on sin balanced. The success of these days of feasting for many people depends on the faithfulness of those offering the *pitrah* of rice which is handled through the religious leader of the village.

On May 9 Lebaran Haji is celebrated as a day of sacrifice. Not only those who have made the hadj but almost all other Moslems who can afford it make the sacrifice by means of an official who is expert in ritual sacrifice of cattle. This is a period which is regarded as lucky, and such family rituals as marriage and circumcision are held some time during the month in which the day falls, that is, the twelfth month of the Mohammedan year. Slametans abound on these occasions.

June 7, or Muharram 10, is the day for venerating Husain,

8. Raden Supatmo, *Animistic Beliefs and Religious Practices of the Javanese* (New York: East Indies Institute of America, 1943).

the grandson of the Prophet, the legitimate head of the Moslem congregation. Only a quiet and nonfestive slametan is offered on that day, but it is a feast day nonetheless.

On August 7 the birthday of Mohammed is celebrated by ceremonial slametan feasts. In some there are fairs held and a great deal of honor shown to the memory of the Prophet.

The last important slametan is held on December 18, commemorating the ascension of Mohammed on a winged steed. The opportunity is taken to review many of the legendary tales attached to the early days of Islam. The religious calendar alone provides almost endless opportunity for the Indonesians to express themselves through their favorite religious vehicle, the slametan.

Slametans are also offered in connection with one's trade, and, if this be the growing of rice, there are slametans at every tension period in the production of rice.

A Moslem character is given to slametans by the recitation of a prayer in Arabic to suit the occasion. As there are over fifty kinds of slametans in common practice and about sixty-five million Indonesians who engage in slametans, and as the person giving the prayer is always paid for his services, it is easy to see what a brisk business there is in slametans. In order to distinguish among the slametans, different types of prayers have been developed, and the official who gives the prayer has to take great care to offer the right one. During the Moslem part of the service the people are very devout and pious in appearance and if asked will insist that this is a regular and important Moslem ceremony. Most of the people who participate understand little that is said in the prayer beyond the *Amin* which terminates the ceremony and is the signal to begin the feast.

Islam conquered a large part of Southeast Asia by providing an attractive form in which to cast many local customary practices. One thing it did was to provide a legal form on which human relations could be organized and regularized. Moslem law was believed at one time to have displaced or swallowed up customary law. Moslem law was in a written form and had the authority behind it of centuries of experience. Local customary law was unstable and varied somewhat from place to place and from time to time. In a competition between adat, or customary law, and Moslem law it seemed inevitable that Moslem law would prevail. Furthermore, as in recent centuries Westerners have dominated the civilian administration, and as Westerners seldom knew the difference between customary law and Moslem law, and in fact probably did not know there was such a difference, it seemed obvious that Moslem law, which was written, would be supported by the Western sovereign, as indeed it was.

Moslem legal terms were well known to Westerners in other parts of the world, and, when they discovered these terms in use in Indonesia, it was natural for them to encourage the practice of Moslem law. Even when native customary law was brought out in a case by local contestants, it was often described by Moslem terms so that it was confused with Moslem law.

The situation as far as the representatives of a Western power were concerned was simple enough. They did not desire to interfere more than they had to with local practices. They thought that Moslem law was accepted by the majority of the native population because the clichés of Islam were used at all times and in all cases. A Mohammedan legal adviser was accordingly attached to every native law court in Indonesia, and he was expected to hand down an opinion not only on matters connected with the Mohammedan religion but on all subjects which fell under the category of native customary law also. The Westerners, it should be repeated, were not aware that there was a difference. The Mohammedan adviser was the penghulu, whom we referred to earlier as the administrator of the affairs of the mosque. The penghulu was regarded by Westerners as a high priest, although he was not one, and the penghulu court was described as a court of priests, although there were no Moslem priests. Marriage and succession were the problems which usually fell within the jurisdiction of the penghulu.

Moslem law of inheritance has frequently been directly contradictory to customary practice and has thus created much confusion. The common people generally settle things of this sort among themselves and so solve their problems by customary law. But in difficult cases which are taken up to the penghulu court the decision is supposed to be made according to Moslem law. Where a considerable inheritance was at stake, the interested persons might strive to have the decision rendered in the sort of court which would favor their own status. Sometimes a person would be favored by Moslem law and not by customary law, and sometimes it would be the other way around. The trend has been to settle inheritance cases according to customary law and not Moslem law.

H. Westra has listed nine points of conflict between Moslem law and customary law of inheritance in Java to show how sharp the differences are.[9] Where customary law may transmit arable land which is only part of an estate to a single heir, Moslem law regards the estate as a whole. Where customary law leaves the estate undivided as long as there are minor children or a widow, Moslem law permits the next of kin to require the distribution of the estate. Where customary law provides that brothers and sisters share alike, Moslem law grants the men twice as much as the women. Where customary law recognizes adoption and permits the ones adopted to inherit, Moslem law does not recognize adoption and denies to the adopted any inheritance. Where customary law gives a daughter precedence over the parents and brothers of the deceased, Moslem law permits her to have only a share of the estate. Where customary law permits children of the deceased to inherit by representation, Moslem law does not recognize representation. Where customary law grants paternal and maternal half-brothers share and share alike, Moslem law grants the larger share to paternal relatives. Where customary law makes a distinction between property inherited from previous ancestors and the inheritance of prop-

9. "Customary and Muslim Law in the Netherlands East Indies," *Transactions of the Grotius Society*, XXV (1940), 151–67.

erty acquired during marriage, Moslem law makes no such distinction. Where customary law provides a widow a reasonable life-interest in the estate, Moslem law permits her to receive only a fourth or even an eighth of the estate, according to circumstances.

In the sharp conflict that naturally arose between Moslem law and customary law, customary law gradually won out in matters of inheritance, which touches on the very welfare of the people involved. In a sense this is a measure of the respective strengths of the native ways and the imported religion. When the issue was met, the customary ways tended to prevail. As a matter of fact, the effectiveness of Moslem law in Indonesia is very limited and feeble, and it has had very slight effect on the law of succession. The sphere of its control has not been extended to land laws, penal laws, laws of obligations, or administrative laws. It has no effect on the wakf or sacred foundation, which cannot be affected.

Almost no study of Indonesian customary law was made until the end of the nineteenth century. Several excellent studies were made then, one of the best of them by C. van Vollenhoven.[10] The system of customary law has wide implications because it has such an extensive application and pertains to the practices of the people in such widely located regions as Madagascar, Malaya, the Philippines, the archipelago, and even Formosa. The adat is not the same in all places and in fact differs from community to community. There are enough factors in common, however, to make it recognizable. In general, it might be said that the people have ignored Moslem law when it came into conflict with their traditional way of life.

With the development of intelligent studies of Moslem and customary law, modern administrators have taken cognizance of the differences. For instance, in some of the islands no Moslem functionary may perform a marriage ceremony without a permit from the head of the community indicating

10. *La Découverte du droit indonésien* (Paris, 1933); *Het adatrecht van Nederlandsch-Indie* (3 vols.; Leiden, 1918–33).

that, according to customary law, there is no objection to the wedding taking place. It thus becomes obvious that the idea of the Moslem adviser, the penghulu, in court affairs was based on an erroneous conception of the effectiveness of Islamization in the archipelago.

From the time of Daendels, in criminal and civil cases, whenever the plaintiff or defendant is a Mohammedan, the advice of the penghulu on the written law is asked. The penghulu is actually never able to advise according to customary law. In a criminal case, under Moslem law he has to recommend horrible punishments which were probably applied in Arabia centuries ago in such a connection. The judges came to the point of listening to but not heeding the advice of the penghulu. In matters of inheritance it is the same. The opinion of the penghulu is recorded, and then the decision rendered in accordance with customary law or adat.

Although there are nominally sixty-five million Moslems in Southeast Asia, there are not that many persons living their lives in accordance with Moslem law. Most people are respectful toward the law, but they are respectfully indifferent. Customary law has steadily won its ascendancy, and religious law has been given a very narrow field of application.

In Malaya the situation is somewhat different, as the Moslems under British guidance accepted the Indian Penal Code in criminal law. Islamic law tends to govern in matters relating to family and inheritance. There is also legislation, for instance, which penalizes Moslem women who consort with infidels and pagans. And Moslems who eat or drink in public during Ramadhan may be fined.

In Siam, when the Civil and Commercial Code was promulgated in 1925, the government provided that the Moslems, who made up 90 per cent of the population in the southern provinces of Yala, Pattani, Naradhivas, and Satul, should be governed in matters of family and inheritance by Moslem law. An official Siamese version of the law was made up by a board of Islamic advisers. This local version included local customary law or adat. The government then appointed an

Islamic board of examiners having five members who selected four Islamic judges, one for each of the provinces, who were to sit with Siamese judges and advise them on matters of family and inheritance. This practice was discontinued for several years, from about 1940 until the end of World War II, during the Phibun regime when there was considerable religious persecution.

As the result of an appeal made by the Moslem people after World War II the usual privileges were granted again and were made official in the *Gazette* of December 3, 1946. There was some advance made over the previous situation, however, because now the decision of the Moslem judge is not merely advisory but final. During the early months of 1947, Moslem leaders in the Siamese provinces began to press for wider application of Islamic law and even to talk about political separation from Buddhist Siam. In Siam, then, the Moslems prefer to be governed by Islamic law, but it is Islamic law heavily larded with customary law or adat. Islamic law has not won a victory over customary law in Siam.

It is clear that the great majority of Moslems in Southeast Asia are less subject to Moslem law than has usually been thought to be the case. They actually look to customary law for guidance in most situations.

Are the Indonesians really Moslems? The answer is certainly "Yes," but they are Moslems of a sort not to be found in other parts of the world. It is obvious that their customary practices are not an expression of the *fiqh* or Moslem dogmatic theology. They are Moslem-minded and have sanctified all their practices with Moslem sayings and prayers. The names of Allah and Mohammed are on their lips daily. They stubbornly resist all attempts to convert them to any other religion. The thing that makes the Indonesian Moslems seem different is that Islam has had to adopt a vast amount of matter which was alien to it but which was indispensable to the multitude of believers. Old customs were sanctioned by new creed.

The Indonesians regard themselves as orthodox Sunnites

of the school of Shāfiʿī, and yet Islam for most of them is a superficial thing. They incompletely fulfil their obligations under the five pillars of Islam. The shape of their mosques is unorthodox. The position of the penghulu in the mosque is unique in the Moslem world. They depend on the magic of the charm and the mystic *dhikr* to ward off evil. Their practice of circumcision is carried out according to local custom. The men use silk and gold and silver ornaments contrary to law. The position of their women is not Moslem in character. They exceed all customary Moslem practice in the veneration of saints. Their practice of slametans has forced Islam to sanctify offerings to spirits and ancestors. And in an issue between Moslem and customary law the customary law usually wins. We are almost forced to conclude that Islam has become their religion without having converted them to a new point of view and without having seriously modified their usual practices. They are Moslems, nonetheless, because they have converted Islam.

VI

WESTERNIZATION AND MODERN TRENDS IN SOUTHEAST ASIA

IT MIGHT seem more appropriate to make the subject of this final chapter "Christianity and Modern Trends in Southeast Asia" rather than "Westernization and Modern Trends in Southeast Asia." This would have been unsatisfactory in view of the fact that under the topics of Hinduization and Islamization this book has not confined itself strictly to Hinduism or Buddhism or Islam in a narrow religious sense but has emphasized the whole way of life imported with those cults.

By "Westernization" is meant the extension of the organized life of the West into Southeast Asia. This includes the products of the science and technology of the West and by that very fact is limited to the influence of the West on the East since the latter part of the nineteenth century. It also includes the concept of government in the West, and as that concept has been emphasized at various times in the direction of democracy, of fascism, or of communism, so the emphasis has shifted in Southeast Asia. When democracy and fascism or democracy and communism clash in the West, there are similar clashes on a limited scale in Southeast Asia over the same general issues. Westernization includes the use of Western languages and of Western literature and the development of native literature on the pattern of Western literature. It includes the drift of native customs and manners toward the patterns of Western customs and manners. It emphasizes the integrity and responsibility of the individual rather than the village or commune. Westernization includes the development of local crops and other raw materials on a commercial basis rather than for personal use. It includes the use of money as a basis of exchange and trade rather than as hoarded wealth and accordingly requires the development of banks. It involves the element of speed and so carries with it the development of fast motor roads, railroads, airfields, telegraph lines, and radio stations. It involves freedom of speech and the other civil liberties which make it possible to broaden the base of government and to make civil administration depend on an enlightened population. It involves in all these things the religious concepts and moral standards of the West as taught by missionaries and as practiced successfully or unsuccessfully by missionaries, merchants, and colonial administrators. It involves the materialism of the West as well as its idealism. In reaffirmation it may be said that Westernization means the extension of the organized life of the West into Southeast Asia with all its conflicts and inconsistencies, its good and its bad.

The Western way of life was made known in Southeast Asia by various means. One of the earliest of these was Christian missions, which rode like a surfboard on the flood tides of the new way of life and beached in every center of any importance in Southeast Asia. In some places it was left high and dry. In others it revealed itself as a fully equipped landing craft with wheels, and its riders proceeded to occupy the surrounding region.

Almost all the early Christian missionaries made statements before they went out that they were going in order to save the souls of the lost. They launched their expeditions on the instruction given by Christ: "Go ye, therefore, and teach all nations, baptizing them in the name of the Father, and of the Son, and of the Holy Ghost, teaching them to observe all things whatsoever I have commanded you: and, lo, I am with you always, even unto the end of the world." The content of the missionary message varied according to church creed, but, in general, emphasis was placed on those texts which expressed the sincere concern of the missionaries, both Protestant and Catholic, for the souls of the people they went to serve. This concern was their dynamic which drove them forth to brave the unknown terrors of a mysterious and dangerous world.

The Catholic church was well organized from the beginning. In the Protestant world the different religious organizations began by competing with one another before they incorporated and organized in cartel fashion for the salvation of Southeast Asia. It developed that Baptists were to save Burmese, Presbyterians were to save Siamese, Methodists were to save Malays, and the Christian and Missionary Alliance missionaries were to save Indochinese.

It is interesting to note what the missionaries actually accomplished in the light of what they said they set out to do. They went to save souls and stayed to open dispensaries, to build modern hospitals, to erect model leper homes, to urge prison reform, to advise on the proper treatment of the insane, to initiate education for females, to lecture on modern science and physics, to invent alphabets for those peoples who had none, to introduce printing, to invent typewriters, to compile dictionaries, to produce in many cases the first written or printed literature, to advise women on new methods of obstetrical treatment, to indoctrinate the public on proper methods of public health such as how to behave during a cholera epidemic, to introduce physical education, and, indeed, to lend a new vocabulary to the languages of the peoples of Southeast Asia. These and many other things were actually done by the missionaries.

In Siam, in 1926, King Prajadhipok made public acknowledgment of the inestimable contribution made by missionaries to the general progress of his nation. Although a Buddhist sovereign, he was a wise enough man to see that what Christian missionaries had worked for was as wide as life and as deep as man's need. The missionaries did not confine themselves to matters of creed but applied themselves to the problem of integrating oriental communities in Southeast Asia into the context of a technological world. Many of the missionaries did not realize that that was what they were doing. They thought that they were accomplishing only what they had come to do. If the success of their work is measured by the numbers of converts recorded in church statistics, which are usually overstatements, then most of them failed, because, even according to their optimistic figures, the converts have been few. If, however, their effort is measured against the total effect they have had on the way of life of the nations they have served, they have achieved enough success to satisfy the most unfriendly and critical observer.

Merchants and traders, the forerunners of colonialism, were also vehicles for the new way of life. When they first began to come to Southeast Asia, they themselves had few of the values which we think of as the values of the West. Beginning with the fifteenth century, Europe had erupted into Asia with all the savagery of the Middle Ages. The sailors and adventurers who sailed the ships to the East for Portugal, Spain, Holland, France, and England were from the lower levels of society. In those days piracy was an honorable trade. They came to Southeast Asia because they were poor and because they hoped to become rich.

The social concepts and practices of the earlier European merchant invaders were not always up to the level of the natives whom they conquered by their superior weapons and organization. The European traders bathed rarely and seldom washed their sweat-soaked garments. They lived in airtight rooms to keep out the bad air. They dumped their garbage and sewage into the streets and canals. And many of them were frequently and constantly drunk. They conquered natives who lived in airy homes, who bathed daily not once but several times, who disposed of their garbage and sewage whenever possible in running water, and who drank little or no alcohol.

The products of the technological and scientific West together with a concomitant materialistic ideology began to come into existence in the nineteenth century and were imported into Southeast Asia to some degree as soon as the West itself began to appreciate them. Trade channels were already established and operating when such things as automobiles, sewing machines, radios, and the works of Darwin, Dewey, and Marx began to appear on the market.

A third agency in Westernizing Southeast Asia was the colonial powers. The Dutch have been in control of the East Indies in some manner for almost three centuries. The Spanish occupied the Philippines as early as 1542 and introduced Roman Catholicism, which was accepted by most of the population. Spain's grip on the Philippines was broken by the United States in 1899, and thus the United States has been chiefly responsible for the introduction of the organized life of the modern West. England achieved administrative control over Burma by three wars in the nineteenth century, the last one occurring in 1885. France moved with power into Indochina in the second half of the nineteenth century and only consolidated her acquisitions of territory as recently as 1907. In Malaya the English completed their colonial organization with the formation of the Federated Malay States in 1896 and with the addition of four Unfederated States in 1909.

In all Southeast Asia only Siam was able to cope with adversity and to save her political identity as an independent nation. This was largely because Siam had on the throne in the nineteenth century one of the most enlightened sovereigns and certainly one of the best educated in the world. King Mongkut altered foreign and domestic policies which had stood for centuries. He felt that the answer to expanding European imperialism was not to isolate but to Westernize his nation. He made a beginning, but it was his son Chulalongkorn who gave vigor to the program by engaging the services of Western experts who could advise him on every department of national life. Although Siam did not become a colony technically, she was thoroughly affected by colonialism because she voluntarily transformed her way of life to match and even to precede the changes taking place in the colonies which surrounded her.

The colonial powers did not have programs which went along evenly, but, in general, in all of them progress was made in the direction of Westernization. Each one of the colonial powers developed its colony in accordance with the economic, social, and political practices and ideologies of the political power. In the Philippines the American emphasized political development and hustled the Filipinos to assume political responsibility for themselves in 1946. No attention was paid to the fact that the Philippines were as economically dependent on the United States as ever. The French stressed cultural assimilation and tried to develop Frenchified indigenous persons. The Catholic church was promoted, with every effort made to replace the Chinese type of religious philosophy with the French type. Economically Indochina was made to exist for the benefit of France, and little heed was paid the development of political independence. The British and the Dutch emphasized economic progress and the general welfare of the people. The Dutch carried out their program firmly with the idea that it was good for the native peoples. The British were probably more easygoing and patient in their application of their economic and general welfare programs. In all these colonial areas the trend has been to create larger administrative units and consequently to draw together on a working basis many diverse peoples.

The colonial powers built railroads and motor highways. They made airfields and put up radio towers. They erected hospitals and dispensaries. Their ships brought in consumer goods from the West. They built electric-light plants and city water systems and even on occasion a sewage-disposal system. They encouraged indigenous education and developed schools along Western lines. Only a few of the indigenous persons went to Westernized schools. But everyone who could do so secured for himself some of the things of the West and mimicked the manners and dress of Westerners as they saw them portrayed in the ubiquitous movies.

On one occasion I stayed unknowingly with the leading gangster of Chaiya in southern Siam. He was the best-dressed man in Western style in the community and, aside from the highest government official there, had the nicest home. He sat respectfully by my side while I as a missionary preached Christianity. I did not discover his profession until I was ready to leave. It was something of a shock to learn that my sponsor in the community was the leading gangster and racketeer. I took him to task for his duplicity and asked him why a man in his profession was so helpful to a man in mine. He said that he was very grateful to Americans because, by a careful study of their methods as shown in gangster films and by a liberal use of American weapons, he had risen to the top of his profession. He had listened carefully to all that I had had to say in my public addresses with the hope of learning more to his advantage.

Ideas are the luxury of the few, but things and practices are available to anyone who has the price and the opportunity. When people begin using the things of another people and mimicking them, they inevitably begin to become like them in some respects regardless of what their ideologies may be.

Those few persons who were successful in the Westernized schools of Southeast Asia were encouraged by scholarships of various sorts to go abroad to secure higher education for themselves. The wealthy sent their sons and daughters abroad anyway. The program of sending students abroad got strongly under way in the twentieth century and has been chiefly responsible for the development of Westernized nationalist leaders in Southeast Asia. It is this Westernized indigenous minority which since World War II has been asserting itself belligerently against the very colonial powers which helped make their training possible. Such students who became Westernized either at home or abroad have been one of the most effective instruments in promoting the Westernization of Southeast Asia. However, they seem to want the things and the ideas of the West without the domination of the Westerner.

Colonialism, as judged from this point of view, has been of immense value in the acculturation process and may be regarded as the scaffolding within which the substantial house is erected. Or it may be compared to the pressure cooker which in terms of the acculturation process is forcing Westernization in one-tenth of the time that Hinduization and Islamization required without such pressure. Or it may be compared to the paternal household which has had a stormy experience between incompatible parents and children in which the relations between parents and children inevitably become more and more strained as the children, for better or for worse, consider themselves mature. We may recall that at one time the United States was a colony, and we may also recall the birth pains, the anguish, and the concern which was experienced by everyone involved as we launched ourselves into nationhood.

We see, then, that Westernization is developing under the influence of missionaries, merchants, colonial powers, and Westernized indigenous persons.

Persons who are being Westernized are in the process of being dispossessed of a great many things which they previously thought necessary for a happy life and are acquiring desires for other things which they wish to obtain but have not yet obtained at all or at best only meagerly.

In education they are losing the religious schools which attempt to preserve the static values of the old ways and are developing secular schools which pay scant attention to any particular formal religion but impartially provide information on the subjects under consideration.

In communications they are losing the use of the footpath from village to village which tended to discourage travel far afield, so that it has been said that, for most of the people, over the hill and beyond the next village was out of the world. They are acquiring high-speed motor roads for bicycles, motorcars, and trucks and airfields on which domestic and international airlines function. They are obtaining the use of fast machine-driven boats and ships to traverse the coastal and deep-river channels. In a few decades they have acquired the mental outlooks of a speed age. World War II has given a tremendous impetus in this direction. New roads were driven through jungle which had never before been penetrated. Airfields were built for military purposes in all parts of Southeast Asia. Indigenous businessmen who had establishments in just one locality have caught on to the value of extension to other areas. It is not unusual to discover businessmen on planes touching at Bangkok, Singapore, Batavia, and Palembang on a monthly checkup of their shops in those cities.

In public health they are being dispossessed of the sense of security obtained by offering incense to a spirit to prevent illness or of tying a charm around the wrist and sprinkling lustral water to ward off evil influence. They are learning that the hypodermic with the appropriate liquid content is the more potent charm. In the Netherlands East Indies, for instance, Western medicine became popular chiefly because of the dramatic success of the neoarsphenamine treatment for syphilis and yaws. In Siam it was largely because of the success of vaccination against smallpox and of quinine against malaria. These were dramatic diseases which Western medicine brought under control and, in so doing, won the confidence of the people.

When Dr. Edwin Cort arrived in Siam after World War II with several tons of medicine as a gift from the churches of America to the Siamese people, he was protected by the guns of the government from marauders who knew the value of these things and who would have robbed him. With the assistance of government officials he was able to make these tons of medicines available in all parts of the country to the common people, who accepted them with grateful eagerness. When he arrived in Chiengmai to reopen his hospital, he was met by a parade of the common people which literally stretched from one suburb to the other of the second largest city in Siam.

The effectiveness of these medicines was not limited to public health. Months later acknowledgment was made in the newspapers of the nation that the medicines had been effective in saving the rice crop in some areas where the people had been too ill to work the fields. The people in many instances were led to realize that offerings to the spirits in behalf of the rice crop were not so effective as modern medicines in making the people able to work their fields.

Furthermore, in agriculture, the old ways of securing a crop by magic and by traditional ceremonial is being displaced by information supplied to the farmers by the various departments of agriculture on the selection of seeds, on the best methods for plowing and sowing, and on modern methods of reaping. Westernized heads of agricultural departments make every effort to keep up to date. They publish farm journals, and, when they have opportunity, they go abroad to become familiar with the latest methods in order to pass the information on to their people.

In commerce and trade the people are being dispossessed of many of the old village crafts and methods of sale and are learning modern methods of making consumer goods and of selling them. Generally speaking, most of these countries are producers of raw materials. Southeast Asia has supplied most of the world's crop of rubber, pepper, teakwood, cinchona bark, kapok, hemp, copra, and tapioca. It has produced an important part of the world's supply of tin, palm oil, and sisal fiber. Other products which were reaching world markets in substantial quantities before World War II were tungsten, tobacco, tea, hides, sugar cane, the insecticide rotenone, and various gums, oils, and resins. Burma, Siam, and Indochina were the three leading rice-exporting nations in the world. In the development of these crops on a commercial basis millions of people have been drawn out of their villages into new communities and into a new independence of life relieved of village supervision.

In entertainment they are being dispossessed of the old ways of village amusement and are turning to the movie, the dance hall, the night club, the Western type of novel and thriller. In none of these areas in Southeast Asia are they producing any modern literature worthy of the name, although they are writing quantities of it. Newspapers in the local languages abound and contain international news, commercial information, and love stories in the Western manner.

In large centers of population in place of the candle or coconut-oil lamp they have set up, or are hoping to set up whenever they can get the equipment, electric lighting systems. This alone is enough to transform the way of life of a people who have always gone to bed with the fall of night because they lacked illumination to carry on evening activities.

In place of the crude norias or other systems of irrigation they are learning about dams and canals and the direction and control of waters which might be used not only for irrigation but also for power. Some form of irrigation using dams has been known in Southeast Asia for centuries. Some of those ancient dams, such as one built by King Airlangga in the eleventh century along the Brantas River in Java, have been so good that they can be included in modern irrigation systems. But the idea of dammed water for power as well as irrigation is being learned from the West.

Instead of the chisel or the stylus for writing purposes they are, whenever possible, buying fountain pens, automatic pencils, printing presses, and mimeograph machines. The mark of the Westernized man is the gold clip of a fountain pen on a shirt pocket.

In place of the homespun cloth, which used to be the only kind available in peasant and royal homes, they are becoming acquainted with cheap cotton textiles imported from abroad. During World War II most of these areas became cloth poor to such a degree that it was not unusual to find a family of five or six with only one good piece of cloth among them to be used in turn for public appearances. The war did not drive them to a complete return to the old forms of weaving. They waited the war out in the expectation of securing cheap cloth from abroad. Home industry is passing.

Instead of raw local tobacco rolled in a palm leaf to form a cheroot they are becoming used to foreign cigarettes. These have begun to enter Southeast Asia by the ton and find ready buyers at the most extravagant prices.

In manners and customs the peoples of Southeast Asia are being dispossessed of the old standards for polite human relations and are assuming the manners of the West. In many regions it is no longer polite to show hospitality toward a visitor with some areca nut and betel leaf. They are learning about shaking hands, about chairs, about hats, about shoes, about Christmas cards and cards of invitation, about knives, forks, and spoons, and all the other things that are generally used by Westerners in polite society. The cocktail party has come to stay in Southeast Asia.

In the fine arts they are learning from Westerners and from students who have gone abroad about new kinds of painting, of sculpture, of architecture, and of literature. The old style of painting without perspective which was so common in Siam a couple of generations ago is now almost a lost art. There is only one painter of the old school left in Siam who is capable of doing a painting without perspective. It is a skill that has fled. The instructor of painting in the Department of Fine Arts in Bangkok is appropriately an Italian.

In the world of thought they are being dispossessed of the idea of the authority of the elder and of the divineness of the king. They have heard a lot about the integrity of the individual and his moral responsibility. This is probably one of the most dynamic concepts the West has given Southeast Asia. It is not the king, the clan, the commune, or the village which is important—but the individual. They are beginning to feel that the social order should exist for the convenience of the individual rather than the individual for the service of the social order. Westernized persons are seeing themselves for the first time as persons with the inalienable right to be as fully developed persons as they are able. This has as many implications as there are facets to the gem of life. To them it means class equality. It means that the individual has the right to select his own lifework and is not bound to follow in the steps of his elders. It means that young people realize the right to select their own mates for life and need not wait upon their elders to choose for them. It means that as responsible individuals they feel that they have the right to choose their own religion, the right of freedom of speech, and the right to organize with those whom they find like-minded in matters of commerce, of society, or even of politics.

As a natural result of all these disturbing changes which are making Southeast Asia a sea of roily waters, the Westernized minorities have begun personalized political movements in the hope that they can put themselves in control of political and economic affairs. Their more general purpose seems to be to broaden the basis of government by educating the general public.

In Indochina there is the Viet Min headed by Ho Chi Minh. In Burma there is the Anti-Fascist League headed by Thakin Nu. In Indonesia there is the National Indonesian party headed by Sukarno. And in all these areas there are numerous lesser parties which give their loyalty to outstanding individuals. There is no such thing as party politics—only personal politics.

The nationalist movements in the various parts of Southeast Asia are aware of what other similar movements are doing. What happens in one area has a direct effect on what happens in other parts of Southeast Asia. For instance, they are sensitive to the achievement of political independence of the Philippines and of Burma.

It is impossible to say what the political forms will be like, because the whole area is in political flux. It requires no gift of prophecy, however, to see that something new representing a blending of the inspiration of the political theories of the West with the genius of the indigenous peoples will result. The political forms of the West can no more be rejected during this period of Westernization than could the Hindu theory of the divine klng have been rejected during the period of Hinduization. Each is an integral part of an organized way of life.

The situation has developed in such a way as to disturb even the most stable element of administration—the village. The revolution of 1932 in Siam is an illustration of how the villages have been shaken by a movement in which in the beginning they had no part. The revolution did not arise out of the unrest of the masses of the people but out of the imaginations of the Westernized minority who wanted to assume responsibility for directing the Westernizing of the nation. The revolution of 1932 was successful not because it had the support of the general population in the villages but because it was smartly engineered by astute Westernized minds supported by a small Westernized military group. In the years since 1932 the governmental program has reached into the most remote villages so that in an election year the candidates campaign for votes according to their understanding of Western methods. The masses of the people have caught on quickly to the ethical and nonethical practices in electing candidates. And the successful candidates themselves from the provinces have learned rapidly.

Persons who formed the first legislative body in Siam were almost completely ignorant of how to proceed. The legislature which I saw in action in 1946 was composed of a body of men who had been through four rough-and-tumble years under the Japanese and had become wily experts in parliamentary procedures. They had even succeeded in throwing out in a constitutional manner a Japanese puppet government under the noses of the Japanese without losing control of their nation. The government begun by a Westernized few in 1932 has developed skill and has put down its roots into the villages of the nation. There is probably not a village in Siam which does not know the issues among the candidates for office in the legislature. In the past the people in the villages might approve or disapprove of the central government, but they did not dare to express an opinion. Majesty was divine. Now they may express their opinion by the ballot.

The village life of Southeast Asia was never profoundly disturbed by Hinduizing, Islamizing, or Sinicizing influences.

This was because the ownership of land was not altered, the tightness of village administration was not broken, new things were not so radically different as to make all the old things obsolete and worthless, and the inflow of money was not great enough to develop a new basis for commercial independence.

Perhaps the alienation of land is as good evidence as any of the effect of Westernization in the villages. John Christian in his *Modern Burma* indicated that 50 per cent of the occupied land in Lower Burma, where the commercial rice crop is grown, is owned by nonagriculturists. Half the people who till the soil do not own the land they cultivate. The result has been social instability expressed by a high crime rate. Just before World War II the chief problem was how to get the land back into the hands of the people who worked it. World War II threw the whole situation into confusion by the flight of Indian moneylenders ahead of Japanese forces, the destruction of official records, the shifting of large elements of the local population, and the almost complete destruction of several of the most important metropolitan centers. There is no question in Burma of being reactionary and of holding on to the old. The only thing possible in the villages where commercial crops are grown is to start a new life on a new basis.

In Siam the government has tried to solve the problem of alienation of land to moneylenders by the co-operative society system. The program of creating co-operative societies went on at a rapid pace in the decade preceding World War II. It seemed as though there was a possibility that those peasant farmers who were in debt could be helped to hold on to the ownership of their land. The problem was not so severe as in Burma, since only about 25 per cent of the commercial rice lands were affected. Although World War II did not drive out the Chinese moneylenders, it did discourage the Siamese growers from planting more rice than they needed themselves, and this in turn deepened their debt and made their hold on their land less secure. Since the war only about

35 per cent of the normal export level has been achieved, and the farmers have, whenever they could do so, sought out new and irregular ways of making a living. The need to survive has driven a large percentage of the population, including the civil official class, into illicit activities which have profoundly disturbed the usual way of life. High Siamese officials are deeply concerned about the corruption which has developed throughout the nation and which is directly related to the insecurity of land tenure and the increase of debt. The situation is aggravated by a monetary inflation.

I have a letter from one well-informed Siamese in which he stated that before World War II he had almost never known of a case of a district official taking a bribe and that now he hardly knew one who did not. Here again there is no question of a return to the good old days. A new life must be begun based on a re-thinking and a restating of the values of life to meet the situation. The problem is at once practical and religious.

In Indochina among the Annamese the village is imperiled by the clan practice of dividing the land estate among the children. This practice has tended to make individual holdings smaller and smaller, especially in Tonkin and Annam, where the Annamese have been settled for more than a millennium. In Cochin China, where the French parceled out large areas to French holders and where the Annamese were less well established on the land, the tendency has been to develop a native tenant worker who served a landlord. The usual practice for tenant farmers is to pay about half of the crop grown, whatever it be, to the landlord. That is the minimum. In some instances a larger share is required, and in others a high interest payment is also demanded. There is also communal village property which is made available to the members of the village for working, which usually amounts to about 20 per cent of the total. Almost all the farmers are in debt, many hopelessly so, with rates of usury as high as 25 per cent per month. A person who once becomes involved cannot escape. The agricultural co-operative credit system has been tried in some areas with small success. But it seems inevitable that with the progressive division of the land as practiced in the clan, and with the constant factor of debt tending to force debtors to become tenant farmers rather than landowners, the security of the village is becoming progressively less certain in Indochina.

Philippine villages in commercial crop areas are similarly disturbed. James J. Halsema reported in the *Chicago Sun* for March 2, 1947, on a visit he made in Central Luzon with the Hukbalahap insurgents led by Luis Taruc. He described the movement as a conflict between four million peasants working the rice granary of the Philippines and the landlords to whom they have lost their land through debt. Halsema estimated that the peasant revolt was activated by about seven thousand peasants supported in spirit by the others involved.

In Indonesia, village life has been less affected by the alienation of land than by other factors. Bernard H. M. Vlekke in *Nusantara* pointed out that village rule as described in the fourteenth century under Hayam Wuruk by the poet Prapancha was still in operation in its essential characteristics shortly before World War II. The description given by Prapancha in his famous *Nagara-Kritagama* as recorded by Vlekke is as follows:

"From a great celebration at the royal court, all the village elders and all of the *wadanas* [district chiefs] returned home, having taken leave of the king. This was the last exhortation given them by the king's uncle; 'Serve faithfully your Lord and King! Take care to neglect nothing that may add to the welfare of your district; take good care of the bridges, the roads, the waringins, the houses, and the sacred monuments, that our ricefields and all that is planted may flourish, be protected, and well tended. Look after the dikes of the sawahs, that the draining water does not run off and the people have to leave for better sites. And, if people have to move to another place, let them follow the royal ordinances on the extension of the village fields. Take care that the kitchens [the number of families] are registered and the lists controlled the last day of each month.' "

Native rule was preserved in Indonesian villages in this general form through the centuries with some slight modifications. And village poverty continued also. The villages were virtually self-sufficient without much if any money income. Income taxes start on incomes of about $50 a year, and only about 5 per cent of the native people earn incomes above that figure. In the village economy Indonesians live virtually without cash. One disturbing factor has been the rising influence of money, the lure of which has drawn young people out of the villages and into areas of activity involving commercial production for money.

An inclination toward disintegration of the village organization was begun by governmental uniting of larger areas for administration, thus destroying the stability and independence of what had been autonomous units. The *desa* chief was allowed to remain, but his power was limited to controlling only the lower courts of justice. Higher courts of appeal, previously unknown, were imposed on him, and he was made the representative of the government, whereas formerly he was the representative of the ancestors of the tribe. Furthermore, village schools were created which offered a three-year elementary course. These schools were supposed to become an integral part of the village life, but they did not do so because the teachers received their salaries not from the village in which they served but from the government. The curriculum was the same everywhere, so that all the children in all the villages wherever they attended these schools learned the same things. The schools were superintended by school inspectors who transferred from district to district and so were impersonal in their supervision. This had a disintegrating effect on village autonomy and isolation. That was how matters stood in Indonesian villages at the outbreak of World War II.

Village life was further disturbed in all parts of Southeast

Asia by the millions of persons who were displaced during and since the war. The Japanese are supposed to have transported for labor purposes about a million Javanese alone. Labor forces were moved hither and yon to serve on the various road and railroad projects of the Japanese. Since the end of the war various factors have been effective in continuing the movement of people. Large numbers of Annamese, Cambodians, and Laos have milled around in Indochina or have moved into Siam. Nationalist exiles have gathered in Bangkok and have continued to conduct their affairs *in absentia.* Large numbers of Indonesians have moved out of areas in which there were disturbances created by disagreement between the Dutch and the Indonesians. The Javanese themselves since the war seem to be in a frame of mind to amplify the movement of persons. Indonesian nationalist leaders have stated that, as soon as they can do so, they expect to move nine million Javanese from overpopulated Java to underpopulated Sumatra. A movement as vast as that would probably be impossible even if planned to take place over the course of a decade. There will certainly be some movement, however, from Java to Sumatra. Sumatra itself is not without a sense of unease, as the Achinese in 1947 started a move southward into Batak territory, and the Bataks began a restless shifting on south along the coast and into the interior. Such movement of people indicates a restlessness in all Southeast Asia and the breakdown of village authority and isolation.

We have been carrying the story ahead faster with words than the actual situation is developing. These things are in motion. The Westernized minorities are still minorities amounting to less than 10 per cent of the total population, but they influence and have the support of large blocks of the population. The masses of the people have not been converted to the mental outlook of Westerners any more than they were converted to the mental outlook of Hindus during the period of Hinduization or to the mental outlook of Moslems as a result of Islamization. They are converted in large numbers to the point of admiring and supporting Westernized leaders and wanting Western products.

This is illustrated by the Batak Christian church members in Sumatra. The Bataks have been furnished by Christian missionaries with churches, hospitals, and schools. Some of the Bataks have developed into Westernized leaders, and most of them have secured as many Western things as possible. They have accepted the forms of Christianity but have not discarded their traditional point of view. They have accepted the new words, the new ritual, and the new magic and have interpreted it within the framework of their own experience.

They believe, for instance, that sin is not a contradiction of God's will but is wrong behavior which exposes a man to the perils of the unknown world of spirits. Sin is thus a transgression of adat or customary law, as it always has been. To stop a run of bad luck in a family, they will confess the sins of their forefathers as well as their own.

The Bataks have always believed in lucky days and have learned how to use the Christian calendar for the selection of such days. They have always sought out omens to indicate whether an ill person will live or die, and now they use the communion for that purpose. If the ceremony goes well, the ill will survive. They have always believed in the prophecies of sorcerers, and now they use scripture verses for prognostication. They have always believed that the only comfort for the loss of a child is to have another, and so, when one Christian speaks to another who is sorrowing over the loss of a child and says, "May God comfort you," what he means is, "May God soon send you another child." They have always believed that a childless marriage is unnatural and incomplete and so hold that God has not blessed such a marriage and that the couple should be divorced.

An ill person after taking the missionary's medicine will call in the sorcerer on the theory that it cannot be wrong to want what is good and that any way to get the desired result is legitimate.

The Bataks have had the custom of having swordsmen accompany a corpse for burial in order to drive away evil spirits. In Christian funerals two men with swords accompany the coffin to the church door and wait with the bier outside while the Christian ceremony is held.

The magic in each instance lies in fulfilling the traditional custom in every detail even though Christian elements have been added.

In matters of religion in a narrow sense Westernization is producing a profound effect. This is evident in the psychology of the people. It is inevitable that the breakup of the traditional isolated social group, the decay of the usual ethical forms, should exert an influence on the psyche of the people. Their sense of right revolts against the process. Where the process has already made great strides, it tends to cause a feeling of distress, a notion of unfair suppression and even of exploitation. This feeling arises out of a sense of impotence and bewilderment in the presence of the complex modern world. This feeling then comes into conflict with the moral foundations underlying the solidarity of the old order. There is a rear-end collision between speeding new ideas and the slow-moving real situation. The old and the new exist in confusion at the same time without being harmonized or reconciled.

The natural result from all this clash and confusion is a sense of maladjustment, of sensitiveness, of irritability, of being wronged by someone. This is a state which cannot last long and must strike fire and flash out in compensation with actions and theories which will re-establish self-esteem and provide a way of salvation. A spiritual revolution in the religion is the inevitable result. It may be nothing more than a scrapping of all the old and now invalid concepts and an acceptance of the materialism of the West. In many cases this is exactly what happens.

The old foundations are destroyed and the only point of view which seems to harmonize with the organized life of the West is some sort of humanism or naturalism or materialism.

In most cases, however, the exchange is not that radical, at least not all at once, and a deliberate effort is made to rationalize the old in terms of the new experience. Whenever this is done, it is always termed a "return to the pristine religion" of Mohammed or of Christ or of Buddha according to the religion under trial. It is not really a return to the original religion at all but a re-thinking and a restating of the religion based on carefully selected scripture texts which can be made to seem to apply to the new situation. No one has ever succeeded in making a clean break with the past. One has to sit down in the midst of all his accumulated religious baggage and proceed from there with his eye on the vital factors in the living situation. In order to illustrate what is taking place, we propose to examine briefly recent developments in Indonesia and Indochina.

In Indonesia there is a deliberate organized attempt to reform Islam and to adjust its beliefs and practices to the Western world. A former Haskell lecturer, H. A. R. Gibb, pointed out four objectives contained in a reform movement in Islam which had been formulated at the beginning of the twentieth century by an Egyptian sheik named Muhammad Abduh.[1] Although Egypt may seem to be geographically distant from Indonesia, it is spiritually close, since the development of orthodoxy in Indonesia has come about as a result of the lines of contact between Indonesia and the more orthodox communities in the Near East. Ideas which are current in the Near East in one decade often appear in a modified form in Indonesia in the next decade.

The four main points of the projected reform in Egyptian Islam were: "(1) the purification of Islam from corrupting influences and practices; (2) the reformation of Muslim higher education; (3) the re-formulation of Islamic doctrine in the light of modern thought; and (4) the defense of Islam against European influence and Christian attacks."

All these four points appear in the literature and projects of the Muhammadiyah movement in Indonesia. The Mu-

1. *Modern Trends in Islam* (Chicago: University of Chicago Press, 1947), p. 33.

hammadiyah movement is an expression of Westernized religious leaders of Islam in Indonesia who are seriously questioning the content of their traditional religious teaching and their local practices. According to R. L. Archer in an article previously referred to, every community of any size in Java and Sumatra has a branch of this organization. Each branch operates under the direction of its own president. They have clubhouses, reading-rooms, organized sports, and Boy Scout and Girl Guide troops. The members of the youth organizations are taught Western ideas of sanitation, education, government, and religion. They seek to improve the elementary schools. They have prepared textbooks on religious education along the lines of those used in Christian Sunday schools. They also have developed Mohammedan catechisms. They have introduced the singing of hymns and have attempted to get the people used to the idea of a sermon as a regular part of the worship service. As the Methodist church in Indonesia has for many years held yearly conferences, the Muhammadiyah inaugurated the same practice in order to coordinate their efforts in all parts of Indonesia.

The members of the Muhammadiyah have great respect for the Koran but attempt to interpret it in the light of the contemporary situation. Great care is taken to emphasize those texts which can be fitted in with modern thought and to avoid those which might cause embarrassment. The Traditions are valued for their contribution to the physical, intellectual, and spiritual improvement of mankind. The members talk about mysticism because they know that that is a popular subject, but they interpret it in an ethical and moral way so that its value is practical and this-worldly. By talking about mysticism and by using all the old familiar clichés, they hope to influence the conservatives, who hold strongly to the usual indigenous mystic practices which developed under the cloak of Islam. Mysticism for the members of the Muhammadiyah is not an other-worldly experience achieved by magical practices but is practical and measurable in human relations. Mysticism is not an immediate communion with God but is the achievement of certain ethical and moral standards which are in good repute in all the world. The *dhikr*, that is, the endless repetition of the name of Allah resulting in a trancelike state, has no place in Muhammadiyah practices.

The Muhammadiyah is, of course, opposed by conservatives who try to deny Muhammadiyah members the right of entry into certain mosques. The conservatives hold to the interpretations of the Koran and of the Traditions found in the old commentaries. They represent the attitude of most of the Indonesians numerically speaking, but they represent few of those who have been Westernized and who are taking the lead in Indonesian affairs. Westernized leaders in the Muhammadiyah movement who are prominent in political affairs are able to influence and to secure the support of many conservatives because they use the same religious clichés, but without definition. The same words mean different things to the conservatives and to those who have been Westernized. The more successful leaders are those who use reified concepts without too much explanation. However, the explanations are available for those who want them.

In order to purify Islam from corrupting influences and anachronistic practices, Westernized religious leaders have pointed out the absurdity of invoking Siva, Vishnu, and Mohammed in the same incantation. They bluntly characterize the ceremonial which revolves around the spirit cult and the cult of ancestors as superstition. They urge the people, as good Moslems, to be more orthodox and to abandon heretical practices. They inform the people that white blood does not flow, as they believe, in the veins of Malay rajas and Moslem saints and point out that this absurd idea was also held by the Hindus in regard to Siva.

Westernized leaders are placing emphasis on the brotherhood of man with a view to allying spiritually Moslems in the Indies with Moslems in Egypt, Arabia, and India. A brotherhood is being created which includes all races which accept the creed, the first pillar of Islam. This is developing a democratic emphasis which was not evident either in the Hinduized period or in the earlier centuries of Islamization. There is also a better attitude being fostered toward non-Moslems, and it is possible to detect the elements of religious tolerance among a people holding a religion which has been famed for its intolerance.

Westernized Indonesians are coping with such a practical problem as usury and have decided that Moslems should be able to take advantage of interest rates without being accused of the sin of usury. Interest from banks, shares, and cooperative societies are now generally regarded as legitimate.

Westernized Indonesians are bringing organized efforts to bear on the old religious attitudes with a view to modifying them. Only a beginning has been made, but it is an evidence of what is happening in religion during the process of Westernization.

R. L. Archer made available in 1937 two Malay documents which give a clear indication of the direction of the thinking of the Westernized minority of Moslems. One was an article which appeared in the *Muhammadiyah Almanak*, written by Dr. H. A. K. Amrullah; the other was a book entitled *Tasawwuf Islam*, written by Siswawijata A. Moersiidoelwadjid.[2]

According to these documents, the purpose of Islamic mysticism is to cleanse the divine service from false accretions and innovations which are not founded on the teaching of the Koran and the Traditions. The false accretions referred to are not the innovations from the West but are obsolete local practices and ideas which have crept into the Islamic fold. The writers speak repeatedly of the need to return to the teaching of the Koran and the Traditions and to follow the example of Mohammed, but not as interpreted in the old commentaries. Reform is necessary.

They condemn those mystics who prostrate themselves in worship, who use large turbans and long coats, who deny themselves the good things of life, who devote themselves to devotional exercises and the endless repetition of the *dhikr*,

2. R. L. Archer, *op. cit.*

and who oppose the Westernization of Islam on the authority of the scriptures. The reformers also cite scripture for their point of view. Here is a typical appeal:

"Brother Muslims! away with such teaching of mysticism which does not agree with, or is not based upon the Qur'an, and remember the way of the Lord which says, 'This is the genuine Qur'an in us [Allah], may you hold it as precious, do not follow some other way which will separate you from the way of your Lord' " (Sura 6:152).

The writers reject the reactionary mystics as false Moslems who make true believers appear ridiculous and stupid and who undermine the position of Islam in the world. They point out, for instance, that some of these mystics claim that, in order to seek holiness, the faithful must despise or at least discount the value and strength of desire. Such mystics say that the nose should not enjoy smells, nor the eyes sights, nor the tongue tastes. In short, when a person has no enjoyment in the things of this world, then they regard him as holy and fit for a seat in heaven.

The Muhammadiyah leaders oppose this point of view by pointing out that the Lord created man with desires and expected him to use them with wisdom. Without the control which religion exercises, these desires and passions will get the upper hand. Islam, when truly understood, can help one make the fullest and best use of his senses and desires. They believe that those who teach otherwise fail to comprehend the true doctrine. Such persons are those who say that "blessed in the life to come are those who are content to lose all their possessions" and that "those who have need for the things of this world and yet hope to enter heaven may be likened unto an elephant attempting to crawl into an anthill." The Westernized leaders do not believe that it is more difficult for a rich man to enter heaven than for an elephant to crawl into an anthill.

The Muhammadiyah claim to be the true mystics and the true followers of Islam. They believe in the molding of character and the altering of bad habits into good by practice.

They believe that conduct can be improved. A stingy person should force himself to give alms. A person who is conceited should deliberately humble himself until he develops the habit of right thinking. A person who is blind to his own faults should make a careful study of them so as to become aware of his own shortcomings. One who is a victim of his passions should practice to control them. Everyone should deliberately engage in good works as required by the Koran and the Traditions, and so develop his character.

If a person is given to anger and if he becomes angry when standing, he should sit. If he is still angry, he should lie down. If he is still angry, he should get some water for religious ablutions and directly worship the Lord. This will certainly cure him of his anger, for who can be angry when in the presence of the Lord?

If a person is given to envy, he should realize that it will cause not only his ruin but possibly his death. A person who is continually envious causes his blood to become heated. This condition induces heart trouble and leads one to an early grave. One should keep in mind the will of the Lord and realize that he who is envious is not in sympathy with the will of the Lord. Practical solutions are also offered by the Muhammadiyah writers for the sins of pride and hypocrisy.

In all their teaching they keep an eye on the good things of this world which the followers of Islam should have. The Muhammadiyah is not a religious movement which requires denial of self. It approves of the full realization of the individual's capacities and desires. The purpose of the movement is to prepare Moslems to meet citizens in the world of science and of international cultural relations without feeling ridiculous or embarrassed by parochial practices.

The Westernized leaders have come to see their own people with the eyes of Europeans, and they feel that they are entangled in obsolete folkway customs and enslaved by anachronistic fears which have no basis in fact and no place in the modern world. They are putting forward an organized effort to overcome those aspects of Islam which they feel bring no credit to their religion and are out of joint with contemporary practice in Western nations. They have not fully accepted the materialism of the West but are drifting in that direction. Some of the leaders would feel at home in a convention of humanists.

The demand which Islam of real life is making on its followers in the archipelago becomes steadily less. As relations with the West increase, those who confess Islam become more cosmopolitan in custom and concept. It is probable that in time to come Moslems in Indonesia will share with followers of other religions those qualities and characteristics which we think of as typical of educated persons in the modern world. In their religious writings they already extol many of those virtues held in high regard in other religions. Even as liberal Baptists, Methodists, and Presbyterians have become difficult to distinguish, so it will probably become difficult to differentiate among liberal Moslems, Christians, and Buddhists. There will be more difference between conservative and liberal Moslems or between conservative and liberal Christians than between liberal Moslems and liberal Christians.

Moslems in Indonesia are observing the five pillars of the law less and less. The daily prayers are regarded with indifference. Even before World War II the hadj was less popular than in preceding decades, and it seems probable that Mecca for the Indonesians will become a tourist's haven, just as Jerusalem has become for most Christians who go there. Indonesian Moslems have not been converted in great numbers to Christianity, but the content of Christian ethics and the techniques of Christian church practice are being converted by Moslems to their own use.

In Indochina the ties which bind the Annamese to their ancestors suffer more by the disturbance of the old order than Annamese belief in spirits and sorcery. The development of new industries such as coal mines and rubber estates, and the creation of schools of higher education with boarding departments attached, tended to break up the family circle before

World War II. Since the war political and military disturbances have aggravated the sense of unease among the Annamese clans by forcing thousands to leave their villages. The foundation of the clan community is shattered when members of the clan migrate.

The ancestors are bound to the place where their bones lie or, at best, are no more mobile than the tablets in which their spirits are supposed to reside on certain occasions. When the Annamese move away, the graves have to be left behind, and they lose one important bond with their ancestors. In these disturbed times it is the fortunate migrant who is able to take the ancestral tablets with him. And, even if he takes them, he lacks the solidarity of the family around him to support the traditional veneration of the ancestors. The old order of justice is also destroyed when contact is broken between the clan chief and the ancestors because the clan chief has traditionally been the judge and administrator of the affairs of the family and has acted in behalf of the ancestors whom he represents.

Sophisticated Annamese attempt to solve the problem of the clan's relations with ancestors by claiming that the cult of ancestors is not a religion at all and that no element of worship is involved in modern times. They say that all they do is hold dear the memory of the deceased and that they do not regard the ancestors as spirit gods. For them the ancestor cult is merely an evidence of affection, and it makes no difference in the new order of things whether the family circle is broken or not. This is an intellectual attempt to meet the problems created by the breakdown of the ancestor cult. Doubtless these Westernized Annamese are describing their own feelings and are pointing the direction of a trend which has begun. They are saying much the same thing that Chinese moderns are saying of the Chinese ancestor cult. These are the arguments of sophisticates who are trying to dodge the implications of ancient practices which are still religiously maintained by over 90 per cent of the Annamese people.

One of the chief supports of the ancestor cult in past centuries has been the imperial family which conducted the various official ceremonies which were supposed to guarantee the security and happiness of the nation. One of the products of the war was the rise of nationalism, culminating on August 22, 1945, with the apparently voluntary abdication of Emperor Bao-Dai.[3] On that day the emperor announced to the nation:

"In the present crisis, Unity is Life, Division is Death.

"Constating that the urge for Democracy of the people in the North has risen too high, and that if I kept waiting until the opening session of the National Congress, friction between North and South would cause more suffering to our countrymen and afford exploitable opportunity to foreigners.

"For these reasons, however painful I may feel when thinking of my ancestors' fighting during four hundred years to develop our country from Thuan-Hoa to Ha-Tien; however painful I may feel when thinking that I have reigned for twenty years but I have really been near my people for only a few months, during which I have not rendered my country any appreciable service.

"I have decided to abdicate and to hand over the rule of the country to the Democratic Republican Government.

"In handing over the rule to the new Government, I desire to express three wishes:

"1. The new Government should take proper care of the temples of my Royal Ancestors.

"2. The new Government should treat kindly all those parties and groups which had fought for the independence of the country, although they were not in line with the popular masses. This will give them the opportunity to contribute in the reconstruction of the country, and will show that the democratic Republican Government of our country is being built upon the absolute Unity of our entire population.

"3. I advise all groups and parties, all the different classes of people, as well as the Royal Family, to be all united, and to

3. *Vietnam-American Friendship Association Review* (Hanoi), November, 1945.

support the Democratic Republic wholeheartedly in order to consolidate our national independence.

"As for myself, during the twenty years of my reign, I have tasted much of bitterness. Now I feel happy to become a free citizen of an independent country. I will never allow anybody to utilize my name or the name of the Royal Family to deceive our Countrymen.

"Long live the independence of Vietnam!

"Long live our Democratic Republic!

[*Signed:*] BAO-DAI"

On the same day Emperor Bao-Dai addressed himself to his royal clan, which was one of the largest and certainly the most important of all the Annamese clans. The Viet Min nationalists were aware of how much stronger they would be if they could secure the support of this numerous and wealthy clan. The emperor's plea was as follows:

"Having adopted the motto: 'The people above everything else' and having declared that I would far rather be a common citizen in an independent state than be the king of a subjugated nation I decided to abdicate in order to hand over the rule to a Government capable of leading the forces of the whole country towards the consolidation of National Independence and the pursuit of happiness for our countrymen.

" 'Independence for our Fatherland. Happiness for the people.'

"Because of these eight words and for over eighty years, so many of our brothers and sisters have sacrificed their lives in the jungle and in the forests, in prison and in jail.

"Compared with the sacrifices of these hundreds and thousands of heroes and heroines, the act of handing over my throne is but a very small thing.

"Therefore, I am sure that, after reading my last Rescript, on the occasion of my abdication, all my relatives will place the debt to our country above the Love of our Family, and will get closely united with all our countrymen, in order to support the Democratic Government, in the common effort of consolidating the independence of our Fatherland. Only by that lofty and idealistic way can they really show their loyalty to me and their love to our ancestors.

[*Signed:*] BAO-DAI"

The royal clan was torn asunder by this declaration. A few of the more democratically minded members did co-operate with the nationalist movement. But most of the clan stood aloof and waited to see what would happen.

The emperor's first concern in his abdication rescript was for the proper care of the temples of his ancestors. The most important service he could render to his nation was to maintain the integrity of his clan and to throw its support behind the nationalist movement. It is not apparent from the documents, nor was it entirely clear to me when I talked with him in Hanoi in 1946, whether the emperor had acted voluntarily or under duress. The fact that he did act can never be recalled because the news was made known to the most remote Annamese villages. To everyone came the stunning realization that the national welfare which for centuries had been guaranteed by the *Nam Giao* and other royal ceremonies, which drew upon the wisdom and good will of the ancestors of the most powerful of all-powerful clans, would no longer be so guaranteed. The royal clan might continue their clan veneration of ancestors as a clan—but no longer were the seasons and the crops and the welfare of over twenty million Annamese dependent on the success of royal clan ceremonial. With the abdication of the emperor and the ending of the significance of the royal clan to the nation, a knife was drawn across the wrists of the ancestor cult system, making it certain that at some time in the future the clan system would be drained of the last drop of vitality. It will not happen in a day; it may require decades; but it is happening.

The Westernized minority among the Annamese put their support behind the declaration of independence signed by their president, Ho Chi Minh. The first three paragraphs of the declaration are interesting because they show some of the ideas which are familiar to the Westernized few. I quote:

" 'All men are created equal. They are endowed by their Creator with certain unalienable rights, among these are Life, Liberty, and the pursuit of happiness.'

"This immortal statement was made in the Declaration of Independence of the United States of America in 1776. Now if we enlarge the sphere of our thoughts, this statement conveys another meaning: 'All peoples on the earth are equal from birth, all the peoples have a right to live, be happy, and free.'

"The 'Declaration of the Rights of Man and of the Citizen' in the French Revolution in 1791 also states: 'All men are born free and with equal rights, and must always be free and have equal rights.'

"These are undeniable truths."[4]

The declaration goes on to review the current situation vis-à-vis the French and the Allied nations. The thoughts in the declaration are familiar only to a few who have set themselves up as leaders. They are followed blindly by their admirers and by all those who have lost the sure foundation of the imperial clan and realize their loss.

There is not space enough here to trace all the developing lines of disintegration in the ancestral cult. The spirit cult remains as strong as ever and is perhaps stronger than before among the people who feel the chill of death in the cult of ancestors. One festival, that of the *Tet*, or New Year's festival, will serve to illustrate the contemporary situation in regard to the cult of ancestors.

The word *Tet* is from the Chinese character meaning a division of time. Among the Annamese the word stands for the festival which takes place on the first day of the new year, the lunar year. It is a religious festival which symbolizes the dawn of new life, love of family, and worship of ancestors. Preparations begin a week in advance on the twenty-third day of the

4. *Ibid.*

twelfth month. On that day the Home Genius who presides over the daily life of the family is supposed to ascend to Heaven to make a detailed report to the Sovereign of the Above on the behavior of the family for which he is responsible. In each family the Home Genius is given a grand send-off banquet and is offered gold and silver paper and a pair of carp fishes which are expected to transport him into the land of the heavens. The fishes are released in some stream near by.

The head of the clan then supervises the preparations of red paper stickers for the doors and windows. The house is cleaned, and embroideries hung. The dusty ancestor tablets are washed, and all brass objects polished. Special glue-rice puddings are cooked which are square like the shape of the earth. A special signal tree is set up in each clan center to show the ancestors the way to come to join the family. On the last day of the old year the doors are closed before nightfall, and the head of the clan in ceremonial costume presents himself before the ancestral altar and invites the ancestors to come and spend the *Tet* with the clan. A little before midnight the head of the family goes to the temple of the Tutelary Genius and other religious places and venerates the Genii, Buddha, and other gods. The family sets up a table with food in the center of the yard in honor of the Sovereign of the Above and the Home Genius, who will come back after making his annual report on the family. Just as the two years shake hands, they set off firecrackers, announcing the new year. The next morning a formal ceremony is held before the ancestral altar. Feasting and offerings of veneration continue for three days, and on the fourth a final meal is offered the ancestors before they return to the land of the dead.

For the majority of the Annamese people this is one of the most important ceremonies of the year in connection with the ancestor cult. What do the Westernized sophisticates have to say about it? A number of comments appeared in a periodical of the Vietnam-American Friendship Association called the *V.A.F.A. Review* in the January-February, 1946, issue.

One comment was to the effect that, although belief in the *Tet* seems to be ill-founded, the *Tet* has contributed greatly to the Vietnam people because it has helped preserve their greatness, their strength, their love for life; it has brought about an annual communion between the living and the dead, whom the Vietnamese believe never really die; and it has given an annual renewal of life. The point seems to be that, however unreal the basis for the *Tet* might appear to be to Westerners, it has rendered excellent service to the Annamese people.

Another comment was to the effect that it would be cruel to suppress the *Tet*, which was admittedly a "nation-wide self-delusion, a periodical self-deception over a thing the concept of which has still to be revised under new lights," because it is a lovely ritual of aesthetic value. The writer stated that most Vietnamese believe that their life and their happiness depend on the right relations between nature and man, that the *Tet* establishes such right relations, and that they fail to realize that man's destiny depends more directly on man's right relations with man. He went on to say that the *Tet* would continue to be gay but that the people would come to realize that happiness cannot be secured by magical means.

A further comment by another writer was to the effect that the Vietnamese should prefer their own civilization and culture to that of the West because such things as the *Tet* were their very life-blood and without them they would lose their spiritual food, their moral principles, and would decline and die as a race. But he urged that the Vietnamese should seek from the West teachers, engineers, and technicians and should re-think their traditional religion and culture in terms of modern developments. It is conceivable that such a person could study the philosophy of Whitehead and then return to his people, who believe that all organized matter is inhabited by spiritual forces, and present them with a rationalization of their spiritism in terms of the forces and planes of energy described by Whitehead.

A Westernized development of Annamese spiritism was begun in 1919 when a governor of an Annamese province on the island of Phu-Quoc in the Gulf of Siam, Ngo-Van-Chieu, claimed to have received a message from a spirit named Cao-Dai. He claimed that Cao-Dai had informed him that he had been selected to make known a new religion on earth which would incorporate the good features of all religions including Buddhism, Confucianism, Taoism, Christianity, the spirit cult, and the cult of ancestors. The new religion, according to Cao-Dai, would be symbolized by an eye surrounded by solar rays indicating that mankind would be guided and enlightened by the eye of God which would have the right views and would always see the light.

Cao-Dai affirmed the existence of the soul and the survival of the physical body after death. He upheld the worship of one God and the veneration of a celestial hierarchy of spirits. He taught the proper understanding of spiritual things and emancipation from servitude to such material things as wealth and honor in order that man might achieve peace of soul. Cao-Dai directed man to face up to his responsibilities to family and humanity.

In order to remind his followers that man should live his life in the presence of the unseen God, they were required to engage in the ritual of worship four times daily.

The founder, Ngo-Van-Chieu, an ardent Taoist, received the message when in company with a group of Taoist mediums who had been attempting to evoke spirits. They tried table rapping and tipping and other methods usual to mediums in other parts of the world. They also used the so-called *corbeille à bec*, or cock's basket, by means of which an energetic spirit could directly write out his message and thus provide extensive specific information. The basket was of almost cylindrical form, rounded on the bottom, covered with yellow silk, to which was attached a long, slender haft of wood, slightly bent, at the end of which was a vertical pin of wood which was the pencil which wrote the messages. The spirit that spoke through the *corbeille à bec* claimed to speak for the

Emperor of Jade, or the Annamese god Ngoc-Hoang-Thuong-De.

The religion did not begin to gather followers until Ngo-Van-Chieu was ordered to Saigon on official business. There he won many followers by organizing séances and establishing communication with Cao-Dai by means of the *corbeille à bec*. In one of these meetings in 1925 the spirit of Cao-Dai convinced a high Annamese official, Le-Van-Trung, member of the council of the government of Indochina, that he should assume the leadership of the new religion and endeavor to make it widely known. He became grand master in 1926. Under his leadership evangelistic missions were sent throughout Cochin China, speeches were made, séances held, and propaganda centers organized. This movement had such success that the annual feast commemorating the advent of Cao-Daism was dated from November, 1926.

The new religion established itself on the base of about a thousand communicants and through them won several hundred thousand followers. Some claimed in 1947 that there were from one to three million Cao-Daists. There were no exact figures. Although most parts of Cochin China proved to be susceptible to the new religion, it won few followers in Annam and almost none at all in Tonkin. It became a southern Annamese religious movement with the holy abode established in the caves of Long-Thanh, province of Tayninh, about fifty miles out of Saigon. There the main temple of the cult was established, and there the Temporal Pope set up his residence.

One of the main purposes of the new religion is to prepare Annamese to mingle with Westerners on a common base of understanding. The eclectic aspect of the religion is strongly emphasized. Some of its advocates are outstanding Westernized leaders. One such is Dr. Le-Van-Hoach, president, in 1947, of the French-supported Provisional Republic of Cochin China. The pope, Phan Oong Tac, is supposed to have functions and controls over his followers similar to those of the Pope of the Catholic church. The Annamese pope of Cao-

Daism was exiled to Madagascar in 1943 by the French, who suspected him of working too zealously with the Japanese occupying Indochina. But the pope returned after the surrender of the Japanese and, as a friend of the French, became for a time governor of Saigon. During the early months of 1947 it was reliably reported that the Cao-Daists in general had declared themselves in support of the French and in opposition to the Viet-Minh. In brief, Cao-Daism is a religious movement headed by Westernized persons who are advocating ideas and practices aimed to make Annamese feel at home in a Westernized world.[5]

A tribute to Westernization was made in 1945 by a Vietnam nationalist, Dr. Nguyen van Luyen, in his book *Le Viet-Nam*. The tribute was remarkable because it was written at a time when there was great tension between the French and the Vietnamese nationalists. He said in effect that the Vietnamese have sought to assimilate French culture and desire that that assimiliation be perfect; that scientific ideas are valid everywhere and that the Vietnamese should study them and use them; that European culture has led the Vietnamese to re-examine their ancient humanities and to attempt to synthesize the old with the new in order to enrich the lives of the people; that the French made the tremendous contribution of a system of romanization into which the Vietnamese have translated the outstanding religious and philosophic literature of the world; and that culturally the French had sown good seed and that a good crop was being produced in cultural affairs.

In summary, Westernization is developing in Southeast Asia, a Westernized minority amounting at present to less than 10 per cent of the population just as Hinduization and Islamization produced similar élite minorities in previous centuries. Those who are Westernized are not completely con-

5. Most of the Cao-Daist library was destroyed during the war. Phan Truong Manh, head of the Cao-Daist Institute at Saigon, has published a few leaflet summaries in French. These are without title except *Résumée sur le caodaisme*. A magazine, *Cao-Dai: Giao-Ly* is published currently by Tuan-Bao in Saigon.

verted to the point of view and mental outlook of Westerners. They are converting Western ideas and Western things to their own use because they are able to understand the West only within the framework of their own experience. Something completely new will accordingly result which will be a product of the inspiration of the West with the genius of the peoples of Southeast Asia. A people who produced Borobudur and Angkor when inspired can rise to great heights again when the spirit stirs within them.

The masses of the people continue, at present, almost as usual in their traditional practices. They are acquiring from the West, just as they previously acquired from India and China, a new format within which to fit the body of their traditional practices and concepts. There is this difference, however, that never before have invading religions penetrated Southeast Asia at a time when the village was so profoundly shaken to its foundations as it is now. It is my expectation that Westernization will affect more people more profoundly than any previous invader. Isolation of the village is no longer possible and cannot be maintained indefinitely.

The peoples of Southeast Asia are caught between two stepping-stones which are so far apart that there is some doubt whether they will be able to complete the transition smoothly. There is the very real possibility that in the attempt either the foot which rests on the foundations of the past or the foot which rests on the foundations of the future will slip and let them down between the two. If such a sad event should occur, there is no question in my mind that they will arise in midstream and ascend, however painfully, onto the foundations of the future.

BIBLIOGRAPHY

ALABASTER, HENRY. *The Wheel of the Law*. London: Trubner & Co., 1871.

ANDERSON, JOHN. *English Intercourse with Siam*. London: Trubner, 1890.

ANGELINO, A. D. A. DE KAT. *Colonial Policy*. 2 vols. Chicago: University of Chicago Press, 1931.

ANUMAN, PHYA. *Ruang Laem Indochine Smai Boran*. Bangkok, 1940.

ARCHER, R. L. "Muhammadan Mysticism in Sumatra," *Journal of the Royal Asiatic Society, Malay Branch*, XV, Part II (1937), 1–126.

BANERJEA, J. N. *Development of Hindu Iconography*. Calcutta: University of Calcutta, 1941.

BANGKOK CALENDAR.

BERNARD, MAURICE and YVONNE. *Lettre aux amis d'Hanoi*.

BEZACIER, L. *Essais sur l'art annamite*. Hanoi: Imprimerie d'Extrême-Orient, 1944.

BIGANDET, PAUL AMBROSE. *The Life or Legend of Gaudama the Buddha of the Burmese*. London: Kegan Paul, Trench, Trubner & Co., 1911.

BIGGS, T. HESKETH. *The Shwe Dagon Pagoda*. Rangoon: Hanthawaddy Press, 1895.

BLAKENEY, RICHARD. *The Journal of an Oriental Voyage*. London: Simpkin, Marshall & Co., 1841.

BOURGEOIS, REMI. *Le Tonkin en 1857*. Hanoi: G. Taupin & Cie., 1943.

BOUSQUET, G. H. "Introduction à l'étude de l'Islam indonésien," *Revue des études islamiques*, XII (1938), 135–260.

BROEK, JAN. O. M. *Economic Development of the Netherlands Indies*. New York: Institute of Pacific Relations, 1942.

Bulletin de l'École Française d'Extrême-Orient. Published at Hanoi since the beginning of the twentieth century.

BURNAY and LINGAT. *Lois Siamoises*. Bangkok: Imprimerie de l'Assomption, 1930.

CADIÈRE, LÉOPOLD. *Croyances et pratiques religieuses des Annamites*. Hanoi: Imprimerie d'Extrême-Orient, 1944.

Cambridge History of India, Vol. IV. Cambridge: Cambridge University Press, 1937.

CARTWRIGHT, B. O. *Turpin's History of the Kingdom of Siam*. Translated from the French. Bangkok: American Presbyterian Mission Press, 1908.

CATOR, W. J. *The Economic Position of the Chinese in the Netherlands Indies*. Oxford: Basil Blackwell, 1936.

CHATTERJI, BIJAN RAJ. *Indian Cultural Influence in Cambodia*. Calcutta: University of Calcutta, 1928.

CHHABRA, B. CH. "Expansion of Indo-Aryan Culture during Pallava Rule as Evidenced by Inscriptions," *Journal of the Asiatic Society of Bengal (Letters)*, Vol. I, No. 1 (1935).

CHRISTIAN, JOHN LEROY. *Modern Burma.* Berkeley: University of California Press, 1942.

CLIFFORD, HUGH. *The Hikayat Raja Budiman (A Malay Folk Tale).* 2 vols. Singapore, 1896.

———. *Studies in Brown Humanity.* Singapore: Federal Rubber Stamp Co., 1898.

———. *Further India.* New York: Stokes Co., 1904.

———. *In Days That Are Dead.* Garden City: Doubleday, Page & Co., 1926.

COCHRANE, WILBURT WILLIS. "The Story of the Shans." Handwritten manuscript on Shan religion and custom. 50 pages on microfilm.

COEDES, GEORGE. *Bronzes Khmers.* Paris: Librairie Nationale d'Art et d'Histoire, 1923.

———. "Documents sur l'histoire politique et religieuse du Laos occidental," *Bulletin de l'École Française d'Extrême-Orient,* Vol. XXV (1925).

———. "Tablettes votives bouddhiques du Siam," *Études asiatiques,* 1925, pp. 145–67.

———. *Prachum Charuk Syam.* 2 vols. Bangkok, 1926.

———. *Boranawathu nai Phiphithaphan.* Bankgok, 1928.

———. *Pour mieux comprendre Angkor.* Hanoi: Imprimerie d'Extrême-Orient, 1943.

———. *Histoire ancienne des états hindouises d'Extrême-Orient.* Hanoi: Imprimerie d'Extrême-Orient, 1944.

COLE, FAY-COOPER. *The Peoples of Malaysia.* New York: D. Van Nostrand Co., 1945.

COLLET, OCTAVE J. A. *L'Île de Java sous la domination française.* Bruxelles: Librairie Falk Filks, 1910.

COLQUHOUN, A. R. *Amongst the Shans.* London: Field & Tuer, 1885.

COOMARASWAMY, A. K. *History of Indian and Indonesian Art.* London, 1927.

CORDIER, GEORGES. *Étude sur la littérature annamite,* Première partie: *Considérations générales.* Saigon: Aux Éditions d'Extrême-Orient. Deuxième partie: *Le Théâtre.* Hanoi: Imprimerie Tan-Dan; Troisième partie: *La Chanson.* Hanoi: Imprimerie Trung-Bac.

CORT, MARY LOVINA. *Siam.* New York: Randolph & Co., 1886.

COVARRUBIAS, MIGUEL. *Island of Bali.* New York: Alfred A. Knopf, 1938.

CRAWFURD, JOHN. *History of the Indian Archipelago.* Edinburgh: Archibald Constable & Co., 1820.

DAMRONG, RACHANUPHAP, KROM PHYA. *Nithan Boranakhadi.* Bangkok: Prachan Press, 1944.

DAMRONG and NARIT. *Tamnan Phrakod lae Hipsopbanndasak.* Bangkok, 1928.

DANGUY, HENRI. *Le Nouveau visage de la Cochinchine.* Saigon: La Rampe Indochinoise, 1929.

DODD, WILLIAM CLIFTON. *The Tai Race.* Cedar Rapids, Iowa: Torch Press, 1923.

Dohring, Karl. *Buddhistische Tempelanlagen in Siam.* 3 vols. Bangkok: Asia Publishing House, 1920.

———. *Siam.* München: Georg Müller, 1923.

Dutch Papers: Extract from the Daily Journal Kept in Batavia Castle, Containing an Account of Events Which Occurred in the Netherlands India, Especially Those concerning Siam, between 1624–1642. Bangkok, 1915.

Eakin, P. A. "Wheels within the Wheel of the Law in Siam," *International Review of Missions*, July, 1931.

Earl, George Windsor. *The Eastern Seas.* London: Wm. H. Allen & Co., 1837.

Emerson, R.; Mills, L.; and Thompson, V. *Government and Nationalism in Southeast Asia.* New York: Institute of Pacific Relations, 1942.

Encyclopaedia of Islam.

Far Eastern Quarterly, "Netherlands Number," February, 1946.

Fauconnier, Henri. *Malaisie*, trans. Eric Sutton. New York: Macmillan Co., 1931.

Ferrand, Gabriel. *Relations de voyages et textes géographiques arabes, persanes et turques relatifs à l'Extrême-Orient du VII au XVIII siècles.* 2 vols. Paris, 1913. (Supposed to contain all known reports on East Indies from Arabian and Persian sources.)

Finot, L.; Parmentier, H.; and Goloubew, V. *Le Temple d'Icvarapura (Bantay Srei, Cambodge).* Paris: G. Van Oest, 1926.

Finot, Louis. "Lokecvara en Indochine," *Études asiatiques*, 1925, pp. 227–56.

———. "Inscriptions d'Angkor," *Bulletin de l'École Française d'Extrême-Orient*, Vol. XXV (1925).

Firth, Raymond. *Malay Fishermen: Their Peasant Economy.* London: Kegan Paul, Trench, Trubner & Co., 1946.

Foreign Policy of the Provisional Government of the Republic of Vietnam. Hanoi: Foreign Office, Republic of Vietnam.

Furnivall, J. S. *Progress and Welfare in Southeast Asia.* New York: Institute of Pacific Relations, 1941.

Getty, Alice. *The Gods of Northern Buddhism.* Oxford: Clarendon Press, 1914.

Ghoshal, U. N. *A History of Hindu Political Theories.* Oxford: Oxford University Press, 1927.

———. *Progress of Greater Indian Research (1917–1942).* Calcutta: Greater India Society, 1943.

Gibb, H. A. R. *Modern Trends in Islam.* Chicago: University of Chicago Press, 1945.

Glaize, Maurice. *Les Monuments du groupe d'Angkor.* Saigon: Portail, 1944.

Goloubew, Victor. " 'Le Harihara de Maha Rosei," *Études asiatiques*, 1925, pp. 286–95.

———. *Religieux et pèlerins en terre d'Asie.* Hanoi: Taupin & Co., 1944.

Graham, W. A. *Siam.* 2 vols. London: Alexander Moring, Ltd., 1924.

Granier, F. *Voix dans la pagode.* Saigon: C. Ardin, 1924.

GRAY, JAMES. *Ancient Proverbs and Maxims; or, the Niti Literature of Burma*. London: Trubner & Co., 1886.

GRIFFIN, ELDON. *Clippers and Consuls*. Ann Arbor, Mich.: Edwards Brothers, Inc., 1938.

GRIGGS, W. C. *Shan Folk Lore Stories*. Philadelphia: American Baptist Publishing Society, 1902.

HALE, A. *The Adventures of John Smith in Malaya, 1600–1605*. Leyden: E. J. Brill, 1909.

HALL, H. FIELDING. *A People at School*. London: Macmillan & Co., 1906.

———. *The Soul of a People*. London: Macmillan & Co., 1909.

Handbook of the Netherlands and Overseas Territories. The Hague: Economic Section of the Ministry of Foreign Affairs, 1931.

HARVEY, G. E. *History of Burma*. London: Longmans, Green & Co., 1925.

———. *British Rule in Burma*. London: Faber & Faber, 1946.

HITTI, PHILIP K. *The History of the Arabs*. London: Macmillan & Co., 1937.

HOBBS, CECIL CARLTON. "Christian Education and the Burmese Family." Unpublished thesis, Department of Education, Colgate-Rochester Divinity School. Rochester, N.Y., 1942.

HONIG, P., and VERDOORN, F. (eds.). *Science and Scientists in the Netherlands Indies*. New York: Board for the Netherlands Indies, Surinam, and Curaçao. 1945.

HURLIMANN, MARTIN. *Burma, Ceylon, Indochina, Siam*. New York: B. Westermann Co., 1930.

INNES, EMILY. *The Chersonese*. London: Richard Bentley & Son, 1885.

JONES, WILLIAM (trans.). *Institutes of Hindu Law*. London: Rivingtons & Cochran, 1825.

Journal of the Greater India Society. Calcutta: Oriental Press.

KEESING, FELIX M. *The South Seas in the Modern World*. New York: John Day Co., 1941.

KEITH, A. BERRIEDALE. *A History of Sanskrit Literature*. Oxford: Clarendon Press, 1928.

KENNEDY, RAYMOND. *The Ageless Indies*. New York: John Day Co., 1942.

KEPPEL, HENRY. *The Expedition to Borneo of H.M.S. Dido*. 2 vols. London: Chapman & Hall, 1847.

KONTSRI SUBAMONKALA. *La Thailande et ses relations avec la France*. Paris: Éditions A. Pedone, 1940.

KROM, N. J. *Barabudur, Archeological Description*. 2 vols. The Hague, 1927.

La République du Viet Nam. Hanoi. (A daily newspaper.)

"La Terreur blanche en Annam." (A typed manuscript concerning an incident at Banmethuet in October, 1938.)

LAJONQUIÈRE, E. LUNET DE. *Inventaire descriptif des monuments du Cambodge*. 3 vols. Paris: Imprimerie Nationale, 1902.

LANDON, KENNETH PERRY. *Siam in Transition*. Chicago: University of Chicago Press, 1939.

LASKER, BRUNO. *Peoples of Southeast Asia*. New York: Alfred A. Knopf, 1944.

Lathithamniamtangtang, Phak 1 to 24.
Lesserteur, E. C. *Rituel domestique des funérailles en Annam.* Paris: Imprimerie Chaix, 1885.
Leuba, Jeanne. *Les Chams et leur art.* Paris: G. Van Oest & Cie., 1923.
Levi, M. Sylvain. *Indochine.* Paris: Exposition Coloniale Internationale de Paris. 1931.
Lingat, R. *Prawat Sat Kotmai Thai.* 2 vols. Bangkok: University of Moral and Political Science, 1935.
Logan, J. R. "The Manners and Customs of the Malays," *Journal of the Indian Archipelago and Eastern Asia* (Singapore), III (1849), 274–84; IV (1849), 433–35.
Louvet, Louis Eugène. *La Cochinchine religieuse.* Paris: E. Leroux, 1885.
Low, James. "The Keddah Annals," *Journal of the Indian Archipelago and Eastern Asia*, Vol. III. Reprinted in 1908.
McFarland, George Bradley. *Historical Sketch of Protestant Missions in Siam, 1828–1928.* Bangkok: Bangkok Times Press, Ltd., 1928.
Madrolle, M. *Tonkin du Sud.* Hanoi: Comité de l'Asie Française, 1907.
———. *Madrolle Guides: Indochine du Nord; Indochine du Sud; Indochina.*
Majumdar, R. C. *Champa*, Books I, II, and III. Lahore: Punjab Sanskrit Book Depot, 1927.
———. "The Sailendra Empire," *Journal of the Greater India Society* (Calcutta), Vol. I (1934); Vol. II (1935).
———. *Suvarnadvipa.* 2 vols. Decca: A. K. Majumdar, 1937–38.
———. *Hindu Colonies in the Far East.* Calcutta: General Printers & Publishers, 1944.
Malayan Branch Royal Asiatic Society, Journal of.
Malleret, Louis. *Pour comprendre la sculpture buddhique et brahmanique en Indochine.* Saigon: Portail, 1942.
Marchal, Henri, "Pavillons d'entrée du Palais Royal d'Angkor Thom," *Études asiatiques*, 1925. pp. 57–78.
———. *L'Architecture comparée dans L'Inde et L'Extrême-Orient.* Paris: Les Éditions d'Art et d'Histoire, 1944.
Marquis, Édouard. *Inde française.* Saigon: Tin-Duc Thu-Xa, 1943.
Marsden, W. *The History of Sumatra.* London, 1783.
Maspero, Georges. "La Géographie politique de l'Indochine aux environs de 960 A.D.," *Études asiatiques*, 1925, pp. 79–125.
———. *Le Royaume de Champa.* Paris: G. Van Oest, 1928.
———. *L'Indochine.* 2 vols. Paris: G. van Oest, 1929.
Maspero, Guy P. and Éveline. *Mœurs et coutumes des Khmers.* Paris: Payot, 1938.
Maung Htin Aung. *Burmese Drama.* Oxford: Oxford University Press, 1937.
May, Reginald le. *An Asian Arcady.* Cambridge: W. Heffer & Sons, 1926.
———. *Buddhist Art in Siam.* Cambridge: University Press, 1938.
Maybon, Charles B. *Lectures sur l'histoire moderne et contemporaine du pays d'Annam.* Hanoi: Imprimerie d'Extrême-Orient, 1930.

MUNDY, RODNEY. *Narrative of Events in Borneo and Celebes.* 2 vols. London: John Murray, 1848.

NAERSSEN, F. H. VAN. *Culture Contacts and Social Conflicts in Indonesia.* Translated from Dutch by A. J. BARNOUW. New York: Southeast Asia Institute, 1947.

NAG, KALIDAS. *India and the Pacfiic World.* Calcutta: Book Company, Ltd., 1941.

NARATHIPPRAPHANPHONG, KROM PHRA. *Phrabaromarachaphisek Sapadamarachamaha Chakriwong of 1925.* 2 vols. Bangkok: Eksawnit, 1929.

NGUYEN VAN LUYEN. *Le Viet-Nam.* Hanoi: Le-Van-Phue. 1945.

NGUYEN VAN TO. "L'Argot annamite de Hanoi," *Études asiatiques*, 1925, pp. 170–97.

PALLEGOIX, MGR. *Description du Royaume Thai ou Siam.* 2 vols. Paris: Vialat & Cie, 1854.

PARMENTIER, H. *Les Sculptures Chames.* Paris: Librairie Nationale d'Art et d'Histoire, 1922.

———. "Origine commune des architectures hindoues dans l'Inde et en Extrême-Orient," *Études asiatiques*, 1925, pp. 199–241.

———. *L'Art Khmer primitif.* 2 vols. Paris: G. Van Oest, 1927.

PE MAUNG TIN and LUCE, G. H. (trans.). *The Glass Palace Chronicle.* Oxford: Oxford University Press, 1923.

PECK, ELLEN M. H. *Travels in the Far East.* New York: Crowell & Co., 1909.

PELLIOT, PAUL. "Deux itinéraires de Chine en Inde à la fin du VIII siècle," *BEFEO*, IV (1904), 131–413.

———. "Quelques textes chinois concernant l'Indochine hindouisée, *Études asiatiques*, 1925, pp.243–63.

——— (trans.). "Mémoires sur les coutumes du Cambodge by Tcheou Ta-Kouan," *BEFEO*, Vol. II (1902).

PHAM DUY KHIEM. *La Jeune femme de Nam Xuong.* Hanoi: Taupin & Co., 1944.

PIERIS, P. E. *Religious Intercourse between Ceylon and Siam.* Translated from the Singhalese. Bangkok: Siam Observer Office, 1908.

PLEYTE, C. M. *Die Buddha Legende in den Skilpturen des Tempels von Boro-Budur.* Amsterdam: J. H. de Bussy, 1901.

PONDER, HARRIET WINIFRED. *Javanese Panorama.* London: Seeley, Service & Co., 1942.

PRATT, J. B. *The Pilgrimage of Buddhism.* New York: Macmillan Co., 1928.

PRZYLUSKI, J. "Indian Colonization in Sumatra before the Seventh Century," *Journal of the Greater India Society* (Calcutta), Vol. I (1934).

———. "The Terminal Stupa of the Barabudur," *ibid.*, Vol. III (1936).

PURCELL, VICTOR. *Malaya.* London: Thomas Nelson & Sons, 1946.

QUANJER, PH. *Mœurs et coutumes de la Malaisie.* Paris: Payot, 1939.

RAFFLES, THOMAS STAMFORD. *History of Java.* 2 vols. London: Henry G. Bohn, 1844.

Rauws, J.; Kraemer, H.; Van Hasselt, F. J. F.; and Slotemaker de Bruine, N. A. C. *The Netherlands Indies.* New York: World Dominion Press, 1935.

Ray, Nihar-Ranjan. *Brahmanical Gods in Burma.* Calcutta: University of Calcutta, 1932.

Remusat, Gilberte de Coral. *L'Art Khmer.* Paris: Les Éditions d'Art et d'Histoire, 1940.

Russier, Henri. *Histoire sommaire du royaume de Cambodge.* Hanoi: Imprimerie d'Extrême-Orient, 1944.

Sangermano, Father. *The Burmese Empire.* Westminster: Constable & Co., 1893.

Sarkar, Himansu Bhusan. *Indian Influences on the Literature of Java and Bali.* Calcutta: Greater India Society, 1934.

Sathien Koset. *Prapheninaokhongthai.* Bangkok, 1946.

Saunders, Kenneth. *Epochs in Buddhist History.* Chicago: University of Chicago Press, 1934.

———. *The Ideals of East and West.* New York: Macmillan Co., 1934.

Schiller, A. Arthur. *Legal and Administrative Problems of the Netherlands Indies.* New York: Institute of Pacific Relations, 1945.

Schrieke, B. J. *The Effect of Western Influence on Native Civilization.* Weltevreden, 1929.

Seidenfaden, Erik. *Guide to Bangkok.* Bangkok: Royal State Railways, 1926.

Shway Yoe. *The Burman, His Life and Notions.* London: Macmillan & Co., 1910.

Siam from Ancient to Present Times: The Souvenir of the Siamese Kingdom Exhibition at Luwbini Park, 1925.

Sice, Eugène. *Le Mariage en pays d'Annam.* (*Selon la tradition ancestrale et les coutumes religieuses.*) Dijon: Imprimerie Bernigaud et Priyat, 1929.

Smith, Samuel J. *The Siam Repository, 1869–1872.*

Snouck, Hurgronje, C. *The Achinese.* 2 vols. London, 1906.

———. *Mohammedanism: Lectures on Its Origin, Its Religious and Political Growth and Its Present State.* New York, 1916.

———. *Mekka in the Latter Part of the Nineteenth Century.* Leiden, 1931.

"Southeastern Asia and the Philippines," *Annals of the American Academy of Political and Social Science,* Vol. CCXXVI (March, 1943).

Souvignet, E. *Variétés tonkinoises.* Hanoi: Imprimerie Schneider, 1903.

Spalding, H. N. *Civilization in East and West.* London: Humphrey Milford, 1939.

Stutterheim, Von Willem. *Rama-Legenden und Rama Reliefs in Indonesien.* 2 vols. München: Georg Müller, 1925.

Stutterheim, W. F. *A Javanese Period in Sumatran History.* Surakarta, 1929.

———. *Indian Influences in the Lands of the Pacific.* Weltevreden, 1929.

———. *Indian Influences in Old Balinese Art.* London: India Society, 1935.

———. "The Meaning of the Hindu-Javanese Caṇḍi," *Journal of American Oriental Society*, LI, No. 1 (March, 1931), 1–15.

Supatmo, Raden. "Animistic Beliefs and Religious Practices." (Mimeographed.)

Swettenham, Frank A. *Malay Sketches*. London: Macmillan & Co., 1895.

———. *British Malaya*. London: John Lane Co., 1907.

———. *The Real Malay*. London: John Lane Co., 1907.

Takakusu, J. (trans.). *A Record of the Buddhist Religion as Practiced in India and the Malay Archipelago (A.D. 671–695) by I-Tsing (I-Ching)*. Oxford, 1896.

Telford, J. H. "Animism in Kengtung State," *Journal of Burma Research Society* (Rangoon), XXXVII, Part II (1937), 86–237.

Témoignages et documents français relatifs à la colonisation française au Viet-Nam. Hanoi: Association Culturelle pour le Salut du Viet-Nam, 1945.

Thoburn, J. M. *India and Malaysia*. New York: Hunt & Eaton, 1892.

Tourism in Netherland India. Batavia, Java. (A periodical issued by the Travellers Official Information Bureau of Netherland India.)

Tran van-Chuong. *Essai sur l'esprit du droit sino-annamite*. Paris: University of Paris Law School, 1922.

Tyerman, D., and Bennet, G. *Journal of Voyages and Travels*. 2 vols. London: Frederick Westley and A. H. Davis, 1831.

Van Goor, M. E. Julius. "Notice sur les ruines de Panataran," *Études asiatiques*, 1925, pp. 375–84.

Van Vollenhoven, C. *La Decouverte du droit indonésien*. Paris, 1933.

Verneuil, M. P. *L'Art à Java: Les Temples de la période classique indo-javanaise*. Paris: Librairie Nationale d'Art et d'Histoire, 1927.

Vietnam-American Friendship Association Review. Published monthly at Hanoi.

Vlekke, Bernard H. M. *Nusantara*. Cambridge, Mass.: Harvard University Press, 1944.

Vogel, J., Ph. "Ganga et Yamuna dans l'iconographie brahmanique," *Études asiatiques*, 1925, pp. 385–402.

Wales, H. G. Quaritch. *Siamese State Ceremonies*. London: Bernard Quaritch, Ltd., 1931.

———. *Ancient Siamese Government and Administration*. London: Bernard Quaritch, Ltd., 1934.

———. *Towards Angkor*. London: Harrap & Co., 1937.

Wallace, Alfred Russel. *The Malay Archipelago*. 2 vols. London: Macmillan & Co., 1869.

Watson, C. R. "The Moslem of Sumatra as a Type," *Moslem World*, III (1913), 159–69.

Weber, Albrecht. *The History of Indian Literature*. London: Trubner & Co., 1878.

Wells, Kenneth E. *Thai Buddhism, Its Rites and Activities*. Bangkok: Bangkok Times Press, 1939.

WESTRA, H. "Custom and Muslim Law in the Netherlands East Indies," *Transactions of the Grotius Society*, XXV (1939), 151–67.

WILLIAM OF SWEDEN, PRINCE. *In the Lands of the Sun*. London: Eveleigh Nash, 1915.

WINDSTEDT, R. O. "Negri Sembilan: The History, Polity, and Beliefs of Nine States," *Journal of the Royal Asiatic Society, Malay Branch*, Vol. XII, Part III (October, 1934).

———. "A History of Selangor," *ibid.*

———. "A History of Malaya," *ibid.*, Vol. VIII, Part I (March, 1935).

———. "The Advent of Muhammadanism in Malay Peninsula and Archipelago," *Journal of the Royal Asiatic Society, Straits Branch*, LXXVII, 171–75; LXXXI, 5–6.

WINDSTEDT R. O., and WILKINSON, R. J. *A History of Perak*. Singapore: Printers, Ltd.

WORSFOLD, W. BASIL. *A Visit to Java*. London: Bentley & Son, 1893.

INDEX

Alexander the Great, 62

Ancestor cult, 192–96; festival of *tet*, 197–99; ritual in, 42–44

Ancestor worship, 45–49, 121, 192, 193

Animism, 25

Annamese: ancestor cult of, 192, 193; cult of Cao-Dai, 200–202

Annamese folkways: ancestor cult of, 42–44, 45; Chinese influences on, 32–60; Taoist shrines in, 34

Annamese religion, 32–60; Chinese format of, 32; Chinese origin of, 32; concept of supreme being in, 56; cult houses in, 34, 35; cult of spirit of agriculture, 54; death offerings in, 42, 43; feminine spirits in, 35; nature spirits in, 55; special ceremonial in, 38; a spirit cult, 33; spirit of Heaven, 56; sun spirit in, 56; trade cults in, 53, 54

Annamese spiritism, Westernized, 200

Asoka, empire of, 62

Bali, religion of, 8

Brahma, 73

Brahman religion, 78, 79

Brahmanism, 102

Britain, control in Burma, 169

Buddha, 67, 72, 73, 77, 78, 85; and Siva, association of, 78

Buddhism, 25, 31, 32, 33, 59, 60, 67, 76, 78, 101, 111, 112, 121, 192, 200; in Annamese religion, 32, 34, 59, 60; in Cambodia, 85–87; decline of, 86; diffusion of, 65; in early Siam, 101, 102, 108; in Farther India, 76, 77

Burma: British control of, 169; Hinayana Buddhism in, 21, 23, 24, 25; and independence from Britain, 7; religious culture of, 21–25; rice-growing in, 9; spiritism in, 21–25

Cambodia: Brahmanism in, 86; Buddhism in, 85–87; height of Indian culture in, 88; Hindu religion in, 84–88; observations on customs in, 89–99; Sanskrit literature in, 88

Cambodian civilization, 84–89

Cao-Daism, 200–202

Caste system, 72

Catholicism: in China, 170; in Philippines, 8, 134, 169

China, Catholicism in, 170

Christianity, 184, 185, 192, 200

Civil Hierarchy, Law of, 125

Code of Manu, 132

Colonialism, as a cultural process, 171–73

Commerce, its role in Hindu expansion, 62, 63

Confucianism, 32, 33, 57–60, 200

Confucius, 34, 50, 57, 58

Cremation, 16, 26; in Siam, 116, 119–20

Cult practices, in Southeast Asia, 11

Darwin, Charles, 169

Death Valley Railroad, 65

Dewey, John, 169

England: colonial organization of Malaya, 169; control in Burma, 169

European imperialism, 169

Federation of Malaya, 7

Fine arts, 176

Five pillars of Islam, 143–46, 192

France, influence of, in Indochina, 169

Golden Chersonese, 63

Harivamsha, 68

Hinayana Buddhist countries, 8

Hindu civilization: in China, 70; in Farther India, 69, 70

Hindu culture: aristocratic nature of, 69, 72; in Cambodia, 84–88; caste intermarriage in, 72; Code of Manu,

132; in Indochina, 68, 71–75; in Indo-Javanese literature, 79; in Indonesia, 68; in Sailendra Empire, 71, 75; spread of, 62–70
Hindu deities, 72, 73
Hindu expansion, 62, 63
Hindu influence in Southeast Asia, 69, 70
Hindu trade, with the Mediterranean, 62
Hindu Trinity, 72, 73, 78
Hinduization: definition of, 61, 62; effects of commerce on, 62; in Farther India, 88, 89; by Indochinese and Indonesians, 68; observance of the dharmashastras, 61; in Siam, 100–133; use of Sanskrit, 62
Hinduized nations, history of, 71–75
Hinduized state, definition of, 128, 129

India: Aryan invasion of, 10; caste system in, 72; Jataka tales of, 64; trade of, with Southeast archipelago, 63, 64
Indochina: abdication of Emperor Bao-Dai, 194–95; Democratic Republican Government in, 194; French influence in, 169; Hindu culture in, 68
Indochina peninsula, Cambodian customs in, 89–99
Indo-Javanese literature, Hindu influence on, 79
Indonesia: Annamese ancestor worship in, 45–49; Annamese folkways in, 32–60; Hindu culture in, 68; indifference to Islamic ritual, 143–46; Moslem culture in, 163–64; Moslem law in, 158–62; Moslem practice in, 143–46; Moslems in, 192; Muhammadiyah movement in, 186–88; pilgrimages to Mecca, 146–47; position of women in, 154–55; religious culture of, 13–21; ritual feats in, 156, 157; United States of, 6, 7; veneration of saints in, 155–56
Islam, 134, 192; and abstention from pork, 153; artistic sterility of, 136, 137; basis of orthodox, 143; call to prayer of, 149; conversion to, 135; early ceremony in, 140–41; focal point for, 137; Hinduized elements in, 136; in Indonesia, 138, 139; pilgrimage to Mecca, 146; position of women in, 154–55; practice of circumcision in, 152–53; prayer ritual of, 144–45; progress of, in Southeast Asia, 137–43; prohibitions concerning dress in, 153; schools of, 149–50
Islamic fasting, 145

Jataka tales, 64
Java, population of, 8, 9
Javanese history and literature, 79–84
Javanese religion, 78

Kanishka, empire of, 62
Koran, 146, 149, 150, 151, 187, 188, 189
Kublai Khan, 101

Language stock: Annamese, 4; Malayo-Polynesian, 3, 4; Mon-Khmer, 4; Thai, 4; Tibeto-Burman, 4
Law of Civil Hierarchy, 125

Mahabharata, 61, 68, 72, 129
Malacca: fall of, 138; focal point for Islam, 137
Malaya: English colony of, 169; Federation of, 7
Malayo-Polynesian language stock, 3, 4
Manu, Code of, 132
Marco Polo, 137
Marx, Karl, 169
Mecca: orientation of mosques toward, 148, 149; pilgrimage to, 146
Mohammed, 135, 188, 189; ascension of, 158; celebration of birth of, 158
Mohammedanism, 147
Mongolian conquests, 69
Moslem call to prayer, 149
Moslem ceremony, 140–41
Moslem law, 158–62
Moslem literature, 136, 137
Moslem practices, contribution of Southeast Asia to, 148
Moslem religion, in Indonesia, 163–64
Moslem ritual, 143–46
Mosque personnel, 149
Muhammadiyah movement, 186–91

Mythology of the puranas, 61

Nat worship in Burma, 21–25
Netherlands-Indonesian Union, 7

Philippine Islands: Catholicism in, 8, 134, 169; political development of, 170; political independence of, 6; Spanish occupation of, 169
Population: in Burma, 2; in East Indies, 2; in Indochina, 2; in Java, 8, 9; in Malaya, 2, 3; in Philippine Islands, 3; and relation to war, 9; in Siam, 2
Purana literature, 61, 68, 69, 70
Puranas, mythology of the, 61, 130

Ramayana, 61, 68, 69, 72, 78, 79, 115, 129, 130, 131
Reincarnation, 18
Religions: belief in reincarnation, 18; importance of prophecy in, 18; practice of cremation in, 16, 26; spiritism in, 13–31, 32–60
Religious ceremonies: at death, 16, 25; importance of lucky days in, 19, 20; of planting and harvesting, 18, 24
Renville Agreements, 7
Ritual, Moslem, 143–46
Ritual bathing, 144, 157
Ritual offerings, 145
Royal Hindu cult, 69

Sailendra Empire, Hindu culture in, 75, 77
Sanskrit, 76; in Siam, 129
Sanskrit language, 62, 66, 77
Sanskrit literature, 67, 72, 88, 130
Selucides, empire of the, 62
Siam: Brahmanism in, 111, 112; Buddhism in, 25, 30, 31, 132; burial practices in, 116, 117; coronation customs in, 112–16; divine kingship in, 106–8, 109–11, 112, 120, 123; government in, 178, 179; a Hinduized nation, 100–133; history of, 100–106; Law of Civil Hierarchy in, 125; legal system in, 131, 132; Moslem law in, 162, 163; political independence of, 169; purana mythology in, 130; religious culture in, 25–31; the royal harem in, 123–25; spiritism in, 25
Siamese literature, 129, 130
Siva, 72, 73, 188; *see also* Buddha
Southeast Asia: agricultural methods in, 174; agriculture of, 5, 7, 11; area included in, 1, 6; Christian missionaries in, 167; Christianity in, 134; climatic nature of, 4, 5; contributions of, to Islam, 134–64; culture similarities in, 10, 11; early Christian influences in, 166; early civilizations of, 1–2, 6, 9, 10; European imperialism in, 169, 170; geographical nature of, 4–6; Hindu influences in, 8, 10, 13, 17, 69; history of Islam in, 134–64; importance of rivers in, 1, 5; maritime nature of, 1, 5; modern social customs in, 176, 177; modern trends in, 165–203; Moslem influences in, 8, 10, 13, 17; population and dialects of, 2, 3; relation of population and war in, 9; rice culture in, 5, 11; Western entertainment in, 174; Westernization of, 165–203; Westernized schools in, 170, 172
Spiritism, absence of priesthood in, 36, 37; ancestor worship in, 45–49; and birth, 20, 27; and death, 16, 19, 25, 27, 42; and disease, 23, 38, 39, 40, 41; importance of charms in, 20, 21, 30, 39; importance of lucky days in, 19, 20, 39; intermediaries in, 38, 39; and marriage, 20; in modern Indochina, 192; omens in, 24; in Siam, 116
Sunda Straits, 64

Taoism, 32, 33, 37, 58, 200
Thai, early Siamese civilization of, 100, 101

United States of Indonesia, 6, 7

Viet Nam Republic, 6
Vishnu, 72, 73, 78, 188

Western medicine, 173
Westernization, definition of, 165–66
Westernized government, 177, 178

PRINTED IN U.S.A.